INDUSTRIAL SUBSIDIES AND FRICTION IN WORLD TRADE

National industrial subsidies are a major irritant in international trading relations. There have been many attempts to curb the perceived deleterious effects of subsidies on the international economics and trading order; most have met with stiff opposition and mixed success. Today the combination of industrial subsidies and the countervailing duties intended to combat them present one of the major threats to the international trading order.

Industrial Subsidies and Friction in World Trade is a comparative analysis of a number of instruments devised to regulate industrial subsidies and lessen the impact of countervailing duties. Some of these, such as the institutions of the newly created European Economic Area, are being analysed for the first time. The study contains a fresh review of the Canada–US FTA and NAFTA in light of their growing body of cases and a closer examination of the lessons of the EU and EEA. Finally, the book takes an early look at the Uruguay Round Subsidies Code in order to determine the long-term prospects for its success. *Industrial Subsidies and Friction in World Trade* clearly shows how the differences in the regulatory mechanisms used in the EU and North America highlight the vast chasm between the two perspectives.

Rambod Behboodi currently teaches international trade law at the University of Copenhagen law school. He is a member of the Bar of Ontario and practises mainly in the area of international trade law.

INDUSTRIAL SUBSIDIES AND FRICTION IN WORLD TRADE

Trade policy or trade politics?

Rambod Behboodi

ROUTLEDGE

London and New York

First published 1994
by Routledge
11 New Fetter Lane, London EC4P 4EE

Simultaneously published in the USA and Canada
by Routledge
29 West 35th Street, New York, NY 10001

Typeset in Garamond by
Ponting–Green Publishing Services,
Chesham, Buckinghamshire
Printed and bound in Great Britain by
TJ Press (Padstow) Ltd, Padstow, Cornwall

British Library Cataloguing in Publication Data

A catalogue record for this book is available from
the British Library

Library of Congress Cataloging in Publication Data
Behboodi, Rambod
Industrial subsidies and friction in world trade: trade policy or trade politics? / Rambod Behboodi.
p. cm.
Includes bibliographical references and index.
1. Subsidies—Law and legislation.
2. Antidumping duties—Law and legislation.
3. International trade. I. Title.
K3205.E3B44 1994
341.7'54—dc20 94-3980

ISBN 0-415-11113-7

To my parents,
Roya Fanian and Khosrow Behboodi,
without whose many sacrifices this
would never have been possible

CONTENTS

Acknowledgements ix
Abbreviations and specialised terms xi

Part I The background

1 INTRODUCTION 3

2 DOMESTIC INDUSTRIAL SUBSIDIES IN INTERNATIONAL TRADE THEORY 7
Introduction 7
Classical free trade theory 8
Subsidies as trade barriers 10
Critique of the classical theory of free trade 15
Critical appraisal of subsidies in an imperfect market 24
The political economy of subsidisation 32
Evaluation: principle or chaos? 41

Part II: International institutions for the regulation of subsidies

INTRODUCTION 47

3 MULTILATERAL REGULATION OF SUBSIDIES 50
Introduction 50
GATT Track II 50
European Free Trade Association 56
The European Economic Area 67
Multi/bilateralism: and they negotiated happily ever after? 78

4 SUPRANATIONAL REGULATION OF SUBSIDIES 81
Introduction 81
The European Economic Area: the false start 82
The European Union 84
Supranationalism: politics by bureaucratic fiat 95

5 UNILATERAL REGULATION OF SUBSIDIES 97
Introduction 97
GATT Subsidies Code Track I 98
The Canada–US Free Trade Agreement 105
Unilateralism: speak loudly and swing a big stick 129

Part III The outlook

6 THE URUGUAY ROUND 133
Introduction 133
Negotiating framework 134
Regulatory and institutional framework 136
Analysis 147

7 CONCLUSION 151

Notes 157
Bibliography 193
Index 208

ACKNOWLEDGEMENTS

It is impossible to list all of the people who have shared in the task of bringing this work together in the past two years. Lack of space and weakness of memory necessitate selectivity. I ask therefore that omission of certain names be forgiven and not construed as a slight.

First I should like to thank Professor William C. Graham, Q.C., M.P., and Professor Michael J. Trebilcock for their help and support throughout my studies in law and particularly in the preparation and finalisation of this work. I am indebted to them for their taking the time out of their busy schedules to meet with me, discuss my progress, make suggestions, review and correct the early drafts of this book, and generally to give me guidance in navigating my way through one of the most difficult areas of international trade law.

I should also like to thank the librarians at the Bora Laskin Law Library, the International Business and Trade Library, the Government Publications Depository at Robarts Library, University of Toronto, the Library of the Delegation of the European Communities at Ottawa, and the Library of the law firm of Cassels Brock & Blackwell. Their help was invaluable in completing the research for this book.

I should like to acknowledge the generous support of the Faculty of Law, University of Toronto, and the people of the Province of Ontario in providing the facilities and the greater part of the financial support required for the completion of this work.

Last, but most certainly not least, I should like to thank all my friends, in particular Mr. Edward Akkawi, who suffered my endless recitations and arguments, and who read and edited my drafts, as I tried to come to an understanding of the issues discussed here.

LIST OF ABBREVIATIONS AND SPECIALISED TERMS

BENELUX	The customs union of Belgium, the Netherlands, and Luxembourg
CEC	Commission of the European Communities
CIT	Court of International Trade (US)
CITT	Canadian International Trade Tribunal
CVD	Countervailing Duty
DMNR	Deputy Minister of National Revenue (Canada)
DRM	Dispute Resolution Mechanism
DSB	Dispute Settlement Body (GATT 1994)
EC	European Community
ECC	Extraordinary Challenge Committee
ECJ	Court of Justice of the European Communities
ECSC	European Coal and Steel Community
ECU	European Currency Unit
EEA	European Economic Area
EEC	European Economic Community
EFTA	European Free Trade Association
EP	European Parliament
ESA	EFTA Surveillance Authority
EU	European Union (EC post Maastricht)
FTA	Free Trade Agreement
GATT	General Agreement on Tariffs and Trade
MNR	Ministry of National Revenue (Canada)
MTN	Multilateral Trade Negotiations
NAFTA	North American Free Trade Agreement
OECD	Organization for Economic Cooperation and Development
OEEC	Organization for European Economic Cooperation

PGE	Permanent Group of Experts (GATT 1994)
SCC	Supreme Court of Canada
SIMA	Special Import Measures Act (Canada)
SIMR	Special Import Measures Regulations (Canada)
USITA	United States International Trade Administration
USITC	United States International Trade Commission
USSC	United States Supreme Court

Part I

THE BACKGROUND

1

INTRODUCTION

> *In the field of trade . . . the spectacular decline in tariff rates has brought into view a variety of trade restriction measures that previously were masked. Unlike tariffs and quotas, many of the remaining barriers are complex and subtle, varying substantially from one country to the next and deeply intertwined in domestic policies and institutions. . . . Schemes to promote laggard regions . . . have taken on increased importance as subtle, yet powerful, barriers to trade. So too have measures justified on the basis of health and safety. . . . Because many of these measures were not explicitly designed to restrict foreign trade, it is difficult to determine how restrictive they may be and even more difficult to fashion appropriate remedies. The adjudication of disputes over such measures, it is becoming evident, requires a fact-finding capability and a degree of shared interest among governments not often found in global organizations.*[1]

This study is about 'subsidies': what they mean and how they are regulated. In this chapter I will argue why, in my view, a new study on this subject needed to be undertaken.

In the past few years I have been troubled by the potential severity of the difficulties Canada faces in its international trade relations. Obstacles faced by Canadian exporters are manifold and complex. On the one hand, the breakdown of trade barriers in Europe – beginning with the Euro-6, and by the end of this year potentially encompassing 18 countries and 380 million people – has forced many European industries to become more efficient and competitive, thus making international competition more difficult for Canadian industries. On the other hand, the persistent protectionist sentiments in the United States – by far the largest market for Canadian goods and services, and probably still the wealthiest single market in the world – most recently manifested in the debates over the passage of the North American Free Trade Agreement, are not likely to be checked, regardless of the Agreement's legislative successes – or, perhaps even because of the high price the Administration of President Clinton was willing to pay to secure the passage of the Agreement through Congress.

The question is how should we respond to these increasingly difficult challenges ahead? Will business and the labour force become more efficient (and suffer dislocation and adjustment costs in the short term), or will they instead rely on government protection and largesse to avoid the strains of competition? How will the choices we make as a society affect our trading partners, and how will they respond? Which responses are legitimate, and which are not? As the international economy moves toward greater integration, these questions increase in importance not just for export-dependent countries such as Canada, but for all countries whose economies will be increasingly interwoven with those of their wealthier, and more powerful, trading partners.

Among the choices open to a government in advancing its objectives, whether domestically or internationally, 'subsidies', especially domestic or non-export related subsidies, have a particular allure. This book will not attempt to question the effectiveness or the economic logic of subsidies: it suffices to say that governments perceive subsidies to be important tools of domestic economic, social and industrial policy. However, they also recognise that subsidies, even domestic subsidies, may have adverse effects on international trade flows and the world economy generally, hence the interest in regulating these practices.

In the past, domestic subsidies have been shielded by reference to 'national sovereignty' and 'domestic policy'. However, in the face of growing global economic integration and the changing economies of industrial countries, dwelling upon a blind defence of national sovereignty may distract us from the key problems of economic and trade policy: industrial subsidies will not halt or reverse the competitive disadvantage in which the industrial world finds itself *vis-à-vis* newly industrialised countries. Nevertheless, subsidies continue to be among the deadliest weapons of international trade war, and both the US and the European Union have shown their willingness to engage their considerable arsenals to advance their trading interests. Of course, neither trade superpower can tolerate a protracted subsidies war for long, but in the meantime a war of measures and countermeasures, subsidies and countervails, will reduce global welfare. It is, therefore, in everyone's best interest to impose limits on subsidies.

How are those limits to be set and who will enforce them? It is in the interest of smaller countries – the bulk of the international community – to have the limits set and enforced multilaterally, and not unilaterally. As many European countries have experienced, disarming powerful interests in international trade can be difficult, but is possible and absolutely necessary, so that comparative and competitive advantage, and not the big stick of industrial subsidies or unilateral measures such as countervailing duties, determine and expand the wealth of nations.

There is little that is novel or even exciting in these observations. Indeed, I do not propose to suggest that this study will be a theoretical groundbreaker, nor will it present *the* solution to the problem of consensus-building in the international trading arena.

The following analysis is worth studying for two reasons. First, though informed by trade theory, it is not a theoretical work; and though mindful of political considerations, it is not a manifesto or a manual. This analysis is concerned with what is practically feasible as well as theoretically sound, politically viable and economically acceptable. If pragmatism tends to be too cynical, theory can become so abstract as to lose its relevance. Part of the value of this work is its frank willingness to recognise the tensions that exist among national ambitions and objectives, and to study the routes that have been taken to diffuse these tensions, removed from theoretical prejudgement and abstract idealism.

Second, this work is focused on a narrow subject, that is, the international regulation of domestic industrial subsidies; it is, however, a comprehensive examination of a wide range of instruments devised and used by the international community to deal with the problem of subsidies. In the following chapters, I examine multilateral mechanisms such as the European Free Trade Association, supranational bodies such as the Commission of the European Union, and unilateral instruments such as countervailing duties (CVDs).

Finally, this is among the earliest attempts at understanding the results of the Uruguay Round of Multilateral Trade Negotiations and the Agreement on Subsidies and Countervailing Measures. It is hoped that by studying this Agreement in conjunction with the other instruments for the regulation of subsidies, a better understanding of the strengths and weaknesses of the Agreement may be achieved.

The study consists of seven chapters (including this introductory chapter and a conclusion) organised into three parts. Part I outlines the theoretical background of the study; it also lays down its analytical framework. This part is necessary to show what is meant by the term 'subsidy', what it is about the practice that is, or may be, problematic in international trade, what considerations exist to justify the continuation of the practice, and what broad assumptions may legitimately be made in assessing the various institutions and mechanisms discussed in Parts II and III.

Part II consists of three chapters, in which I discuss three broad approaches to the definition and regulation of industrial domestic subsidies. These I call the multilateral, supranational, and unilateral approaches. The multilateral approach is used in the GATT Subsidies Code Track II mechanism, the European Free Trade Association (before the creation of the Surveillance Authority), the EC–EFTA Free Trade Agreements, and the second European Economic Area Agreement. The Supranational approach was adopted by the Treaty of Rome Articles 92–3, and the First EEA Agreement before it was struck down by the European Court of Justice. The unilateral approach is simply the countervailing duty approach. This is in the GATT Track I provisions, or somewhat modified, in the Canada–US FTA and the proposed North American Free Trade Agreement (NAFTA). Part III consists of an analysis of the Uruguay Round Agreement on Subsidies and Countervailing Measures and a concluding chapter.

Before I began to write this book, I believed that given the political nature of the question of subsidies, disputes in this area should be resolved through political mechanisms. The concluding chapter, however, takes a different approach. I argue that precisely because of the sensitive nature of subsidies, a political dispute resolution mechanism increases the chances of a stalemate in disputes and possibly even encourages bullying by economically stronger nations. A judicial or supranational mechanism, although perhaps illusory in the present economic and political atmosphere, reduces the possibility of such bullying. At the same time, such a mechanism need not be blind to political interests; as long as these interests are incorporated into the mandate of a supranational dispute resolution mechanism, it is possible to envisage long-term international trade peace in the area of subsidies.

2

DOMESTIC INDUSTRIAL SUBSIDIES IN INTERNATIONAL TRADE THEORY

INTRODUCTION

There is a tendency among practitioners to treat theoretical analysis with a measure of derision; theoreticians tend to aim for theoretical coherence regardless of practical difficulties. The most workable balance, however, lies somewhere in between. Theory untempered by pragmatism is but shallow idealism; pragmatism unguided by theory is incoherent and short-sighted. In many ways the problem of subsidies in international trade suffers from the worst of both worlds. Much analysis is done in the abstract and in the world of pure economic theory; practical negotiations and applications of international trade rules are so politicised and are conducted with such overwhelming cynicism as to mock the very idea that a coherent philosophy underlies the exercise. It probably does not. As Cantin and Lowenfeld observe with respect to the Canada–US FTA and NAFTA,

> even reading one chapter of each agreement is enough to make one forget what the agreement was about, as one searches for clues to rules within rules, exceptions to exceptions, and bewildering cross references.[1]

The observation is equally applicable to most other trade agreements.

There is, of course, very little use decrying the cynicism of politics if the theory itself is not realistic and does not lend itself to pragmatic application. Therefore, my concern here is with the extent to which the theory of free trade, and specifically its analysis of the role of subsidies in international trade and commerce, takes note of the realities of modern economics. For too long, misguided by abstract theory and exasperated by politics, trade negotiators have groped in the dark for solutions to an increasingly complicated set of problems in trade among nations. I will try to show that traditional free trade theory is much too problematic a guide for negotiations in the area of subsidies.

Part of the problem is the lack of a universally agreed upon definition for subsidies. But the problem is deeper than that. As will be shown in the following discussion, there is little consensus among advocates of freer trade as to the precise effect of 'subsidies', however defined, on world economic and trade patterns. Nor does there seem to be a macroethical framework in which subsidies can be defined or defended (or attacked) with any degree of certitude or conceptual coherence.

The following analysis is divided into six parts. The first and second parts will discuss the classical theory of free trade and the effect of subsidies in that framework. The third and fourth part will question the relevance of the classical theory of free trade and comparative advantage to the modern world, and will refine the classical critique of subsidies and the role of government in today's international economy. The fifth part contains a brief discussion of public choice theory and its relevance in analysing the political economy of subsidies. In the final part, I will set out the analytical framework in which the subsequent comparative analysis will be conducted. The reader is forewarned that the following theoretical discussion is of necessity no more than a sketch. The scope of this work does not allow a comprehensive study of various schools of trade theory, and I will not attempt to present a new analysis in the area of trade theory or the economic or trade effects of subsidies. The point here is to devise a framework for, and provide a background to, the comparative institutional analysis that will follow.

CLASSICAL FREE TRADE THEORY

The classical theory of free trade among nations is simply the theory of market economy writ large, with one or two slight modifications. It postulates that in the absence of significant transaction costs and given international immobility of labour and capital, but full national mobility of both labour and capital, each country will specialise in the production of goods and materials in which it has an advantage (it is more efficient) relative to other countries (absolute advantage), or which are more profitable to produce than other products, even if all products can be produced more cheaply than in other countries (comparative advantage). In a free trade environment, then, the country that produces certain goods more efficiently than others will gain a comparative advantage over other countries in those goods and will allocate its resources to the production of those goods. Other products it needs it will buy from countries that have a comparative advantage in their production. As a result, each country will direct its resources to activities which yield the greatest return; world resources will thus be used by the most efficient users, and there will be an increase in national and world welfare.[2]

The classical Smith–Ricardo model was further developed by Heckscher and Ohlin. The Heckscher–Ohlin Theorem postulates that a country's trading relations with the rest of the world depend on its endowments of productive factors, usually identified as land, labour and capital.[3] This, in turn, rests on two fundamental hypotheses: 1) there are factors of production that are immobile between countries, and 2) these factors are used in different combinations to produce different goods. In their model, as in the Smith–Ricardo model, capital and labour are considered to be immobile across borders, but fairly mobile within each country. Thus, a country with abundant natural resources will have a resource based economy, while one with a large labour pool will tilt away from capital intensive industries and toward labour intensive production.[4] The theory operates on the assumption that with growing specialisation, the growth industries will become more efficient and increasingly successful, while industries in decline will give way to foreign competition and go out of business. The capital and labour thus freed from declining and inefficient industries will be attracted to the growth industries, contributing further to their growth and development. Meanwhile, consumers will benefit from cheap foreign products.

Although the Smith–Ricardo model was based on a two-country, two-product model, it seemed to work throughout the nineteenth century British-led growth in industrial capacity and economy in Western Europe. The massive social movements and political reforms of the first half of the nineteenth century were largely brought about by the change in investment patterns caused by the importation of cheap foodstuff and exportation of cotton and manufactured products that had been made possible by global free trade. This pattern continued beyond the nineteenth century. The 1906 watershed election in Britain which brought the Liberal Party back into power was partly fought over free trade; the Liberal arguments for continued importation of cheap food and certain goods, as well as a more vigorous export policy, was favoured by the British electorate.[5] This is not surprising, given the *Pax Britannica* that dominated the world economic order until the Great Depression. It was believed that utmost 'competition, unrestricted by national [protectionist] considerations alone assured the fullest effect of the principle of economy of production'.[6]

The Empire of Her Britannic Majesty has disintegrated, but the classical theory of free trade, the legacy of the Industrial Revolution and Imperialism, lives on. Even today, the classical concepts of comparative advantage, free trade, and fair competition in a market unfettered by government regulation or involvement have a great deal of persuasive power in certain circles. The US Senate, for example, argued recently that 'natural advantages possessed by one country ought not to be offset by artificial aids afforded by another'.[7] Rivers and Greenwald point out that the United States has an 'attachment to the principles of free market economics greater than that of most other countries,' even though they concede that the US Government does not always shun involvement in the market.[8] Interestingly enough the attachment is no less strong on part of the European Union, the European Free Trade Association, or any other free trade area.[9]

But free trade – freedom of the marketplace beyond the domestic market – is not just about the dismantling of visible (tariff) barriers to trade. The removal of tariffs is valuable only if 'the parties do not turn around and impose new non-tariff barriers' to trade among nations.[10] The range of available tools to impede trade (reduce imports) or artificially to enhance the attractiveness of exports is limitless. One such perceived impediment is industrial subsidies, or government *largesse* in one way or another to domestic industries. This is one method, among many, by which sectoral advantages may be artificially created, whereby efficient allocation of resources by the marketplace may be distorted.

SUBSIDIES AS TRADE BARRIERS

Industrial subsidies or state aids to industry may be broadly defined as government initiatives or programmes that have the purpose, effect, or potential of conferring a benefit on an industry, group of industries, or industrial sector.[11] Theoretically, since subsidies are defined as programmes benefiting *specific* industries, they are considered to be different from infrastructure spending, most social programmes, and almost all cultural activities.[12] It is based on this broad and somewhat out of focus definition that I conduct the following enquiry.

The question of subsidies has assumed a peculiar allure among practitioners and theoreticians of international trade. While much of the discussion centres on agricultural subsidies, industrial export and domestic, or export-enhancing and import-substituting (they are not synonymous), subsidies have also figured prominently in the debates over the proper definition and scope of limitations on state aids. Although the debate has become especially vociferous in the past two decades, it has been an issue of even longer standing in US trade politics. The difficulty seems to revolve around two sets of concerns: subsidies as economic and trade distortions, and subsidies as unfair trade practices.

Subsidies as distortive of efficient allocation of resources

According to classical free trade theory, subsidies can be expected to have two principal effects in the domestic market: they will reduce either the costs of the manufacturer with respect to a product or a product line, or the cost of a product to the consumer. In either case, more of the product will be sold or produced than an efficient marketplace would have allowed without the distortive subsidies. Thus, resources will be diverted from efficient manufacturing concerns, where they yield the highest returns *through the market*, to the subsidised industry, where they will yield an *artificially* high return. The subsidising country will be poorer, because its resources are not being used efficiently and because its other efficient producers are being taxed (thus increasing their net costs and reducing their market share of goods and investment) to pay for the subsidisation of an inefficient industry or sector.[13]

The difficulty, from an international perspective, is not the internal diseconomies and distortions of the subsidising country. At least two other concerns are at issue here. The first is that a country's subsidies 'significantly distort . . . the economies of other societies'.[14] This happens when the lower costs of subsidised products cause a misallocation of output between the foreign and domestic markets, whereby resources are diverted to less efficient producers.[15] Whether the effect of the subsidy is to substitute domestic products for imported goods or to expand exports, foreign producers could be harmed as a result of shrinking markets. Even in the case of export subsidies, where there is a net (and perverse) redistribution of wealth from the taxpayers of the exporting country to the consumers of the importing country, the resulting misallocation of productive resources in the importing country could be problematic enough to be of concern internationally.

Second, subsidies can be effective tools of protectionism; protectionism is seen as inherently harmful and distortive by the advocates of free trade. As Johns points out, the escalating use of subsidies can replace tariffs as the central distortion of international trade and commerce.[16] Just like the tariff wars of the years past, the

> adverse effect of subsidies upon worldwide economic welfare can be compounded if political forces compel governments to engage in "competitive subsidization" to match the subsidies that are granted by the governments of other trading nations.[17]

Hufbauer and Shelton Erb also argue that any reduction in world prosperity caused by 'unbridled and competing national subsidies' is chiefly the result of the protectionist nature of the practice, and not, presumably, of other possibly distortive effects.[18]

Subsidies as unfair trade practices

The fairness argument revolves around the almost Quixotic quest of the United States for a 'fair' international trading order. The essence of it is that American firms can be competitive in a 'fair' trading environment or on a 'level playing field', but cannot compete against the treasuries of foreign governments.[19] The argument is that 'US exporters have no unfair advantages . . . only disadvantages which require a bit of help to offset them'.[20]

Unfair foreign advantages take many forms, but one of the most important tools of market penetration is domestic or export subsidisation. According to Sykes

> in theory, foreign governments may use subsidies to help their industries to earn supra-competitive returns at the expense of US industries and consumers. . . . In its simplest form, the analysis supposes that foreign governments may provide the financing for predatory campaigns to monopolize US or world markets[21]

or to enhance the strategic position of their producers.[22] That these motivations do not underlie most foreign subsidy programmes targetted by American criticism (and trade remedy actions) seems to be of little consequence. Instead, American arguments for a 'fair' international trading environment exhibits an almost spiritual attachment, a sort of mystical faith, in a marketplace in which private actors are not assisted by the state, but rather thrive on the fruits of their own labour.

The moral argument against subsidies is a curious Americanism that 'is so vague, it is even hard to articulate'.[23] Hudec argues that the concept of fairness is essentially indeterminate and depends on the definition each government wishes to put on the word.[24] Of course, as with any other article of faith, this is nebulous and impossible to define clearly. Jackson suggests that the objection to subsidies in this context may have to do with the 'additional layer of risk involved in competing in a world trade environment when other than market and profit maximising considerations of foreign firms are motivating those firms' exports'.[25] It seems to me, however, that Jackson over-explains the phenomenon. The belief in a 'level playing field' goes back to what Rivers and Greenwald identified as the American attachment to the principles of a market economy. Hudec observes that the

> core content of . . . unfairness claims derives from a concept known as "fair competition". The normative assertion behind the idea of fair competition is that merit should determine business outcomes – that businesses should succeed or fail according to their respective merit as competitors.[26]

This is based on an idealised attachment, for few American businesses in this century or the last have thrived, or even survived, without some government help, ranging from tariff protection to direct or indirect financial assistance;[27] it is an ideal, and not an idea, to which America is attached, for markets do not operate in an efficiency-driven, economics-governed abstract. As Fallows puts it, the Anglo–American attachment to a 'fair' trading regime is political economy turned into 'an essentially religious question, subject to the standard drawback of any religion – the failure to understand why people outside the faith might act as they do'. Hence the reaction of the Anglo–American world to unfamiliar trading practices: countries that disagree with the Smith–Ricardo paradigm do more than disagree, they 'cheat'; they are morally culpable.[28]

The fairness argument becomes even more problematic when put in macroeconomic terms. In the first place, where there is a dispute over the adverse effects of a subsidised product, it should be noted that countries do not trade only in the product in issue. In most trade relationships there are a range of products that are traded between the partners, some of which are subsidised and some of which are not. Second, money for 'unfair' subsidies is usually not found by governments in a pot of gold at the end of a rainbow. Governments fund sectoral subsidies that give (or could give) a competitive edge to certain industries out of taxes imposed on other sectors, or even individuals, or worse, by deficit-spending. While it could be argued that the costs of subsidies are spread among a large population while the subsidies are more concentrated and thus of more immediate effect than taxes, little analysis is done to show the extent to which the competitive advantage of the taxed but not subsidised industries is affected (worsened) by a generous subsidies programme, or how the added burden of a growing national debt load adversely affects the subsidised country's terms of trade. The importing country, some of whose industries may be harmed by the subsidised imports, may in fact gain a competitive advantage in the non-subsidised sectors. As Hindley observes, the practice of trade remedy law administering agencies has been to examine only the gross amount of an alleged subsidy.[29] However, he points out,

> the relevant question about an activity is whether the total of government actions with respect to it (including the taxes it pays to finance subsidies to other activities . . .) increases the volume of output as compared with some referential state.[30]

Given the multitude of ways in which taxes affect industrial costs and competitiveness, a counterfactual model to show the balance of advantage may be difficult to construct. In this context, a fairness argument becomes meaningless in the abstract: depending on the 'referential state', an importing country may observe competitive gains in non-subsidised sectors, or a subsidised exporter may not experience an increase in its volume of production.

Third, for the most part subsidies are not simple outlays of money by governments to the private sector. Very little analysis has been undertaken to evaluate the costs (other than general taxes or costs imposed by deficit spending, such as higher interest rates and weaker currencies) governments impose on their industries that may make a subsidy necessary in the first place. While not all subsidies are created to offset government-imposed costs such as relocation to outlying regions, environmental controls, or workplace regulation, some can be seen to have precisely that objective in mind. If so, the effect of the impugned subsidy will not be to increase output, but rather to avert an artificial and government-induced drop in output. While the proper economic response to these costs may be a lowering of the regulatory burden on domestic industries, once a decision has been made to regulate, it is not immediately clear why it would be 'unfair' for a government to pay, in the form of subsidies, for the stringent requirements it chooses to impose on its industries.

As Hudec observes, 'eliminating a subsidy will produce a level playing field only when the playing field is otherwise level'.[31] But whether a level playing field actually exists is another matter. Subsidies are rarely analysed in the context of the national socio-economic structure in which they are granted. There are significant differences in the benefits and burdens which foreign competitors of US corporations enjoy or bear. Subsidies are just one part of the complex socio-economic structure of a country. Ultimately, according to Bhagwati and Hudec, arguments of fairness must extend to every difference in foreign governments' policies or institutions.[32] Unless the aim is complete harmonisation of national socio-economic objectives and policies among trading partners, this is hardly a recipe for co-operative trading relations.

CRITIQUE OF THE CLASSICAL THEORY OF FREE TRADE

Johns argues that the classical approach, which confined itself to the analysis of trade between two usually anonymous countries and two generic products, 'produced a body of theory which is at worst positively misleading and at best merely vacuous'.[33] He also criticises classical free trade theory for having a purely materialistic view of welfare as consumption of goods, and all but ignoring such intangibles as the 'quality of life'.[34] In this part, I will concern myself with an economic critique of abstract free trade theory. Three sets of arguments will be discussed. First, the existence of market failure factors such as imperfect competition and non-market allocated costs such as externalities will be examined to identify the limits of the *laissez-faire laissez-passer* theory. Second, I will discuss theories of modified comparative advantage, which have a less deterministic view of comparative advantage and allow for government management or even creation of advantage. Third, I will discuss a further refinement of comparative advantage which has been termed 'competitive advantage'.

Imperfect markets

Free trade theory is based on the operation of an unfettered international market in 'circumstances of perfect competition and internal labour mobility, within an analytical structure that is essentially static'.[35] Price and consumer demand alone are to determine the efficient allocation of resources within the market. However, this cannot adequately explain the operation of the market and the allocation of resources in practice. First, not all the costs of the allocation or use of resources are captured by the market price of those resources. Second, the differences in market conditions among nations gives rise to conflicting resource allocation bases that could distort an internationally efficient allocation of resources and thwart specialisation among nations, a basic premise of free trade theory.

Externalities

The oft-stated problem of externalities in the market place has been well argued by others and does not require a thorough exposition here. Essentially, the problem is the extent to which the actual market cost/price of a product captures the true social costs of its production. If, for example, a lake is polluted by a manufacturer and governments step in to pay for the clean-up, the manufacturer has effectively transferred the costs of the pollution from the price of the product to the taxpayers. As a result, more resources are allocated to the polluting product than would have been if all the costs of the clean-up were borne by the polluter.[36]

The problem of externalities is not restricted to pollution, of course, and may involve renewal of natural resources, education and infrastructure paid for by the public and exploited by business, and the like. Externalities can be created by different legal regimes, or be modified, or eradicated by them. For example, in the case of Research and Development (R&D) expenditure by corporate entities, spending may be reflected in the accounts of a corporation that may be unable to capture the full benefits of its investment in research because of lax intellectual property laws. Meanwhile other corporations may benefit from the results of the research without having had to do any work. In this case, the nature of the intellectual property regime can determine the extent to which the researching corporation may benefit from the results of its own research, the extent to which it can limit the positive externalities for other firms, and thus, the optimum allocation of resources to research and development in that particular economy by private actors. Therefore, the operation of a 'free market' in the abstract is not entirely helpful in determining the most efficient allocation of resources

Imperfect competition

More problematic than externalities, however, are the imperfections in competition endemic to post-industrial economies. Johns points out that in the development of free trade theory very little attention was paid to certain national economic factors and conditions and their influence in international trade relations.[37] These include increasing returns to scale,[38] the growing dependence of large corporations on global markets,[39] non-factor costs such as taxes and social security payments, risk elements, some aspects of location, agglomeration, and short-term movements in demand.

For example, one of the most important market imperfections is the problem of imperfect information. While contingency markets such as insurance or futures markets can be expected to cover the risk of information failure to some extent, it is not certain that all risks will be covered by the market regardless of their economic or social value, or that the risk premium will be at a social optimum. Innovative but highly risky enterprises, long-term investments, or other high-risk market players may not be able to take advantage of the market and the economy might suffer as a result. As the Commission of the European Union recognises, the private sector cannot be relied on to undertake or underwrite *all* socially desirable, but risky, economic activities.[40]

Malmgren notes the tendency for economists and lawyers alike to argue that market inefficiencies as well as most structural differences among national economies are usually reflected in exchange rate adjustments, thereby obviating the need for a thorough analysis of the distortive impact of these inefficiencies and differences. However, he argues, the obsession with the importance of the trade economy in determining the exchange rate is misplaced, and other factors, such as a country's capital accounts, may have as important a role in determining the exchange rate as trade factors.[41] Therefore, free trade theory is at a basic level oblivious to some economic conditions that may affect the workings of an efficient marketplace.

Recognising the limitations of an abstract theory of free trade is crucial in understanding the operation of the modern market. Barceló argues, for example, that market imperfections in some instances may cancel each other out. In these cases, a single theoretically liberalising move, such as the removal of a tax, duty, or a government programme, may in fact further distort, rather than correct, an already distorted market.[42] Free trade, comparative advantage, and efficient allocation of resources involve more than just deregulation of the market and the removal of trade barriers.

Modified comparative advantage

Recognising the existence of these market failures gives rise to an interesting modification to the theory of comparative advantage. There is a move away from viewing advantage as necessarily naturally bestowed. Instead, government programmes, large market agents, and domestic consumer demand variations are seen as important elements in the development and maintenance of the comparative advantage of a nation in the international market. This is a key modification to the classical theory and needs to be elaborated further.

Let us take three countries with similar levels of development (educational and industrial), natural endowments, distance and risk factors, political institutions and economic orientation. For historical reasons, however, each country has developed a distinct ideological attitude toward natural resources and industrial development. Country A believes in an unregulated, unfettered free market including, among other things, no regulation of trusts and cartels. Country B believes in heavy regulation of its natural resources industry, but is otherwise open to market competition. Country C pays little attention to natural resources, but has a restrictive market environment, with strict limits on the size of domestic corporations and market participation by foreign companies. The three countries agree to enter into a free trade agreement that covers manufactured as well as natural resource products.

A number of developments can be expected. Despite the absence of comparative advantage in the resource sector given unregulated markets, it is likely that B will become a net importer of resources from A and C, due to A and C's regulatory environment. Also, depending on the ability of companies in A to exploit economies of scale, C may become a net importer of resources as well. A growth in A's exports of natural resources will divert capital and labour away from other industries into the resources sector, while B and C may be expected to specialise in the manufacturing sector. However, if companies in B can grow large enough to take advantage of increasing returns to scale (which companies in C cannot do because of stringent competition laws), then C will become a net importer of certain manufactured products as well. Affected by the growth of large scale resource and manufacturing industries, companies in C may be encouraged by their government, through R&D grants, to specialise in small scale luxuries, or high-technology products. Educational programmes or tax incentives may alter the balance of advantage in favour of C in sectors other than resources or manufacturing, such as services.

There may even be other factors at work. A change in consumer demand may make looking for alternative sources or uses of raw materials feasible, thus affecting the trade advantages of A. An extraterritorial application of competition laws may make A and B's products less attractive to C. In short, it can be seen that a change in tastes, environmental or conservation laws, or the competition regime in a market economy could have serious implications in the development of the comparative advantage of nations. If this is true among countries with similar endowments, it is *a fortiori* applicable to dissimilar economies.

Comparative advantage, then, is more than just a function of natural endowments in resources and labour. By judicious and well planned investment in infrastructure and 'key' sectors of the economy, natural endowments may be enhanced and other endowments may be developed. Moreover, comparative advantage may be created or destroyed in certain sectors even without a coherent programme aimed at the alteration of the balance of resources in the economy. Other goals and objectives of a society or its cultural attitudes, habits, and values may interact positively or negatively with the existing endowments of its economy. As Porter points out, factor conditions are affected through government policies toward the capital market, education and the like. Governments can affect buyer demands through regulation; they can shape producer strategies through large scale purchases. The US defence procurement programmes throughout the 1940s, 1950s, and 1960s, for example, were instrumental in establishing US high-technology firms in leading positions in civilian markets.[43]

Competitive advantage

Porter, however, takes a more expansive view of what constitutes or shapes national 'advantage' in international trade than the theorists of modified comparative advantage. He questions the relevance of the tendency among trade theorists 'to gravitate to clean, simple explanations and to believe in them as an act of faith in the face of numerous exceptions'.[44] He argues that natural endowments, management style, or government intervention in the economy (or lack of it) do not seem to account for a nation's pattern of export.[45] What then accounts for the success of some economies and not others? An exploration of his critique may give us a sounder appreciation of the underlying rationale of freer trade in the post-industrial global economy. He suggests that nations

> succeed where country circumstances support the pursuit of the proper strategy for a particular industry or segment. . . . Many national attributes affect the ease or difficulty of pursuing a particular strategy, from the norms of behaviour that shape the way firms are managed to the availability of certain types of skilled personnel, the nature of home demand, and goals of local investors.[46]

These national attributes may be placed in three categories: classical advantages, modified advantages, and competitive advantages. The classical advantages are basic human resources (raw population numbers), physical resources and, in some instances, capital resources. But such things as the knowledge base of a nation and the level of skill of its workers (modified advantages), and its infrastructure are not factors that are inherited by a nation. Most, according to Porter, must be developed through long-term investment.[47] Thus, governments 'can improve or detract from the national advantage'.[48]

It must not be assumed that this is a modern, or even unique analysis. Continental economists have long been critical of the principal thrust of the Anglo–American *laissez-faire* world view. As early as 1837 the German economist Friedrich List argued that

> the lessons of history justify our opposition to the assertion

> that states reach economic maturity most rapidly if left to their own devices. . . . The growth of industries is a process that may take hundeds of years to complete and one should not ascribe to sheer chance what a nation has achieved through *its laws and institutions*. In England Edward III created the manufacture of woolen cloth and Elizabeth founded the mercantile marine and foreign trade. . . . Following these examples every responsible government should . . . stimulate the growth of those economic forces that a nation carries in its bosom.[49]

The third category is the one that sets Porter's analysis apart from all previous analyses and brings early theories of industrial strategy forward to the global post-industrial economy of the late twentieth century. That rests on the basic premise that firms, not nations, compete in international markets. According to Porter, in 'modern international competition, firms need not be confined to their home nation. They can compete with global strategies in which activities are located in many countries'.[50] An internationally successful firm is one that locates each aspect of its activities in the country best suited to advance those particular industrial interests. Even if the entire production line of a firm is located in one country, the firm must be able to take advantage of these state–industry synergies to be successful internationally. Porter himself gives the example of shipbuilding.

Case study: shipbuilding and competitive advantage

Shipbuilding is one of the industrial world's most troubled industries. Increasing costs, over-capacity, and increasing competition from newly industrialised countries have driven many shipyards in the West into near bankruptcy, most of which shipyards are maintained only by the infusion of massive periodic subsidies.[51] However, some shipyards are doing well and, Porter suggests, their success is, to a great extent, due to what he terms the 'influence of nation', the state–industrial synergy, that gives a competitive advantage to a firm, sector, or a nation.

Korean shipyards, for example, are cost leaders. They maintain competitiveness by building a vast array of ships at relatively low cost; they have inherited the mantle of Japan in this market and will probably pass it on to an even lower cost newly industrialised country such as Malaysia in the near future. Scandinavian shipyards (mostly Finnish) have very high labour costs, strong unions, union participation in management, high safety regulations, and high taxes (relative to Korea), which factors make competition on the basis of cost alone impossible. However, these shipyards have developed a strategy of 'focused differentiation', whereby they build high quality icebreakers and cruise ships. Japanese shipyards, which have also remained competitive, produce a wide variety of high-end, high-quality ships that are sold at premium prices. On the losing side of the spectrum, however, Spanish and British shipyards have high costs but not a differentiated product.[52]

The classical theory of comparative advantage might have some difficulty explaining the strength of the Finnish and Korean shipyards in the face of the decline of the industry in two of largest seafaring countries in the world, Britain and the US. Their success and Japan's remarkable ability to hold on to a *niche* in the market are particularly interesting because none of the successful countries has an abundance of the key raw materials for shipbuilding (iron ore and coal, for steel). It can be surmised that due to a combination of national culture, industrial factors, infrastructure, and the regulatory regime of the host country, shipbuilding 'works well' in Finland, Korea and Japan in such a way that it does not in Britain and the US. In fact, years of subsidisation and restructuring by the latter countries have not been able to revive the industry in either.

This is where 'influence of the nation' becomes important. Shipbuilding in Korea and Finland, the service industry in the US, luxury wool products in Britain, appliances and ski boots in Italy, mining tools in Sweden, and, arguably, telecommunications in Canada – each of these product lines have developed in countries where state–industry synergies have been exploited most efficiently. In some countries such as Sweden and Japan, Porter argues, industries have had the benefit of strong support from national governments, mostly as a result of a sound industrial policy. But, Porter suggests, the role of government must not be exaggerated. The growth of the service industry in the US was not entirely due to a specific government policy, while the competitiveness of certain sectors of the Italian industry developed *in spite of* misguided and wasteful government management of the economy.[53]

Analysis

As Nyerges notes, the thesis that complete economic freedom prevails in market economies is empirically and conceptually untenable.[54] Whether in capturing externalities or correcting market imperfections, creating or maintaining comparative advantage, or developing a socio-political order to foster competitive advantage, governments have an important role to play in the regulation and the direction of the market. At the very least, Nyerges points out, in many countries the government is the largest consumer of some of the most important sectors of the economy. In fact, nowhere is this more pronounced than in the US, where the 'economic strength of many big . . . companies . . . rests on government spending', principally, but not entirely, through defence expenditure.[55]

Thus, the market is not an abstract economic entity. Phelps Brown and Diaz-Alejandro argue that the market is a creature of the social conditions, political realities and vested interests of a state.[56] Whitman argues that 'the economic justification of the nation state must lie in the existence of public or collective goods . . . and of differences of national consumption preferences of such goods. . .'.[57] Governments express and manage these collective goods. Johns finds classical free trade theory problematic because it treats 'the market processes of production, distribution, consumption and exchange . . . in isolation from other motivational and socio-cultural factors'.[58] Mundheim and Ehrenraft argue that the way each country 'finances the values and structures it favours will affect production costs and profits of specific industries. . .'.[59] Governments bring together these socio-cultural factors and provide the mechanism to finance societal values. Trade among nations is more than a private transfer of commodities across boundaries; it is also a trade in moral goods and values, sociological conditions, and political systems and choices. The trade advantages of each nation are determined by a confluence of these factors and not in abstraction therefrom.

Moreover, the belief in the 'fairness' of *laissez-faire* trade necessarily rests on the principal postulate that the *ex ante* 'distribution of income and property is just and, in the international context of the post-trade situation, remains so. . .'.[60] There is no reason why this should be taken as an article of faith. Advantages in trade have been developing over many decades – indeed, centuries – and have been influenced by strategic considerations, colonisation, warfare (especially third country involuntary involvement), and other factors in international relations. A state may legitimately question the present allocation of resources and justly strive by any means, including subsidisation, to alter and enhance its comparative advantage.

A rethinking of the role of subsidies in the international economic order is therefore necessary. If markets are not perfect, and if the classical theory of comparative advantage cannot provide a sound basis for understanding the advantages of a free flow of goods in the international market, then the question of subsidies as trade barriers needs to be revisited. In the following section subsidies will be re-evaluated from a number of different perspectives. First, the role of subsidies as market correcting mechanisms will be studied. Second, I will examine the extra-economic considerations that may go into funding state aid schemes, such as distributive or political goals. Third, I will discuss what I have termed the pursuit of strategic economic objectives, or macroeconomic management through subsidies. Fourth, I will provide a case study of the long-standing dispute between the US and the EC over alleged subsidies to the Airbus consortium. That case, in my judgement, provides a clear practical example of many of the key arguments regarding industrial subsidies. Finally, in the subsequent part I will examine the literature on public choice theory, which questions the attempts to cleanse subsidies and argues that subsidies, as with other government programmes, are manifestations of 'rent-seeking' behaviour by private interest groups in the market for government *largesse*. Analysing this critique is crucial, for if accurate, public choice theory presents a serious challenge to much of the rationale for subsidies in the context of imperfect markets.

CRITICAL APPRAISAL OF SUBSIDIES IN AN IMPERFECT MARKET

A distinction must be made at the outset between general social expenditure and subsidies specific to an industry or group of industries. Specific subsidies are considered to be distortive because they are devised to redistribute and reallocate resources according to non-market criteria and thus will result, at least in theory, in an economically inefficient allocation of resources. General expenditures do not, in theory, affect the allocation of resources as among industries or sectors.[61]

Of course, it must be recognised that this distinction, however sound theoretically, is empirically problematic. Comparative advantage is 'not entirely externally determined'.[62] According to Trebilcock, many industrial countries

> owe a significant part of their international comparative advantage to social investments in health, education, law and order, basic research, and physical infrastructure,[63]

all of which are general expenditures that help industrial development and, depending on the choice of infrastructure and basic research, may determine the distribution of investment across industries. However, since most of the literature seems to have accepted this distinction as a valid one, the following analysis will be based on industry-specific subsidies.

Subsidies as market corrective mechanisms

The United States International Trade Administration said in *Carbon Steel Wire Rod from Poland* that

> we believe a subsidy . . . is definitionally any action that distorts or subverts the market process and results in a misallocation of resources encouraging inefficient production, and lessening world welfare.[64]

However, Sykes points out that

> international consensus is wholly lacking as to the proper distinction between "inefficient" or market distorting subsidy programs and other government activities. . . . Existing national laws . . . make no effort to distinguish efficient from inefficient subsidies, even by some set of controversial, unilaterally announced criteria.[65]

This is understandable. In discussing the Hungarian state-run economy in 1978, Nyerges outlines some of the problems in viewing subsidies in the abstract. In particular, for example, he points to the high rate of consumption subsidies that is funded primarily by heavy taxation of domestic industries. Some industrial subsidies in Hungary, he suggests, are simply intended to correct distortions caused by the state pricing mechanism, or to offset the effects of internal industrial taxation.[66] While market economies do not suffer from the same difficulties, it is not impossible to envisage subsidisation programmes intended to offset market-distortive costs imposed on industries due to, for example, environmental, workplace safety, or competition or regulatory objectives.[67]

Moreover, as Schwartz and Harper argue, the model under which all subsidies are seen as necessarily distortive takes no account of the existence of a public sector.[68] Every industrial activity is subject to taxation and benefits from government expenditure. To the extent that different taxation or spending objectives create distortions in the market, a government may choose to establish corrective mechanisms, including domestic subsidies. In fact, it is suggested, 'much (perhaps all) government support can be defended as being a "correction" rather than a "distortion" of the market process'.[69] These distortions may be strictly market based, such as externalities or imperfect information,[70] or extra-market considerations.

Extra-economic considerations in economic management

Hudec observes that whether the market produces a better allocation of resources is a question-begging statement. According to him, 'it produces a better allocation of resources only if one assumes that the way we want to allocate resources is according to the desires of the consumers who make up the market demand.'[71] However, in a market economy allocative and distributive decisions are made by a multitude of actors, ostensibly for economic, but probably also for political, moral, or social, reasons.[72] Which externalities we want to capture, the nature of our ideal market, which social goods we want to protect or advance, and the type of industrial economy we want to foster (low wage, unskilled, non-unionised labour v. a high wage, skilled and unionised workforce) are value choices that have to be made through the appropriate socio-political – and not necessarily economic or consumer-driven – channels. However blunt, inefficient, or ineffective, subsidies are one tool among many that the state may use to advance these goals and to distribute, or redistribute, a society's resources. In this paradigm, whether subsidies are distortive is a question of political values and not of abstract economics.

It is an uncontestable statement of fact that there are situations 'where the market mechanism alone fails to achieve a socially desirable allocation' of resources.[73] When structural poverty, unemployment, and inflation persist with all the attendant costs such as crime or social unrest, or when, as a result of economic change, there is mass movement across regions, thus creating problems for the host as well as for the home regions, 'it is not unusual for government assistance and government procurement to be undertaken without considering associated non-tariff distortive effects [in international trade]. . .'.[74] Therefore, recognising the complex national objectives that give rise to these protective programmes is 'essential to the normative evaluation of non-tariff distortions to international trade'.[75]

What must also be recognised in evaluating subsidy programmes is that economic criteria of efficient resource allocation cannot be imposed on domestic industrial or adjustment programmes, many of which are driven by quite different considerations, without adequate reflection. As Barceló points out, a government policy advancing non-economic objectives is 'inefficient'

> only if the goal is nationally undesirable or if the cost is excessive. But the existence of a subsidy *per se* cannot establish, or even suggest, either of these conclusions. Since any government can defend a domestic subsidy as a collective payment for a public good its people desire and "consume" collectively, notions of presumptive inefficiency seem untenable.[76]

If domestic allocation of resources may be governed by extra-economic considerations, it is not clear why international trade, which is in essence trade in nationally produced goods, should be viewed only from an economic perspective. If, for example, there is an injury to the US steel industry as a result of Canada's desire to protect its steel workers through subsidies, it is no different from the damage the US industry may sustain if the injury occurred as a result of an increase in the comparative advantage of the Canadian steel industry. The conceptual difference between subsidies and increasing comparative advantage is, in this context, a sterile one.[77]

As a general rule, subsidies are not aimed at a particular third country, but at political and social targets within the subsidising country.[78] Despite the abstract domestic allocative inefficiencies observed in economic models (and the consequent trade distortion), and regardless of some obvious ethical difficulties with the choice of certain subsidies,[79] third country interest in domestic programmes is problematic and lies primarily in the domestic politics of the third country. A concern for global welfare in this context, according to Hindley, is a 'shallow hypocrisy.'[80] Thus, an *erga omnes* enforcement of international, or in the case of the US, national, rules on subsidies tends to disregard the 'impact of international pluralism on the international validity of domestic concept'.[81]

Herein lies one of the thorniest problems of international trade theory. Absolute free trade 'by definition subordinates all other policy. . .' to the economic imperatives of free flow of goods across international boundaries.[82] However, whether that is domestically politically feasible or internationally desirable is another matter altogether. Pelkmans argues that given this problem, the theory of free trade may be modified to recognise this reality, for example, by treating income redistribution as non-distortive in trade matters.[83] The question then becomes why income redistribution and not other domestic objectives? Why subsidies and not other domestic economic instruments? There is no point at which a logically tenable line can be drawn to separate the feasible and desirable instruments and outcomes from unacceptable ones. Ultimately, as Trebilcock *et al.* argue, it is not clear why subsidies and other domestic programmes should not be treated as aspects of a country's comparative advantage or, as most traditional theorists would argue, disadvantage.[84]

Pursuit of strategic objectives through subsidies

This is really a subset of the previous points, but on a larger scale. Essentially, the argument is that a number of desirable *economic* outcomes may not be achieved through the market mechanism, mainly because of monopolisation by earlier entrants, high entry costs, information failure, or other market failures. These outcomes may be desirable either for economic reasons or for extra-economic considerations, such as a country's defence requirements.[85] This is more than just a question of distributive or allocative objectives; the very survival – military or economic – of a state may hinge upon the type of national investment it may carry out in this area regardless of abstract notions of market efficiency or allocative concerns. Research and Development funding, subsidies to high-technology industries, certain subsidies to high-wage industries such as steel and automobile manufacturing, and certain defence procurement practices may be grouped in this category.

For example, better accessibility to post-secondary education, especially scientific or research oriented disciplines, through government spending or better grant and loan structure for students is likely to increase interest and involvement in basic research. This, in a world highly dependent upon innovation and specialisation, is likely to help the competitive advantage of the country. Aside from being a socially desirable outcome from a democratic or egalitarian perspective, then, spending on education can be seen as a strategic instrument of economic development. As another example, a small R&D grant can, under the right circumstances, lead to the creation of an industrial empire.[86] While, as Hufbauer argues, it is not easy in these circumstances to determine the importance of government intervention,[87] a number of economic strategies may be pursued through subsidisation to enhance the competitive advantage of a nation. Aside from R&D spending, Porter mentions focused social investment, the returns on which are likely to be higher than generalised infrastructure spending, and which may in fact target a single sector or industry.[88] Such an analysis considers the strategic economic returns on social investments as being more important than the diseconomies, distortions, or inefficiencies that, in theory, may arise from subsidisation.

The economic strategy of a nation does not reside only in its pursuit of a higher national wealth measured by higher levels of output. A high standard of living may be achieved by having low output in high-wage industries. 'Industrial Policy' advocates such as Lester Thurow and Robert Reich, for example, encourage subsidies for 'high value added production', or industries that pay high wages.[89] Growth in these products will cause a shift of resources (including workers) from low-wage industries to higher-paying ones. While subsidising already high-wage industries, such as the steel or aircraft industry, may seem perverse and anti-egalitarian, the shift of resources and expansion of high-paying production will allow low-wage workers to move up and collect industrial rents, thus justifying the subsidisation programme.[90] This rests on the economic premise that in open economies, 'the marginal welfare gained per dollar of subsidy will be greater the greater is the world price of the subsidised product, which is a high-wage (value-added) product'.[91] As Porter argues, industrialised countries cannot compete with Mexico and India for low wage products, nor should they want to.[92] A strategically sound industrial policy will divert resources from these industries to more advantageous ones, and may use subsidies to achieve its objective.

Whether each and every subsidy programme that purports to achieve such an objective actually does so is debatable. Empirically, the value of 'strategic' subsidisation is, as yet, uncertain. For example, based on the above argument, governmental R&D expenditure in areas of 'strategic' importance such as electronics should be directly proportional to the subsidising countries' export performance in those sectors. However, that has not been the case. Despite being the largest R&D spender, both in absolute terms and in the government's share of total national expenditure, the US has consistently run a negative trade imbalance in high-technology goods. Ireland, on the other hand, runs a healthy trade surplus in high-tech goods despite relatively low R&D expenditure. Switzerland, where government high-tech R&D is proportionately less than one-tenth of the US figure, consistently runs a trade surplus in high- and medium-tech goods.[93] This illustrates the difficulty of making categorical statements about the value or effectiveness of strategic subsidies.[94]

Nevertheless, if one accepts that there are instances where the market may fail to achieve certain strategic goals, subsidies may be used to correct such market failures. That there may be other reasons, such as 'rent-seeking' behaviour by market players, for the subsidies or certain adverse consequences to the subsidies, is indisputable; undoubtedly, no government programme has a single aim, a single constituency, or a single consequence. The point here is to show the intellectual viability of theories that attempt to paint a different picture of subsidies than the one painted by traditional free trade arguments based on market distortions and inefficiencies caused by subsidies.

Case study: conflict and irresolution in the Airbus–Boeing war

The policy conflict between the US and the EU over industrial subsidies granted to the Airbus consortium is a good example of the theoretical conflict between the advocates of a classical theory of trade and those with a broader understanding of the elements involved in the formation of advantage in trade among nations. It is also instructive in showing how abstracted trade theory is from reality and how even the strongest advocates of classical *laissez-faire laissez-passer* rarely come to the bargaining table with clean hands.

Aircraft production is widely regarded as a 'strategic' industry.[95] It has long been a target of industrial policy in Europe and, through defence R&D expenditure and government procurement, in the US. The reasons for this are manifold and obvious: the most important are the enormous start-up costs involved in aircraft production, the unusually slow learning curve, and the difficulty of finding large enough markets to reach a profitable scale of production, all of which adversely affect the working of the market in allowing for the development of an aircraft industry in smaller markets. In fact, as Baldwin and Krugman observe, but for the presence of Airbus, 'the manufacture of wide-bodied aircraft would be essentially a Boeing monopoly'.[96]

This is where the difficulty lies. Unquestionably, without extensive government financial support in the form of equity infusions, loans, soft loans, grants, exchange rate guarantees, or regulatory support in allowing the development of the multinational consortium, Airbus would not have thrived. On the other hand, it is arguable that without the close connection between Boeing and the US Department of Defense and the concomitant secure market, R&D support, and generous depreciation tax allowances, the commercial aircraft industry in the US would not have developed to the degree it now has.[97] Even the US International Trade Commission (ITC) concedes that military contracts and government-sponsored R&D have had a positive impact, albeit indirect and incidental, on the development of the wide-bodied aircraft industry in the US.[98] According to the ITC,

> this support contributed to the development of a skilled aeronautical workforce and helped establish an extensive R&D infrastructure. Over decades, this support may have benefited the US industry by lowering costs and improving production efficiencies.[99]

If so, how can 'subsidies' to Airbus be said to have distorted the market or assisted in the development of a product that a *laissez-faire laissez-passer* market could not have sustained? Distortion of an otherwise distorted market may in fact lead to efficiencies.

Baldwin and Krugman disagree. They argue that

> if one country subsidises the entry of a monopolist into an otherwise unprofitable market, the effect will be a gain for all other countries, a possible gain for the world as a whole, and a possible gain for the subsidising country.[100]

On the other hand, they suggest that the subsidisation of a duopoly, as took place with the development of Airbus, would represent a net decrease in world welfare, even though the consumers might benefit overall. However, while this may be accurate for a narrow view of welfare, pure economic considerations may not be the best indicators of the success or failure of a government programme in achieving welfare objectives.

For example, how is one to determine the success of the US defence procurement policy? Aside from obvious cases of mismanagement, corruption, and inefficiency in the administration of defence procurement programmes, the underlying motivations of these programmes are not restricted to the US national defence. Barnes' article on the new procurement policy talks as much about helping the industrial base of the US to become more competitive as ensuring that the government gets the best value for its money.[101] It would not be inaccurate to suggest that defence procurement is an important aspect of the US industrial policy (if not the entirety of the policy itself).[102] Seen in this light, defence spending by the US government is hardly different from various EU industrial policy initiatives.

As the ITC points out and various studies of the Airbus–Boeing case have confirmed, there are clear positive technological externalities to be gained as a result of defence expenditure and, in the case of Airbus, direct subsidies to the aircraft industry: For example, Boeing 707, 757 and 747 are the civilian versions of, or use technology originally designed for, the KC-135 (as well as the 367–80),[103] the B-1 bomber, and the military cargo plane C-5A, respectively.[104] It has been argued that 'technology synergies are the most important way in which the military side of the aerospace industry has advanced the commercial side.'[105] These positive results must be considered in conjunction with employment gains, strategic competitive gains, and other non-economic gains before a complete assessment of welfare gains of a subsidy programme can be made.

Thus, it can be seen that on the one hand, subsidies in this sector may have made possible industrial development that the market itself could not have sustained. This development is important for the concerned countries from a strategic as well as a microeconomic (and perhaps even an ethical) standpoint. National programmes are also so bound up with a host of other policies and objectives, such as legitimate defence requirements, that it becomes extremely difficult to gauge accurately the success, welfare gains, or even the effects of those programmes in an abstract economic world. The difficulties inherent in this area even catch many expert observers off guard: Baldwin and Krugman imply that Boeing has not been subsidised, an assumption that Harris justifiably calls 'a bit peculiar'.[106]

THE POLITICAL ECONOMY OF SUBSIDISATION

It was noted above that in many instances, subsidies are devoted to political and social objectives within the subsidising country. It was suggested also that subsidies may be used to advance a number of economic or non-economic objectives that the market, left to itself, might not be able to achieve. Whether subsidies actually achieve their objectives, or whether they do so in the most economically efficient and ethically acceptable way, is of course debatable. It was pointed out that the classical theory of free trade views subsidies with a great deal of suspicion. Moreover, aside from the international allocative inefficiencies caused by subsidies, these government instruments are seen as inherently deleterious to a nation's competitiveness and national welfare. And, as if the direct welfare-reducing effects of subsidies were not bad enough, the international repercussions of competitive subsidisation, that is, retaliation and countervail, may offset whatever benefits that may be conferred by such government programmes. These problems may lead us to ask why, when governments are charged with protecting and enhancing the national welfare of their constituents, welfare-reducing subsidies are granted, how decisions with respect to subsidies are arrived at, and how the success or failure of these government programmes are evaluated.

A growing body of work in the area of public choice theory has advanced the argument that 'subsidies are granted and administered by a political process in which the actors, politicians and administrators are not neutral but act according to their own preferences and the constraints they face'.[107] Political actors are described as 'entrepreneurs selling policies for votes'.[108] Such 'non-neutrality' causes allocative inefficiencies and ethical problems, for example, by encouraging enterprises to engage in 'rent-seeking' behaviour[109] with all its attendant costs,[110] or by perversely reallocating tax revenues to small groups organised for the express purpose of obtaining economic rents.[111] By questioning the willingness or ability of governments to assess appropriately the needs of the polity and to devise the appropriate measures to address its needs – ranging from strategic subsidisation to correcting market failures – public choice theory offers a direct challenge to the critical appraisal of subsidies outlined in the previous section. In the following section I will attempt a brief examination of public choice theory in order to determine the strength of the challenge.

Public choice theory

The basic premise of public choice theory is that faced with a series of choices, 'the individual acting rationally will maximise personal utility and choose the highest ranking alternative'.[112] The political process, then, is simply an economic system in which 'actual political choices are determined by efforts of individuals and groups to further their own [economic] interests. . .'.[113] Individual self-interest may be translated into policies by the political process in one of two ways: either directly, though electoral mechanisms and direct appeals to voters' self-interest by politicians, or through interest groups. To use Olson's colourful metaphor, voters do not 'slice the social pie', but wrestle over the contents of a china shop.[114]

In this context, all legislation consist of wealth transfers 'from those who are least capable of resisting the demands for [such transfers to] those who are best organised for pressing their demands'.[115] Thus, the net transfer of wealth will be to large enterprises, politically strategic regions, powerful industrial organisations, trade unions, or other highly concentrated interests from small or newly established enterprises, or large and diffuse groups such as consumers or non-unionized wage-labourers.[116] Subsidies and other political instruments that are used to 'raise the welfare of more influential pressure groups' result from, and further encourage, 'rent-seeking' behaviour by market actors.[117]

'Rent-seeking' behaviour can take many forms. The most basic is lobbying, but depending on the objective, it may include investment in plants by the company seeking rents (to obtain valuable import licences or quotas), donations to political parties, the promise of jobs upon retirement to political or bureaucratic actors, or in the extreme, blackmail and bribery.[118] The prospect of such benefits accruing to political parties or government employees causes the parties or employees to engage in a similar rent-seeking behaviour: parties may include certain issues in their platforms,[119] or people might channel their investment in human capital in expectation of obtaining government jobs and the greater official and unofficial remunerations they entail.[120] The success of a group's rent-seeking behaviour will lead to 'third party distortions', that is, involvement by other groups to capture some of the available rents.[121]

'Rent-seeking' behaviour by political parties and prospective government workers is not limited to opportunistic pronouncements or investments before obtaining power. Rather, once the party does gain power and the employee is hired by government, they engage anew in a different form of 'rent-seeking' behaviour. According to public choice theory, in the war of pressure groups over the spoils of legislation, the government is not a neutral bystander. This is not to say that politicians or the political system are inherently 'corrupt'.

Rather, the exigencies of politics require such behaviour as a matter of course.

For example, whatever a politician's views and objectives, short of using force she cannot attain her policy objectives if she does not win and/or retain power. Election, or re-election, therefore, becomes the primary concern of parties or governments.[122] The result, as Trebilcock *et al.* observe, is that

> neither the effects nor intent of most government policies is to advance the common good, but rather to construct minimum winning coalitions, often through redistributional policies, even though the impact of such policies will often, perhaps mostly, be to reduce aggregate social welfare.[123]

It is in the attempt to put together a 'minimum winning coalition' that a maximum opportunity for rent-seeking behaviour develops.

It is not necessary to go through the many different models developed by public choice theorists to explain this phenomenon. Most public choice models share a few key features that tend to explain the often inefficient choices arrived at by our leaders: first, an amorphous group, the 'voters' or the 'consumers', rationally ignorant[124] or handicapped by imperfect information, unable to organise, and hampered by free-riderism, bearing small portions of each rent obtained by various interest and pressure groups; second, the interest or pressure group itself, usually highly concentrated, powerful, able to affect policy, influence or even 'buy' legislation,[125] and in the process obtain rents that are of immense value to the rent-seeker, but only marginally affect the voter or consumer;[126] and finally, a government that is a captive of these interests, or at best, has to accommodate these interests because they provide it with, among other things, campaign finances, electoral blocs, or specialised knowledge or assistance upon coming into power.[127]

The role of the government is complicated by the fact that to win or retain power (at least in single-member, first past the post, plurality electoral systems), a party need only put together a plurality of votes in a majority of seats. Strategic campaigning in this context would involve transferring benefits to marginal voters in a majority of seats (those voters who are not core supporters of any party and who may be swayed by these redistributive policies) while imposing the costs on 'infra-marginal' voters (those voters who are committed to a party and who are not likely to change their votes unless faced with extreme behaviour by the party in power).[128] Thus, agricultural interests, steel and auto workers, shipbuilders, and coal-miners receive subsidies and protection, while consumers pay through higher taxes and higher prices (monopoly or protection rents), regardless of the allocative inefficiencies and ethical inequities of such programmes.[129]

Empirical evidence

Superficially, the evidence in support of the public choice theory is compelling. If we are to accept that most redistributional and protectionist policies are inefficient and welfare reducing, given that the function of government is to enhance social welfare at the least cost to the society, the only other explanations for the course of welfare-reducing action pursued by modern governments are that they are either blind or ignorant. In either of these cases, however, costs and benefits would be more randomly distributed than seems to be the case. On the contrary, many specific redistributional programmes fit more closely in a public choice model than the random operation of governmental ignorance or stupidity. The 'public choice connections' of many of these programmes seem to be empirically verifiable.

As can be expected, permanent programmes such as certain regional, industry-specific and agricultural subsidies are usually championed by concentrated groups (regional groups in the case of farming and some industries such as coal-mining, and 'common interest' in the case of certain industries, such as auto manufacturing) that are able to overcome free-riderism and obtain large benefits from governments. Obtaining *ad hoc* programmes such as help for failing firms or R&D expenditures often requires specialised knowledge, detailed submissions and expert analyses. Since the benefits of these programmes tend to be highly concentrated, 'rent-seeking' behaviour by interested parties is usually well rewarded, which fact would justify expenditure – indeed, investment – on research, experts and lobbyists. On the other hand, the return-for-effort ratio for programmes for the general public is often infinitesimal. Moreover, the costs of subsidies are borne by widely diffuse and often ill-informed groups – tax-payers and consumers. There is little incentive to organise and, in the absence of proper funding and expertise, little chance of success in countering the lobbying of well-funded and concentrated interested groups.

Recent studies of interest group politics by political scientists support, at least to some extent, the conclusions of the economic analysis of public choice theorists. Schlozman and Tierney have concluded, for example, that interest group politics continue to be 'skewed dramatically toward narrow economic interests'.[130] Not surprisingly, producer lobbies were found to be plentiful and well-financed, whereas there were few lobbyists for consumer interests. Lobbyists were actively involved in electoral politics and engaged in 'sophisticated political strategies'.[131] While they reject the simple-minded view that politicians are in the control of interest groups,[132] Schlozman and Tierney nevertheless confirm the central role of interest groups in not only introducing or killing legislation, but also shaping its details and influencing its implementation.

The result of such behaviour can be globally devastating. According to Reynolds, growing awareness on part of the victimised public led to the development of an increasingly complex web of 'rent-seeking' programmes by governments. Removal of tariffs was compensated by the introduction of much more opaque barriers such as quotas and voluntary export restraints (VERs). Between 1966 and 1986 the proportion of exports covered by broadly defined non-tariff barriers rose from 36.4 per cent to 45 per cent in the US, from 20.8 per cent to 54.1 per cent in Europe, and from 31.4 per cent to 43.5 per cent in Japan.[133] This shows the perseverance of rent-seekers in protecting their privileged position, and the difficulty of uprooting these interests once they have taken hold in the decision-making process.

'Rent-seeking' behaviour is not restricted to interest group politics. As noted above, one of the central premises of public choice theory is that voters vote according to their economic self-interest. Some studies of voting patterns of politicians seem to bear this out. As Farber and Frickey observe, legislators from affluent neighbourhoods and those from poorer ones tend to vote differently; there is also a difference in the voting pattern of representatives from rural and urban areas.[134] Thus, in evaluating their options and making their electoral choices, voters will seek to maximise their own wealth with little regard to the greater good of society. They will expect their representatives to seek rents on their behalf, and will punish those politicians who may wish to advance policies that are beneficial to society but not specifically beneficial to the representative's constituents. Pork-barrelling, in this context, becomes a detrimental side-effect of the 'rent-seeking' and rationally self-maximising voting behaviour.

Analysis

While helpful in understanding interest group dynamics, public choice theory cannot account for many policies and programmes that *do* have characteristics of public goods, that involve transfers of wealth from the politically and economically strong to the politically and economically weak, or that are simply contradictory or overlapping. More importantly, like all other reductionist theories, public choice theory is at times simplistic and tautological. For these reasons, its predictive value is questionable. It is, therefore, doubtful whether public choice theory can fully explain why subsidies are granted, and what the real costs of subsidies are.

Trebilcock *et al.* observe that, in the area of trade, for example, public choice theory does not predict any equilibrium in the political process, 'short of a corner solution entailing infinite protection for the affected industries (a total ban on imports)'.[135] The reality, however, is that there has been a steady decrease in the level of protection in the past 50 years.[136] Public choice models simply fail to take into account the multitude of competing interests that may influence public policy, some of which interests may not necessarily be cohesive or concentrated enough to bid for or capture legislation.

Since few countries are completely self-sufficient in resources and materials, especially in the emerging global marketplace, many industries will rely on imports for inputs into their manufacturing processes. Many export industries may forego mercantilist policies in fear of retaliation from their target markets. Retailers, particularly large-scale low cost retailers such as department stores and retail chains, may not favour protection. In fact, in Canada throughout the negotiations for free trade with the United States, 'Big Business' *favoured* free trade. While this episode, particularly the aggressive marketing of the Canada–US Free Trade Agreement by business lobbies, may present an interesting case study of the power of the Big Business lobby, it is not clear what kind of economic 'rents' can be obtained by freeing up markets and imposing international limits on the regulatory capacity of domestic governments. This is not to say that Canadian businesses were anything other than business-minded in their support for free trade. Rather, the pursuit of competition over the allure of protectionist 'rents' may have been a direct result of the increasing dependence of national economies on the global market. Growth oriented industries would do better gaining competitive advantages in a market of 250 million than protectionist rents in one of only 25 million.

The contradictory forces of protection versus competition operate in the area of subsidies as well. While many firms have been relentless in pursuing 'rents' through subsidies – ranging from high-tech R&D grants to basic 'community-based' industries such as steel and coal-mining – increasingly the costs of subsidies are obtaining as much attention as their benefits. Whether this is due to the aggressive anti-subsidy stance of the US or the growing pressure of mounting debts on governments to reduce spending is not relevant at this point. Based on a pure public choice analysis we should not only see infinitely high tariffs, but where such tariffs cannot be imposed, infinitely high rates of subsidisation. In later chapters, however, we will see that at least in the past seven years, there has been a net decrease in rates of subsidisation in all the Western industrial economies.

But if public choice theory is problematic because it is unable to predict future patterns of protection or explain certain anomalies in the behaviour of ostensibly 'rent-seeking' market players,[137] its reductionist methodology makes it an impoverished paradigm in which to study and appreciate human behaviour.

In their critique of the public choice theory approach to voting, Farber and Frickey ask 'why is it so difficult to admit that people vote out of political commitment, not personal satisfaction?'[138] Indeed, why is it so difficult to admit that some proponents of subsidies – be they high-tech R&D spending or farm-support payments, or even politicians and academics – do so not because it will maximise their own benefits, but because they truly believe in the societal benefits derived from such subsidies? For, while politicians may be self-interested in seeking re-election, some do not seek re-election as an end, but as a means to achieve policy objectives such as a more equitable redistribution of wealth. Also, political activists of all stripes often pursue causes from which they do not hope to derive any immediate or substantive benefit, sometimes at great cost to themselves, be they urban anti-logging activists or elderly pro- or anti-abortion crusaders. It is not enough to answer that the *emotional* or *psychological* benefit they derive is a form of self-interest, since such a postulate can never be falsified, but would be mere tautology.

But the problem with public choice theory is deeper than this. McLean argues that the public choice model seems to 'forget about politics'.[139] Indeed, Reynolds concedes that 'public choice theorists tend to emphasize the importance of interests and downplay the impact of ideas'.[140] He views ideas as relevant only in 'generating the necessary public support or opposition for policies that are, in reality, a matter of producer exploitation of consumers'.[141] However, this is an impoverished view of the terms of debate in important questions of public policy. As well, this one-dimensional approach to public policy, that is, the argument that certain policies are 'in reality' aimed at specific 'rent-seeking' objectives without admitting the complexity of public policies and their impact on the post-industrial state, once again highlights the reductionism and intellectual paucity of most public choice models.

This is not to argue that ideas or ideology or the public interest are the only influences on policy-making. McLean agrees with public choice theorists that voters and lobby groups often pull in different directions, but he argues that 'we should not have any predetermined ideas about which pull is stronger'.[142] Farber and Frickey argue that public choice theory fails to explain how voters and interest groups interact.[143] When a piece of legislation or regulation is passed, it is often difficult to determine its beneficiaries in the long run. Even where legislation can be shown clearly to benefit an interest, it is not logically possible to draw the inference that it was the support of the interest in question, and not other factors, that led to the passage of the legislation. Other factors such as ideology could equally as convincingly explain the reasons for the legislative success of certain policies.[144] Indeed, they note the empirical evidence that supports the conclusion that ideology is a better factor for predicting the voting behaviour of legislators and voters than economic interests,[145] that sometimes legislators do advance policies that benefit the public interest,[146] and that where the position of powerful interest groups such as the business lobby is at variance with the interests of the voters, it can be expected that politicians will be influenced by what they perceive to be the will of the voters more than by powerful and concentrated interests.[147]

Empirical evidence is inconclusive, but Farber and Frickey's normative critique is particularly helpful in understanding the weaknesses of public choice theory. Many of the models developed by the opponents of 'rent-seeking' behaviour purport to be 'positive theories', aiming to explain and predict decision-making in the public domain. However, aside from the empirical difficulties already discussed, there are serious *normative* problems in the propositions advanced by public choice theorists. Reference was made earlier to Hudec's observation that eliminating subsidies will create a level playing field only if the playing field was level to begin with.[148] Applying a similar principle to public choice theory's condemnation of 'rent-seeking' as unjustifiable on a cost-benefit analysis, Farber and Frickey observe that 'cost benefit analysis . . . cannot be applied until a prior decision is made about how to distribute social entitlements'.[149] Depending on the prior allocation of resources, any number of 'efficient' results are possible, none of which are normatively superior to the others.[150] Therefore, to determine whether a group engages in 'rent-seeking' behaviour and whether that behaviour is undesirable, factors other than mere economic cost-benefit analysis must be examined.

Public choice theory is an interesting and useful tool in dissecting and analysing how decisions in the public domain, including the decision to grant subsidies, are made. As well, it poses pertinent and penetrating questions as to the validity of the extra-economic and strategic justifications for subsidies. Nevertheless, the theory's less than rigorous exploration and understanding of the influence of politics, its ideology and its mechanics, and its inability to predict policy outcomes given a set of political and economic variables render it less than optimal as a positive theory of governmental and legislative decision-making. At best, it can stand for the proposition that *some* politicians and *some* voters do not seek to advance the public good, *some* pressure groups have a disproportionate amount of influence on governmental decision-making, *some* interest groups actively seek to channel public policy to their own benefit regardless of obvious and predictable detriments to the public interest, *some* of these detriments are empirically verifiable and normatively unjustifiable, and finally, *some* subsidies that arise pursuant to *some* of these 'rent-seeking' activities *may* have deleterious consequences for the public good. This may seem inordinately tentative, but public choice theory is not capable of greater certitude.

EVALUATION: PRINCIPLE OR CHAOS?

> *"If everyone minded their own business", the Duchess said, in a hoarse growl, "the world would go round a deal faster than it does".*[151]

The role and shape of subsidies in international trade is more complex than classical free trade theory allows; this proposition forms one of the basic analytical premises of this work. At least two principal difficulties in theoretical analysis inform the institutional analysis that will follow.

Subsidies do not do what they are presumed to do

It can be surmised from the above discussion that at least practically speaking, no *ex ante* condemnation of subsidies is logically sound and methodologically acceptable. There are at least two reasons for this. First, at a macroeconomic level, subsidies result from the domestic interaction of a complex web of socio-political decision-making practices, economic management, national and international market forces, and natural endowments. In a two country, two product model with fixed transaction costs, labour and capital immobility, and other conventional assumptions of economists, it might be easy to prove the distortive effects of subsidies, or economically gratuitous (assuming no real extra-economic objectives) transfers of money from the government to specific industries or sectors. However, this model is at best sterile. A model that could take into account all the factors mentioned above, on the other hand, must construct a hypothetical scenario based on cultural and political, as well as economic, indicia that would be so riddled with speculative assumptions, predictions and projections as to be no less problematic than simple economic models.

Second, at a microeconomic level, subsidies can be said to be economically distortive or harmful to competition only if producers behave in a manner consistent with economists' presumptions. It would not be a novel observation to say that few business decisions, large or small, are made by entirely rational and economically-motivated market actors. Hunches, intuitive responses, self-interest, megalomania, hubris, ambition, rivalry and many other 'irrational' factors affect the development of economically sound decisions to varying degrees. Moreover, as Trebilcock *et al.* observe, 'the behaviour of firms [is often] motivated by complex interests that do not necessarily point to a pro-protectionist rent-seeking outcome'.[152] Thus, even if a strictly 'economic' macro-model of subsidies were acceptable, the distortive effects of subsidies can only be gauged against a counterfactual that will try to construct the minds of industrial managers, boards of directors, labour unions and other participants without subsidies, or given higher or lower levels of subsidisation. Such an analysis would be fraught with inaccuracies.

These two problems, of course, assume a static concept of comparative advantage. The introduction of other economic factors would further complicate the analysis and make the counterfactual far too nuanced to be of any practical or theoretical use. If, for example, comparative advantage in modern industrial economies can be engendered, where does advantage end and distortion begin? If competitive advantage, as Porter suggests, is determined by non-economic as well as economic patterns in a state, by what criteria can the international trade distortion effects of non-economic factors in economic decision-making be judged?

Subsidies do not mean what they are taken to mean

> *"When I use a word", Humpty Dumpty said, in rather a scornful tone, "it means just what I choose it to mean – neither more nor less".*
>
> *"The question is", said Alice, "whether you can make words mean so many different things."*
>
> *"The question is", said Humpty Dumpty, "which is to be master – that is all".*[153]

Further complications arise when we consider that no single comprehensive definition exists for the practice of subsidies. While the definition with which I began this chapter is workable for theoretical analysis, it begs the question of what exactly is a government benefit to a firm or an industry. The number of ways industries may be helped by their government is, without exaggeration, infinite. Accordingly, the number of government programmes that can be characterised as subsidies does not seem to have any limits.

To close the argument it may be helpful to draw a rough sketch of the extent to which the term 'subsidy' can be stretched; all of the following programmes may be, or have been, considered a subsidy under current international rules. Governments may provide tied aid grants to third world countries, thus indirectly benefiting their own industries.[154] There may be border tax adjustments, for imports and exports, that may simulate exchange rate adjustments[155] or, like the Brazilian IPI tax exemptions on imported industrial machinery for export industries, subsidise domestic producers.[156] Lax environmental or social security regulations, or exemptions may be considered subsidies, however difficult the determination of the rate of subsidisation may be.[157] A public education programme aimed at producing highly skilled workers may be considered a subsidy if offered through specified private enterprises, but not a subsidy if through traditional channels, however similar the results.[158] The regulatory environment for banks and other financial institutions may determine the type of loan or equity structures industries pursue or can obtain, and the types of industries or sectors in which this can be done. As Malmgren has observed, if banks can make loans on lenient terms to weak firms, and are in turn watched over leniently by central banks, 'then where can it be said that commercial lending ends and public subsidy begins?'.[159] Targeted social programmes, regional development programmes, government land ownership, state ownership of industry,[160] and many other variables contribute considerably to the confusion surrounding exactly what is a subsidy, that is, a non-market involvement in the market, and what is not, and what sort of non-market involvements can be justified. Even restraints on the export of natural resources may be seen as subsidies.[161]

This is only a brief outline of a much larger problem. I mention it here and in passing only to alert the reader that, as the cliché goes, things are not always what they seem. To paraphrase another cliché, one country's subsidy is another country's most fundamental social programme. According to Malmgren, when government programmes are seen to affect the market

> it is difficult to distinguish between what is due to direct [government] intervention [in the market], what is due to the "co-operative spirit" [in Japan, for example] between government and business and what is due to the stability of expectation in the private sector

that has been made possible and maintained by a variety of institutions and laws.[162] In short, determining exactly what sort of practices can be lumped into the opprobrious term 'subsidy' is a value-laden task. Issues of socio-political choice, political and cultural institutions, and economic management, among others, play themselves out in sorting out a problem that is chiefly one of morals and politics and not of economics.

To critique classical free trade and its single-minded reliance on the supremacy of the market is not to capitulate to the nihilism of the so-called pragmatists. Rather, the analysis in this part merely highlights the illogic of taking a strictly classical economic line in discussing domestic industrial subsidies. This is important in understanding the reasons for the success of some of the regulatory institutions that will be examined in the following chapters.

Part II

INTERNATIONAL INSTITUTIONS FOR THE REGULATION OF SUBSIDIES

INTRODUCTION

Despite the theoretical difficulty of defining 'subsidies' and determining their effects, it has been generally accepted that an unconstrained use of subsidies tends to be harmful to the economic interests of trading nations – if harm is defined broadly in the narrow context of nations' economic interests. For example, the first reaction to foreign government subsidies was in the late nineteenth century by the US, when countervailing duties were imposed on Russian imports. However, the Russians had subsidised their sugar to offset the distortive effects of American tariffs on sugar imports. So it is not clear whose economic interests were harmed, in what way, and what the harmful effects of subsidies were in that context.[1]

The US concern with subsidisation, which by the time of the Great Depression was being characterised as an 'unfair' trade practice, found its way into the negotiations that led to the General Agreement on Tariffs and Trade (GATT) (Articles VI and XVI). However, the GATT did not provide enough protection against either subsidies or the imposition of countervailing duties. The Subsidies Code,[2] signed in 1979 at the end of the Tokyo Round of trade negotiations, was intended to provide guidelines for the granting of subsidies and the imposition of countervailing duties. It was not successful. The US concern with subsidies has not subsided and its enthusiasm to regulate other countries' domestic economic practices has not been checked. In fact, other countries have moved to enact countervailing duty laws to benefit from the permissiveness of the Subsidies Code, and the international debate on the scope of subsidies continues to poison trade relations among nations.

By no means can it be asserted that, at least since the inception of the GATT, subsidies have been solely a US concern. The treaties establishing the European Coal and Steel Community (ECSC), the

European Economic Community (the Treaty of Rome; the ECSC, the EEC and Euratom now form the European Union (EU)), and the European Free Trade Association (EFTA, the Stockholm Convention), all concluded in the 1950s, had mechanisms to deal with state aid to industry. The problem received brief attention in the EC–EFTA Free Trade Agreements (FTAs),[3] concluded in the early 1970s in the first major realignment of European trade relations since the Stockholm Convention. More recently, lack of agreement in the area of subsidies almost caused the breakdown of negotiations for a Canada–US FTA; the Uruguay Round of Multilateral Trade Negotiations (MTNs) nearly unravelled over the issue of agricultural subsidies.

Each of these trade instruments has taken a distinctive approach to the concern about curbing the deleterious effects of subsidies (and, by extension, countervailing duties). The institutional solutions in each case reflect a number of factors, of which the actual problem of subsidisation is not an important one. More important is the extent of economic, social, and political integration and harmonisation that the parties expect from the agreement, or are willing to accept as an outcome. In this context, international institutions concerned with the definition and regulation of subsidies can be placed into three groups: multilateral, supranational, and unilateral mechanisms. Multilateral institutions, such as the GATT and EFTA, rely on consensus among Contracting Parties (which normally means unanimous voting in Councils or Committees), negotiation and political solutions, voluntary adherence to rules, and international diplomatic institutions for regulating the behaviour of the parties. Supranational institutions are more constraining of the parties' sovereignty, and may impose rules and regulations on the parties through majority voting, or by bureaucratic or judicial institutions (such as the EU Commission). Unilateral approaches rely chiefly on national laws for definitions and regulations, and unilateral instruments such as countervailing duties to correct market distortive behaviour by parties' trade partners.

Each of these instruments has had to grapple with the paradox inherent in theories of subsidies, as set out in the previous chapter. The paradox is this: subsidies, however defined, are important tools for the achievement of certain economic, social, cultural, and political objectives. On the other hand, international conflicts over economic and social values, and competition for scarce resources and limited markets have meant that the operation of subsidies in the modern economy could be very harmful to the subsidising countries' trading partners, or even third countries.[4] Some theories have relied primarily on the socio-political role of subsidies to justify a more relaxed regulatory environment and fewer constraints on the 'sovereign' power of economic and social management through subsidisation. Others emphasise the harmful effects of subsidies or their potential for harm in order to justify a more structural approach to curbing the harmful effects of subsidies. Yet others have tried a more balanced approach, weighing the political and social advantages of subsidies against their trade effects before passing judgement on the acceptability of specific practices. The paradox of subsidies will be a recurrent theme in the following institutional analysis and will form a central foundation for the analysis of the Uruguay Round proposals.

A note to the reader: In this study, only a selected group of institutions will be examined; these govern and regulate well over three-quarters of the total volume of international trade. The approach is admittedly Eurocentric, but this is so for obvious methodological reasons. There is no doubt that the development of the European Union from a limited common market in steel and coal into the largest common market in the world bears closer scrutiny than more recent trade agreements that have been modelled, often unsuccessfully, after the EU. The European Economic Area, which is expected to come into existence at the end of this year, will expand the boundaries of the common market to encompass 18 countries, 15 languages (not counting regional dialects and linguistic minorities), and a population of nearly 380 million; the European Union itself is the most ambitious voluntary nation-building exercise since American independence, if not in history. Not only is there more material to study in Europe, but the progress of the Union and the development of institutions in the EEA provide almost daily intellectual nourishment for the interested scholar.

3

MULTILATERAL REGULATION OF SUBSIDIES

INTRODUCTION

A multilateral or bilateral mechanism is usually based upon a council, commission or a committee that is composed of the political representatives of the contracting parties in which the trade disputes of the parties are to be resolved through negotiation, consensus and compromise. The principal political body may be assisted in its task by a secretariat or a panel of experts, but the panel or the secretariat does not have binding decision-making powers. The parties may approve the decisions of the panels or the secretariat, but the onus is on each party to carry out the accepted decisions of the political body. If the decisions are not carried out, certain measures may be sanctioned by the political body and imposed by the other parties to the agreement.

The multilateral institution is based on the classical model of relations among nations in the international arena. It protects (however nominally, as will be seen) the sovereignty of the parties, while providing a formal mechanism through which influence and power can be exercised to impose discipline on practices in dispute and to bring the disputants to an agreement. Although often operating within a specified paradigm and concrete rules, the political dispute–resolution framework is based on bargaining among interested parties, thus allowing parties to determine for themselves the extent to which they will barter trade advantages with constraints on their sovereign actions.

GATT TRACK II[5]

The GATT embodies the largest, and the first, multilateral international trade dispute resolution institution. Much has already been written about the GATT, its history, its successes, and its failures; I do not propose to revisit well-trodden ground. Rather, my purpose in discussing the GATT is to provide a background for the analysis of other multilateral and unilateral instruments that will follow. This part is, therefore, an overview and by no means can it serve as a guide to the GATT dispute settlement mechanism for subsidies.

I will discuss the GATT subsidies mechanism in two parts. The first part is concerned with what is known as the GATT Track II dispute resolution mechanism. I categorise it as a 'multilateral' instrument, and I hope that in the course of my analysis the reasons for this characterisation will become apparent. The GATT Track I dispute resolution mechanism (DRM) will be discussed in a separate part, *infra*. First, however, I propose to set out the conceptual and regulatory framework of the GATT discipline on subsidies.

Conceptual and regulatory framework

The principal GATT document on subsidies, the result of the Tokyo Round of Multilateral Trade Negotiations, is the Subsidies Code. The Code begins by setting out the paradox of subsidies in its preamble. The Signatories recognise that 'subsidies are used by governments to promote important objectives of national policy'.[6] They also recognise that 'subsidies may have harmful effects on trade and production'.[7] The solution that the Code purports to provide for this paradox is no less enigmatic. It suggests that the 'emphasis of this Agreement should be on the effects of subsidies and that these effects are to be assessed in giving due account to the internal economic situation of the signatories'.[8]

Article 8 contains the general provisions of the Code on the topic of subsidies. It too restates the paradox, but goes on to say that the signatories 'shall seek to avoid causing, through the use of any subsidy', injury to the domestic industries, nullification of benefits, or prejudice to the interests of other signatories.[9] Article 11.1 reiterates the importance of subsidies as instruments of social and economic policy, and states that the signatories 'do not intend to restrict the right of [other] signatories to use' subsidies for the advancement of such policy objectives.[10] It goes on to list a number of 'desirable' objectives that, although inexhaustive, exclude internal wealth redistribution programmes. The parties are nevertheless obligated by article 11.2 to 'weigh, as far as practicable . . . possible adverse effects on trade' of proposed subsidy programmes.[11] This is probably as tentative an obligation as one can imagine in an agreement.

The difficulty with this approach is the lack of a serious substantive discipline on the provision of subsidies.[12] At no point are domestic 'subsidies' defined or identified.[13] Moreover, as will be seen, nothing in the institutional make-up of the GATT allows it to develop new definitions or interpretations for certain key terms such as a subsidy. As a result, according to Völker, the Code did not help reduce the number or scope of disputes involving subsidies and 'hardly contributed to a more workable definition of legitimate and actionable subsidies, except for the annex giving an exemplary list of *export* subsidies'.[14]

Institutional framework

The GATT Subsidies Code has two tracks of disciplinary institutions. The first, contained in Article 4, relies primarily on the unilateral use of countervailing duties to discourage member states from subsidisation. The other track is based on the GATT's general dispute resolution mechanism and relies chiefly on multilateral negotiations to resolve matters in dispute; in the case of failure or breakdown in the negotiations, the GATT permits imposition of sanctions or suspension of benefits by the complaining party(ies). The GATT Track II DRM has four components: notification, consultation, conciliation, and dispute settlement.

Notification

Article XVI of the General Agreement provides that

> if any contracting party grants or maintains any subsidy, . . . it shall notify the Contracting Parties in writing of the extent and nature of the subsidization, of the estimated effect of the subsidization on the quantity of the affected product or products imported into or exported from its territory and of the circumstances making the subsidization necessary.[15]

Few countries have voluntarily disclosed the nature and the economic impacts of their subsidy programmes.

Article 7 of the Subsidies Code imposes further notification obligations on the signatories. It requires the signatories to the Code to provide, on the written request of any signatory, 'information on the nature and extent of any subsidy granted or maintained . . .'.[16] If the information is not provided, the matter may be referred to the Committee on Subsidies and Countervailing Measures of the GATT. The Committee is formed under Article 16 of the Subsidies Code. Its membership consists of representatives from state signatories. The responsibilities of the Committee are set out throughout the Code and include involvement in the consultation, conciliation and dispute settlement procedures of the Subsidies Code.

Consultation

Article 12.3 states that if a signatory believes that its interests under the GATT are being injured by the subsidy practices of another signatory, it may request consultations with that signatory. The signatory against which a complaint has been registered is required to enter into consultations with the complaining party as quickly as possible. According to the Code, the 'purpose of the consultations shall be to clarify the facts of the situation and to arrive at a mutually acceptable solution'. If, according to Article 13.2, consultations are not successful, then the matter may be referred to the Committee 'for conciliation in accordance with the provisions of Part IV'.

Conciliation

The attempt here is to involve the 'good offices' of the Committee in bringing the parties to a dispute to an agreement. The onus, under Article 17, is still on the parties to arrive at a solution to their problem, and the task of the Committee will simply be to 'encourage' the parties in this respect. The signatories are obliged[17] to make their best effort to reach a 'mutually satisfactory' conclusion to their dispute. Not surprisingly, though, the signatories often fail to carry out even this basic 'good will' obligation. As a result, the Code contains a DRM to operate in case of the parties' failure to come to agreement on a solution.

Dispute settlement

The GATT Track II DRM is composed of two bodies: the Committee and an expert panel. Panels are established by the Committee when parties to a dispute are unable to resolve their dispute through conciliation. The members are appointed from among experts who are not citizens of the disputant countries. Unlike Committee members, they 'would serve in their individual capacities and not as government representatives, nor as representatives of any organization'. Therefore, they 'should be selected with a view to ensuring the independence of [the panels'] members, a sufficiently diverse background and a wide spectrum of experience'.[18]

The report prepared by the panel is submitted to the Committee, which 'shall consider the report' and make recommendations to the parties. If the recommendations of the Committee are not followed, the Committee may 'authorize appropriate countermeasures . . .'.[19] This is similar to the operation of the main GATT dispute settlement mechanism under Article XXIII of the General Agreement. Like the GATT Council, the Committee is a political body and serves a dual function as adjudicator and mediator. Also, since traditionally the Council has adopted its decisions by consensus,[20] the Committee has not so far followed a majoritarian rule, even though nothing in the Code precludes it from doing so. Therefore, the party against which a complaint has been lodged may in fact block the adoption of the recommendations of the expert Panel, thereby frustrating the entire dispute settlement process.

Evaluation

The GATT Subsidies Code Track II dispute resolution mechanism is, for lack of a better word, a non-system. There are two reasons for this assessment. First, the regulatory framework of the GATT Subsidies Code lacks substance. Not only is there no definition of 'subsidy' in the Code, but the expert Panels have also failed to provide any guidance as to what may be considered a subsidy. This is *ipso facto* a serious weakness and does not require further elaboration.

Second, the institutions of the Code are devoid of any coherence of purpose. Simply put, it is not clear whether the GATT Subsidies Code DRM, or even the Article XXIII procedure, is an adjudicative system or one based on negotiation. This is more than a philosophical question and lies at the very core of the difficulties of the Subsidies Code. It is also responsible for the failure of the GATT to arrive at a satisfactory definition for 'subsidy'.

The main protagonists in the argument over the nature of the GATT DRM are the EU and the US. Not surprisingly, the US takes the view – supported by most developing and smaller countries – that 'panel decisions are adjudicative interpretations of GATT terms which, upon adoption by the Contracting Parties [or the Committee, as the case may be], are binding on all Contracting Parties'.[21] This approach is particularly attractive to smaller countries, for the perception is that given the extreme asymmetry in power among nations, an adjudicative model protects the weak better than one based on raw bargaining power. Multilateral trade negotiations are often dominated by trade superpowers, and the interests of smaller countries are always in danger of being overwhelmed (or are in fact being overwhelmed) by the interests of the strong. An adjudicative model, however, does have its drawbacks.

The most active GATT litigant is the US. However, whether this is motivated by a real intellectual commitment to an adjudicative structure (unbound, incidentally, by any coherent definition) is questionable. Hudec, for example, is sceptical about the US's legalistic approach. He observes that the

> timing of US lawsuits is quite closely related to events in Congress, with a majority of the lawsuits occurring either just before the Congress was to vote on new trade legislation, or seemingly in response to demands made by Congress when passing such legislation.[22]

GATT complaints, or as Hudec calls them, 'lawsuits', buy time for the US government. By bringing lawsuits before the GATT, however meritless they may be, the US government can avoid for a time domestic pressures to adopt protectionist measures against its foreign trading partners.[23] Thus, it seems, the US favours an adjudicative system to satisfy certain 'domestic imperatives'.[24]

The EU has taken a different approach. It argues that 'the GATT is an institution dedicated to the negotiation of trade issues among countries', and that disputes should be resolved by 'diplomacy and negotiation'.[25] The EU argues that lawsuits could not 'solve the economic and social problems at the root of most trade problems'.[26] Moreover, the EU is concerned about the fact that panels may 'in effect make law by establishing precedents'.[27] This is particularly troubling given the lack of a detailed or agreed upon definition for most of the prohibited practices.

The institutional framework of the Subsidies Code Track II mechanism supports the EU position. There is strong emphasis throughout on consultation and conciliation. The primary task of the Committee is to find common ground between the parties and not to adjudicate. As Hudec observes, the GATT legal structure does not rest on 'conventional ideas of legal obligations *per se*, but on a root concept of mutual and reciprocal "benefits". . .'.[28] Indeed, Trebilcock argues that

> Track II of the Code sets in place the bargaining framework where, as with tariffs, Pareto-superior deals can be struck between states to moderate subsidy practices in return, if necessary, for offsetting trade concessions.[29]

This is patently at odds with an adjudicative model.

Thus, the fundamental divergence in approach between the two largest trading entities in the world, as well as the system's inherent institutional weaknesses, have marginalised the Subsidies Code Track II as an abused and ineffective international regime for the regulation of subsidies. On the one hand, the US files meritless lawsuits for domestic purposes, while the EU files its own lawsuits against the US to teach it 'legal humility'.[30] On the other hand, even if the system were not abused and were conceptually coherent, it is institutionally not given to producing results. First, intransigent disputant countries involved in politically sensitive disputes may be unable or unwilling to settle their differences through negotiations or mediation. Second, according to Hudec, the parties to a GATT dispute not only pack the jury in the Committee, but they can hang the judge by vetoing the adoption of a panel's recommendations. The result is that, according to Völker,

> the consultation mechanisms set up under the Agreement hardly have a conciliatory role; it is rather considered an act of trade war to open negotiations within the GATT framework.[31]

The vehement response of the European Union to an American request for consultation concerning the Boeing dispute (see above) is just one example of the failure of the GATT system to deal properly with the problem of subsidies.

EUROPEAN FREE TRADE ASSOCIATION

The European Free Trade Association (EFTA) was at its inception, and in many ways continues to be, a reaction against the EU. The historical roots of both the EU and EFTA can be found in the Organization for European Economic Co-operation (OEEC; also a forerunner of the Organization for Economic Co-operation and Development, OECD), which had the task of managing and distributing Marshall Aid to war-torn Europe. After the formation of the European Coal and Steel Community (ECSC) by six major European coal producers (the Benelux countries, Italy, France and Germany), the OEEC established a working party to explore the ways in which the ECSC customs union and other European countries could associate. Formal negotiations began in 1957 and three more working parties were struck. However, the negotiations broke down a year later when Jacques Soustelle, the French Minister of Information, argued for a common external tariff and harmonisation in the economic and social spheres in the proposed Common Market.[32]

Britain, Switzerland and the Nordic countries were not prepared for a common market with the ECSC six, who formed the EEC by the Treaty of Rome. They felt that 'a meaningful level of economic integration could be achieved . . . without much harmonization, and without loss of sovereignty or identity'.[33] Following a number of meetings hosted by the Swiss and the Norwegians, the Convention establishing the European Free Trade Association was signed in Stockholm and came into force on 3 May 1960 (the Stockholm Convention).[34]

The state aid provisions of the Stockholm Convention are contained in the competition section of the Convention, specifically in Article 13. There have been two interpretations of Article 13 by the EFTA Council: in 1968 and 1988. To some extent, in formulating its interpretations the EFTA Council seemed to be responding to developments in the EU; however, the first EFTA survey on state aids came a few years before the EU could compile a comprehensive survey of its own. The EFTA Council and the secretariat have promised more action in this front and may in fact have to move faster than anticipated if the proposed European Economic Area (EEA) comes into being. In the following section, I will review institutional developments in EFTA and its responses to the problem of subsidies in Member States. But first, it is necessary to set out the conceptual considerations that underlie the development of EFTA's responses to subsidies.

Conceptual framework

An early EFTA Council interpretation based the Convention's prohibition on subsidies on classical free trade theory grounds. According to the Council Agreement of 3 July 1968,

> the aim of the rules contained in Article 13 is to ensure that government aids do not constitute barriers to trade or promote unfair conditions of competition between Member States.[35]

In subsequent paragraphs, however, the Council admitted that aids compatible with Article 13 are 'legitimate instruments of economic policy' and that the purpose of Article 13 was not to 'inhibit the freedom of Member States to introduce government aid measures as elements in the internal economic policy'.[36] This paradox is, as mentioned above, inherent in any discussion of subsidies. While EFTA was not set up to co-ordinate social and economic policies of its Members,[37] the Member States recognised in Article 30 of the Convention that 'the economic and financial policies of each of them affect the economies of other Member States'.[38] Thus, it was deemed necessary for the EFTA Council to reiterate its belief in the distortive nature of subsidies, while accepting their legitimacy in limited circumstances.

Nearly fifteen years passed before the issue was revisited. In 1982, the Finnish Foreign Minister stated that 'liberalized trade, especially free trade, must be based on the premise that all those taking part in it play by the rules.'[39] He recognised the tension between the classical free trade theory and social, political, and environmental demands on modern governments. But, he argued, subsidies that are aimed at protecting uncompetitive industries are not consonant with EFTA's requirement for 'fair and equal conditions of competition'.[40]

In December, 1984 a Working Party of the Economic Committee of EFTA was set up to examine the extent of subsidisation in the EFTA countries and to submit a report to EFTA. It is significant that the issue was raised following the economic turmoil of the 1970s and the early 1980s, for the Working Party seemed more willing than Rekola to accept arguments in favour of subsidies. It found, for example, that government support in the form of subsidies for environmental protection or for research and development may be economically justified. Nevertheless, the Working Party did not go beyond economic analysis and finally came to the conclusion that despite the possibility of positive results, 'many aids may have distortive effects on domestic economic efficiency and on international trade flows'.[41] Completion of an internal market, the Working Party concluded, required a rigorous state aid policy.[42]

Fairness and free market are the catch phrases of the EFTA; the EFTA position tends to reflect the Smith–Ricardo model at times.

However, there is an attempt to refine the classical model by introducing a small twist, 'competitive health'. Rekola,[43] Pono[44] and Lanner[45] stressed the dangers of subsidies that are aimed at maintaining or tend to maintain uncompetitive industries. Lanner observed, however, that some subsidies programmes have a completely different objective: they may aim at reducing industrial capacity, or restructuring employment in a sector.[46] As Trebilcock, Howse and Chandler have also recognised, such industrial adjustment programmes may be justified economically in the context of a *laissez-passer* market.[47]

Thus, unlike the approach of the ITA,[48] there is no *ex ante* and blanket condemnation of subsidies as distortive or unfair. The tentative approach of the Working Party to the distortive effects of subsidies indicates a conceptually open mind. EFTA's emphasis on the competitive health of its industries not only necessitates a contextual and analytical approach to state aids, but indicates the need to persuade countries of the detriments of subsidies to their own economies before multilateral consequences of state aids are discussed. Consequently, national state aid programmes will go through a more comprehensive and in-depth analysis by the Secretariat and the Council than under a conceptually inflexible system.[49]

Regulatory framework

Article 13 of the Stockholm Convention prohibits export subsidies and other forms of aid

> the purpose or effect of which is to frustrate the benefits expected from the removal or absence of duties and quantitative restrictions on trade between Member States.[50]

The prohibited export subsidies are set out in Annex C of the Convention and may be revised from time to time, but 'other forms of aid' have not been defined in the Convention, neither has, in fact, the requirement 'frustration of benefits expected'. The 1968 and 1988 interpretations intended not only to make the institutions of the subsidies regime more effective, but to give some substance to the terms of the Convention.

'Other forms of aid'

The 1968 Council meeting agreed that four types of government aid would be covered by Article 13: grants, loans, guarantees and equity.

According to the Working Party, the amount of government aid is calculated on the basis of the net cost principle, that is, the amount of the subsidy in each instance is the cost to the government of providing the aid.[51] For example, the net costs of loans and equity are calculated as the amounts of subsidised interest or foregone dividends.[52]

Perhaps as important as what forms of aid are covered are the forms of aid that are not covered by the Convention. Aids generally available to research and technological development are deemed consistent with Article 13, as are aids given 'within the framework of overall economic policy to rationalise the structure of the industry and so to improve its efficiency', as long as they are not directed at exports or used for import-substitution. Regional development aids consistent with 'fair competition' are allowed, as are aids in the form of general public service to trade and industry. Finally, production subsidies are permitted in goods that are not traded widely among EFTA countries.[53]

The 1988 reinterpretation restricted, to some extent, the application of Article 13. Contrary to the general approach argued and adopted by the US (see *infra*), the EFTA Council agreed that 'only those measures can be classified as government aids which result in a net transfer of funds from state resources to the recipient'.[54] The list of subsidies not covered by Article 13 was further expanded to include, among other things, 'aid for the creation of employment opportunities in sectors not suffering from over-capacity, environmental aid, and aid to small and medium sized enterprises'.[55] On the other hand, tax concessions were to be considered state aids, even though the Working Party and the Economic Committee had not included tax concessions in their surveys on state aids.[56]

'Frustration of benefits'

Curzon Price argues that the frustration clause of the Stockholm Convention is like the GATT 'nullification and impairment' of benefits clause. As such, it 'concentrates on the practical *effects* of national support policies to various industries'.[57] She further argues that 'frustration' covers 'all acts of state intervention in the economic domain, the only limitations being a) aids to products bearing no MFN duty prior to integration, and b) direct or indirect aids to exports sold in third countries.'[58] Moreover, EFTA's concern with providing fair conditions of competition in the internal market could mean that the frustration clause was directed at not just indirect subsidies to exported products, but also import-substituting state aids.[59]

The EFTA regulatory framework suffers from two problems. First, it is difficult to determine exactly what is meant by 'frustration of benefits'. Unlike the definition of subsidies, which was followed by a survey of reported and planned state aids, there has been no report of state aids that constitute a 'frustration of benefits' within the meaning of Article 13. This is understandable. Middleton observes that the only basis for concluding that frustration has occurred would be 'speculative projections about future trends in supply and demand', which would be analytically unacceptable. Even more difficult is trying to determine what the 'expected' benefits were at the time of entry into the Convention and the extent to which they have been 'frustrated'.[60] Middleton considers the frustration clause unworkable as a criterion.[61]

Secondly, the formal dispute resolution mechanism, discussed below, has been used only six times since the inception of EFTA: the last time was in 1967, before the first interpretation of Article 13 by the EFTA Council.[62] In addition, the lack of a litigious culture among EFTA countries has resulted in a dearth of case law on the interpretation and application of the Stockholm Convention.[63] There have been no updated analyses or commentaries on what little case law exists in light of the two interpretations of Article 13 since 1968, nor has the Council provided a coherent clarification of the frustration clause. As Hufbauer observes, the latest interpretation failed 'to provide the clear, self-enforcing guidelines that the topic requires'.[64]

Institutional framework

A regime for the definition and regulation of subsidies must be able to do three things: define what is meant by a subsidy, separate objectionable subsidies from acceptable programmes and discipline the wrongdoer. The Stockholm Convention does not provide a strong institutional framework for a subsidies regulation regime. As a result, the EFTA Council has shouldered the responsibility for supplementing the substantive provisions of the Convention, including the subsidies provision. The two interpretations of 1968 and 1988 have gone a long way toward putting some flesh on the Article 13 skeleton. One of the key improvements was the establishment of a notification procedure, which was to form the nucleus of a much stronger regime in the future.

Notification procedure

The 1968 Agreement called for greater transparency of state aid to industry, planned or on-going. This was to allow for speedier identification of subsidies and prompter response to concerns and complaints. The 1985 report reiterated this point, recommending the establishment of a stronger (mandatory) notification procedure and the compilation of an inventory of government aids by the Secretariat for closer scrutiny of distortive programmes by Member States.[65] Following these recommendations, a new notification procedure was put in place in 1987 and Member States were required to provide full and timely disclosure of their aid measures to the EFTA Secretariat. The system was not as successful as had been hoped. As Hufbauer observes, the efficacy of the notification procedure depended entirely on the readiness of the Member States to communicate their aid programmes to the Secretariat, as the Secretariat did not have the resources to monitor and verify the information it received, nor – unlike the EU Commission – could it launch an investigation of its own; in any event, such readiness did not exist. Surveillance by a Committee of Trade Experts was intended to fortify the notification procedure, but it was provided with limited enforcement powers and was of little value.[66]

The EFTA Dispute Resolution Mechanism (DRM)

Disciplining a wrongdoer has three elements: 1) a complaint or an allegation, 2) an investigation, and 3) imposition of punitive measures. Since the criterion of incompatibility with the Convention is 'frustration of benefits', it is up to aggrieved Member States to bring their complaints and concerns about an actual or potential frustration to the Council. Since this involves a dispute between two or more Members, the dispute resolution mechanism of the Convention will be the ultimate arbiter of the compatibility of a state aid scheme with Article 13 and the nature of the disciplinary measure if the scheme is found incompatible.

The General Consultation and Complaints Procedure of EFTA is outlined in Article 31 of the Stockholm Convention. Clause 31.1 states that

> if any Member State considers that any benefit conferred upon it by this Convention or any objective of the Association is being or may be frustrated and if no satisfactory settlement is reached between the Member States concerned, any of those Member States may refer the matter to the Council.[67]

The Council is a political body, composed of representatives from Member States, each of whom has one vote.[68] Decisions and Recommendation of the Council are to be made unanimously, except where indicated in the Convention.[69] The dispute may be resolved by the Council alone, or by the Council with the help of an Examining Committee.

Once the Council has decided, by majority vote, to examine a matter referred to it by a Member(s), it *may* send it to an Examining Committee. According to Article 33, the members of the Examining Committee shall

> consist of persons selected for their competence and integrity, who, in the performance of their duties, shall neither seek nor receive instructions from any State, or from any authority or organisation other than the Association.[70]

The Council is under an obligation to refer the matter to a Committee if requested by a Member State. Once a recommendation has been made by the Committee, or once the Council has considered the matter to determine whether and to what extent a benefit is being or may be frustrated, the Council may make 'such recommendation as it considers appropriate' by a majority vote. If the recommendations of the Council are not followed, the Council may decide, by majority vote, to authorise any Member State to suspend to the Member State in default 'the application of such obligations under this Convention as the Council considers appropriate'.[71] Aggrieved Member States may, while the Council considers the matter, ask for the imposition of interim measures.[72] Under the new reforms (in December of 1989) to the surveillance procedure, the Council may order a Member to retrieve the subsidy from the recipient.

In many respects the EFTA complaints procedure is similar to the GATT Subsidies Code Track II dispute resolution mechanism and suffers from many of the same deficiencies. However, the similarities between the two regimes are mitigated by the following factors.

First, the disparity in wealth and power among the seven nations of EFTA is not as large as that among GATT members. Second, the volume of trade among EFTA countries is not very large: trade among EFTA members constitutes only about 14 per cent of the total exports of EFTA Member States.[73] Third, EFTA's relative cultural homogeneity (compared with the GATT or even the EU), as well as the consociational and consensual elements common to all EFTA members, has meant that few matters are put to a formal vote in the Council. Also, there is always an attempt by the parties to arrive at a consensus, even if it means abandoning the issue if no consensus emerges.[74] In case a dispute arises between two Member States, they are encouraged to arrive at a solution outside the formal procedure of the Convention.[75] But some disputes require resolution of a different nature and do not go away through negotiation and consensus building. This is where the similarity of the EFTA DRM to the GATT has caused major problems for EFTA.

Hufbauer argues that part of the reason for the under-utilisation of the EFTA DRM lies in the fact that 'if invoked, the frustration criterion could lead to long and disputatious proceedings', with little chance of an amicable outcome.[76] Initiating a complaint, as the GATT procedure has shown, may be interpreted as a hostile act. The British Aluminium Smelters case is an excellent example of this problem. It showed the EFTA dispute resolution mechanism at its most impotent and should act at least as a sound caution to the advocates of political (negotiated or consensual) dispute resolution.

The case involved the subsidisation of three aluminium smelters by the British government in the mid-1960s. Norway, a large aluminium producer, objected to the British investment grants, and brought the matter to the EFTA Council. After three years of bilateral negotiations, many working parties, and gentle persuasion by other Members of EFTA, the matter remained unresolved.[77] Curzon Price observes that the case 'was not a particularly edifying episode, and it certainly highlighted the problems of asymmetrical power relationships in even as easygoing a club as EFTA'.[78] Britain kept her smelter and investment grants, and Norway lost. The strengthening of the discipline procedure may avoid a similar final outcome, but it will do little to avert the type of damage that the Britain–Norway trade dispute inflicted on the collegiality of EFTA, or to ameliorate the harm done to Norwegian interests by British subsidies.

Evaluation

EFTA is one of the most successful trade association of the post-war era,[79] but little in its institutional or legal make-up could shed light on the reasons for its success. Rather, the strength of EFTA is due to the relative low volume of trade among its Members, the much higher volume of trade with an accommodating EU, similar cultural backgrounds of its members (save perhaps Portugal; but it was treated almost as a wayward cousin until the April 1974 Revolution, and thereafter as a needy one), a willingness to compromise on key conceptual issues (which is aided by the relatively low volume of trade), and the high per capita income of most of its members. Its dispute resolution mechanism and the subsidies regime it has devised are, as a result, of little analytical value in themselves. The interest in EFTA should lie elsewhere: in its failures and the course it eventually followed.

First, the failures. The British aluminium smelter case is more than a simple breakdown of an otherwise successful mechanism. Its value lies in the fact that *despite* the collegiality of EFTA, and despite the lore of consensus-building among its Members, the system failed to resolve a highly charged dispute, EFTA's only real subsidies dispute in its 30-year history. The British investment grants were clearly subsidies, and Norway was clearly losing its market in Britain. But EFTA was helpless. The Council failed to move Britain and Norway finally gave up. It may be argued that the success of EFTA lies in not having allowed many issues to get to the dispute resolution level. However, a viable DRM should be able to deal with difficult as well as easy cases, intractable as well as pliant disputant countries. It should be able to resolve disputes justly and efficiently; in the smelters case the Council did not do so. But how many more disputes would have arisen if, for example, the volume of trade within EFTA were as high as that between Canada and the US? How would the Article 31 mechanism have dealt with them? The susceptibility of a political mechanism to breakdown increases with the volume of interaction (trade) and the depth of the entrenched conceptual and cultural differences between and among the parties.

EFTA learnt its lesson from the smelter case. The second point, the course of action EFTA followed in the 1980s, is quite instructive for the advocates of freer trade. The surveillance mechanism of EFTA was strengthened substantially following reforms in December of 1989. Currently, a majority vote by the Council can order the repayment of illegal aid by the recipient.[80] This can no longer be considered a purely 'multilateral' instrument. Despite the early desire to maintain full control over national economic policies, it is clear that growing economic and market integration made EFTA members increasingly sensitive to each other's national economic policies. As Curzon Price observes, EFTA's notification and surveillance procedure for government aid creates a right for each partner to participate in the formative stages of domestic policy making.[81] Increasing internationalisation and integration of domestic markets and economies, and growing volumes of trade can make a potent and highly intrusive tool out of the Articles 30–31 mechanism and 1989 surveillance procedure. In certain contexts, when volume of trade is high and the partners are geographically close, freer trade and economic integration go hand in hand. The formation of the European Economic Area and its consequences for EFTA bear witness to this point, and will be discussed in detail in the following part.

It must be recognised, of course, that the strengthening of the surveillance mechanism has been made possible only by restricting the ambit of Article 13 through periodic redefinitions. It is not certain how far EFTA countries would have gone if they had not been willing to recognise deep seated concerns about economic development and readjustment peculiar to each. For example, driven primarily by the heavily underdeveloped Portugal and supported by the primary resource sectors of Finland and Norway, regional development programmes were received more favourably than traditional free trade theory allowed. EFTA understood that in certain instances, a 'supplement to the traditional economy is . . . needed' by way of industrial or regional policy.[82] Whether in the form of loan guarantees, municipal investment in industry, labour mobility and retraining programmes, general programmes aimed at regional industrialisation, or even direct aid to industry, EFTA countries have moved politically to accommodate each other's concerns before adopting a judicial or bureaucratic discipline mechanism.

In the EFTA the paradox of subsidies could only be solved by an institutional paradox: the new institutions are stronger, but they have a smaller scope of action. The old institutions, based on consensus and negotiation, could agree on the basics but not on individual cases. In spite of the limited objectives and range of issues considered by the Council, it failed to resolve major disputes or to discipline the granting of subsidies through its political mechanism. Also, the mixed success of the collegial atmosphere of EFTA needs to be evaluated in the context of inevitable integration and, as the case may be, asymmetry of bargaining power. It is not clear how a multilateral or bilateral system could be useful if there is a greater degree of disharmony in concepts, objectives, or socio-economic programmes between Member State, or the agreement has a wider scope.

THE EUROPEAN ECONOMIC AREA

The European Economic Area (EEA) brought the process of European economic and political integration since 1957 to a full circle. With Austria, Sweden, Norway,[83] Finland and even isolationist Switzerland resolved to join the EU,[84] EFTA and the EEA are increasingly taking the role of an airlock for eventual EU membership.[85] This is not surprising. The European market-building that began with the ECSC nearly forty years ago is poised to become the largest single market in the world, commanding some 46 per cent of international trade and 30 per cent of the wealth of the world. The EU will be discussed in the following chapter, but the relationship between EFTA and the EU, and the final outcome in the shape of the EEA are particularly important for students of international trade institutions. The institutional history of the relationship goes back to the early days of both treaties, and they illustrate in no uncertain terms the pitfalls and strengths of political solutions, unequal bargaining power, and dependence on a larger market. The route that EFTA was eventually required to take should also serve to highlight the concerns about subsidies and institutional responses that are raised throughout this study.

An attempt will be made in this part to provide a historical context for the EEA by discussing the EC–EFTA Free Trade Agreements. This may seem of minor relevance, or even superfluous, but this is not the case. Should any of the EFTA seven fail to ratify the EEA treaty, they will continue to be governed by the terms of their FTAs with the EC.[86] Moreover, the EEA was conceived following the success of the FTAs in eradicating tariffs by the deadline of 1984. At the same time, however, the FTAs were not completely without problems, and the structure of the EEA to some extent highlights the concerns of the EFTA countries over the weaknesses of the FTAs in resolving some of the major trade irritations in their relations. One of these was the problem of subsidies. As will be shown, the FTAs had failed to provide an adequate mechanism for dealing with this issue, and the EEA agreement sought to resolve it once and for all. This failure will be examined in detail in the following part.

Also, the EEA is still subject to ratification by 18 Parliaments (the European Parliament, EU12, and five EFTA states).[87] While the rejection of the EEA by the Swiss has caused some problems for the EU and EFTA, these problems have not been insuperable. The parties have negotiated a new Protocol to incorporate the changes to the EEA Agreement that will be necessary following the Swiss vote. It is not clear, however, what would happen if more EFTA countries fail to ratify the treaty. The point is admittedly speculative, but bears recognition, for the EEA can still be aborted.

What is important here, though, is not the operation of the EEA, but the institutional mechanisms devised by countries trying to protect their trade interests. This is why the first, and aborted EEA agreement will also be discussed in a later chapter. There will be an attempt to learn some lessons from institutions that are the result of compromises deemed valuable or even necessary by international actors.

A last point I should like to raise is my own recognition of the artificiality of classifying international institutions as 'multilateral', 'supranational' or any other category. The present EEA Agreement does not, in many ways, fit into any of the models discussed here. What is important is the broad approach of the parties to the Agreement in devising a mechanism for the settlement of their disputes in these areas. The EFTA and the EU continued, in the EEA, to seek negotiated settlements to their concerns before the imposition of unilateral or even multilateral sanctions. To the extent that the emphasis is on negotiation and development of definitions and regulations through bilateral talks, then, the EEA can be fitted in the same category as the present EFTA mechanism.

The EC–EFTA Free Trade Agreements[88]

EFTA Member States are highly dependant on trade with the EU: 53 per cent of all EFTA exports are to the EU, and 58 per cent of their imports are from the EU. This simple fact could explain the vigour with which the small EFTA countries have pursued a more liberal trading relationship with their giant neighbour.[89] The Free Trade Agreements (FTAs) are also beneficial for the EU. The EFTA countries are the market for more than a quarter of the EU's external trade – more than North America, a market with nearly eight times the population.

The EC–EFTA FTAs came into being in the aftermath of the decision of Britain, Denmark and Norway (later withdrawn) to join the EU in the early 1970s. On the insistence of the EU[90] and partly due to the institutional limitations of EFTA, the remaining Members of the EFTA negotiated bilateral free trade agreements with the EU. All FTAs came into force by the end of 1974, and the target for complete liberalisation of trade was met ten years later. The FTAs liberalise only trade in manufactured goods. The chief concern of the parties was removal of tariffs, but there are provisions dealing with non-tariff barriers such as state aid to industry. However, the scope of these provisions is quite limited, and the institutional arrangement of the FTAs reflects the desire of the parties to maintain almost complete control over their trade, economic, and industrial policy (if such distinctions can be made); the parties to the FTAs have not ceded any sovereign power to a supranational body such as the Commission of the EU.[91] The regulatory and institutional framework of the FTAs reflect this well.

Regulatory framework

Subclause 23(1)(iii) of the FTAs[92] constitutes the entire regulatory framework of the state aid regime of the FTAs. It declares incompatible with the proper functioning of the agreements 'any public aid which distorts or threatens to distort competition by favouring certain undertakings or the production of certain goods'. There have been no further clarifications of this subclause by the organs of the FTAs. Part of the difficulty is the ambiguity of the declaration. As a Swiss court stated in *The (Swiss) Adams* case, the Article does not prohibit any measures. Rather, the court argued incisively, 'it merely lays down what practices are incompatible with the proper functioning of the Agreement'.[93] The Swiss court thus declined to give effect or substance to Article 23.[94] The EU, on the other hand, stated in a declaration its intention to 'assess any practice contrary to Article 23 of the FTA on the basis of criteria arising from the application of the rules of Articles 85, 86, 90 and 92' of the Treaty of Rome.[95]

EFTA did not challenge the definition; neither did it introduce an interpretation of its own. This one-sided policy-making culminated in the unilateral introduction of CVD regulations by the EU

Council. The regulations were not aimed at EFTA, but EFTA countries are not explicitly excluded from their application. Therefore, there may be new problems with the interpretation of subclause 23(1)(iii). More importantly, the CVD regulations do not necessarily cohere with the rules on subsidies under Article 92. While on the surface they address similar problems, the solutions they provide, and the contexts in which the problem of subsidies is dealt with are substantially different. As a result, the question of what a subsidy is under the terms of the FTAs continues to be unresolved.

Institutional framework

The institutional structure of the FTAs is based on diplomacy and negotiation. Therefore, as long as the EU and EFTA countries maintain diplomatic channels and attempt to resolve their differences through negotiation the confusion in regulatory interpretation is not important. Indeed no significant dispute has found its way into the formal dispute settlement procedure of the FTAs.

The Agreements are administered by Joint Committees composed of representatives of the Contracting Parties through recommendations or unanimous decisions; the Committees may also serve as fora for consultation.[96] The Joint Committees may consider, on the application of a Contracting Party, whether a practice is 'incompatible with the proper functioning of the Agreement'.[97] The Joint Committee may examine a case and require the elimination of the objectionable practice. If no action is taken, the aggrieved Party may adopt safeguard measures to deal with the 'serious difficulties resulting from the practices in question'.[98]

The Committees have not been used extensively by the parties and seem to be of little practical value. In fact in the area of subsidies only two cases have been brought to the attention of the Committee, neither of which was of much importance.[99] According to Curzon Price, the reason for this dearth of activity can be found in the harsh reality of the EU–EFTA relation. She argues that

> in the context of the EC–EFTA free trade areas, the absence of an arbitration procedure to settle disputes meant that the EFTA countries were quite helpless to stop the progress of subsidization in the EC, however detrimental it was to their trade.[100]

The problem of asymmetry in the EU-EFTA relationship can

perhaps be better understood by examining an example. Switzerland has a population of 6 million, and trade with the EC involves nearly 50 per cent of its total exports. The EC, on the other hand, has a population of well over 320 million, and only 3.5 per cent of its exports go to Switzerland.[101] As Curzon Price notes, the two parties have 'vastly differing abilities to inflict harm on each other'.[102] Therefore, a political mechanism that relied on the adoption of safeguard measures to counter subsidies would not adequately protect the interests of the smaller party.

Analysis

By 1984 all tariffs on manufactured goods were abolished between EFTA countries and the EU, and the search for a mechanism to deepen the economic integration of Western Europe began in earnest. With the EEA on the verge of becoming a reality nearly ten years later, it may be argued that the EC–EFTA FTAs were successful. The success, however, has not been unqualified, at least in the area of state aids.

There are few data on the significance of subsidisation in the EU–EFTA trade. There is very little discussion in the literature of arguments over subsidies between the Parties. It is conceivable, however, that a number of important trade irritants in this field existed throughout the life of the FTAs, a time of expansion for state aids to industry. While the EU may have negotiated in good faith in each instance, the significant imbalance in power between the trading partners cannot have been absent from the minds of the negotiators. Indeed, it had not been at the very inception of the FTAs: when the agreements were being negotiated in the early 1970s, Sweden and Switzerland sought a system of judicial review to govern the application of the FTAs; the EU opposed such a solution.[103] Twenty years later, in negotiating the treaty establishing the European Economic Area, EFTA once again asked for a system of judicial review. This time the EU Commission relented, but the ECJ rejected the treaty. The EEA agreement was renegotiated, and a modified multilateral dispute resolution mechanism was put in place. In evaluating dispute resolution mechanisms based on negotiation and diplomacy, it is important to note that the smaller Party almost always asks for a judicial mechanism, and rarely gets it.

The European Economic Area

The negotiations over the EEA Agreements were marked by more than the usual breakdowns and stalemates; the final stages of the negotiations saw the unusually active participation of the Court of Justice of the European Union (ECJ) and the European Parliament (EP) in trying to protect the autonomy of European institutions. As a result, the end product was the second agreement to be initialed by the EU and EFTA negotiators; the first agreement was held incompatible with the Treaty of Rome by the ECJ late in 1991. In the following part I will examine the second agreement, which will likely be the final EEA Agreement.

Regulatory framework

The EEA Agreement has a much wider scope than the EC–EFTA FTAs. The EU and EFTA sought in the EEA a comprehensive agreement that would include not only the 'four freedoms' of the Common Market (the free movement of goods, services, capital and person), but also non-economic fields of co-operation, such as research and development, education, and consumer policy. They also sought a legal system that 'would ensure the enforcement of common rules and regulations. . .'.[104]

A key area for developing regulations was that of state aid to industry. The EEA Agreement includes a general prohibition on any state aid which may distort trade. Article 61.1 states that

> Save as otherwise provided in this Agreement, any aid granted by EC Member States, EFTA States or through State resources in any form whatsoever which distorts or threatens to distort competition by favouring certain undertakings or the production of certain goods shall, in so far as it affects trade between Contracting Parties, be incompatible with the functioning of this Agreement.

In its generality, therefore, the prohibition differs little from the FTAs. It is, however, qualified by the possibility of taking certain political, economic and social considerations into account.[105] This is an important qualification. As has been noted above and as will be seen in the section dealing with the EU state aid regimes, the qualification has precedents in both the EU and EFTA regulatory regimes and gives a wide ambit of discretion to monitoring authorities in regulating and disciplining state aid. Under Article 61.3, for example, regional aid and job creation programmes, industrial adjustment schemes, defence and research and development spending, 'aid to promote the execution of an important project of common European interest', and even 'aid to facilitate the development of certain economic areas' may be exempted from the prohibition. The continuation of the present trend in the EU and EFTA under the EEA rules is all the more probable because of the creation of the 'two pillar' system for the administration of the EEA Agreement.

Institutional framework

The EEA does not have a unified institution to monitor state aid schemes. Instead, it relies on EU and EFTA institutions to enforce the common rules on state aid measures. In reaching this solution two principal difficulties had to be overcome. First, EFTA did not have adequate tools to develop, monitor and enforce a coherent and specific set of regulations on state aid. Second, the principle of legal homogeneity within the EEA had to be reconciled with the autonomy of the Contracting Parties, especially after the pointed objection of the ECJ to any encroachment on its powers.[106]

EFTA countries proposed to resolve the impasse in the negotiations by binding themselves to the decisions of the ECJ in cases involving state aid and competition.[107] This proposal, however, did not adequately deal with the question of the ECJ's legal autonomy. The solution, proposed by the EU, was the creation of a 'two pillar' system, wherein the task of administering the EEA Agreement would be divided territorially between the Commission (and the ECJ) and an EFTA monitoring body (the Surveillance Authority). Under Article 62.1,

> All existing systems of State aid in the territory of the Contracting Parties, as well as any plans to grant or alter State aid, shall be subject to constant review as to their compatibility with Article 61.

The review will be carried out by the EU according to the rules laid out in Article 93 of the Treaty of Rome in matter concerning EU Member States (Article 62.1(a)), and for EFTA countries, by the EFTA Surveillance Authority. A joint committee operating within a political framework would settle any differences arising between the two pillars. The authority of the Commission of the European Union to monitor and regulate EU Members' state aid schemes will be discussed in the next section. In the following part I will set out the additional institutions required and therefore created by the EEA Agreement to allow for an area-wide regulation of subsidies.

The EFTA Surveillance Authority

The EEA created three new institutions for the EFTA: the EFTA Standing Committee, the EFTA Court, and the EFTA Surveillance Authority (the ESA). The Surveillance Authority and the EFTA Court will have the task of regulating state aid within EFTA. These are part of the surveillance mechanisms of the EEA.

All signatories to the Agreement, as well as natural and legal persons, may bring a complaint regarding the implementation of EEA rules to the ESA or the EU Commission. The composition of the ESA is modelled after the EU Commission. It will be an independent body and consist of one appointee from each country. Members of the ESA may not take instructions from any government, including their own.[108] The ESA has, among other things, a specific responsibility for ensuring that EFTA countries comply with the state aid and competition provisions of the EEA Agreement. Protocol 26 sets out the powers and functions of the EFTA Surveillance Authority in the field of state aid. It states that the ESA will be

> entrusted with equivalent powers and similar functions to those of the EC Commission, at the time of the signature of this Agreement, for the application of the competition rules applicable to State aid of [the EEA] Agreement.[109]

It will make its decisions by majority voting.

The ESA may initiate infringement proceeding against EFTA states in the EFTA Court. The EFTA Court and the ECJ will oversee the proper functioning of the Agreement. The EFTA Court is composed of one judge from each EFTA country. The primary task of the Court is to 'decide upon cases when the EFTA Surveillance Authority challenges an EFTA state before the Court for not having fulfilled its obligations under the EEA Agreement'.[110] The Court will also be competent to settle disputes between two or more EFTA countries in matters involving the interpretation or application of the EEA Agreement.

The Joint Committee

The EFTA Court is only one half of the judicial mechanism of the EEA. Therefore, there is a possibility that difficulties may arise if interpretations by the EFTA Court and the ECJ are inconsistent. This is mitigated by the co-operation clause of Article 62.2, which states that

> with a view to ensuring a uniform surveillance in the field of State aid throughout the territory covered by this Agreement, the EC Commission and the EFTA Surveillance Authority shall co-operate in accordance with the provisions set out in Protocol 27.

The Parties are bound under Protocol 27 to 'exchange information and views on general policy issues',[111] periodic preparation of surveys, provision of information on a case-by-case basis, and exchange of views on individual state aid programmes.[112] As well, the Parties agree to take 'due account of' a number of framework analyses, decisions, letters, communiqués and opinions by the EU Commission and the EU Council, in developing EEA jurisprudence.

However, the possibility of conflicting or inconsistent interpretation cannot be ruled out. Therefore, a Joint Committee has been set up by the Agreement to arrive at political solutions to problems of inconsistency. In case of an inconsistency, that is, if one of the surveillance authorities questions the decision of the other, the matter may be referred to the Joint Committee, which may decide to retain a uniform interpretation of the agreement.[113] This political solution was a key development in persuading the ECJ of the validity of the second EEA Agreement. The EU Court noted that the powers of the Joint Committee 'do not affect the binding nature of the Court's jurisprudence or the autonomy of the Community legal order.'[114]

Two further points are significant. First, the interpretation of the rules of competition, including the regulation of state aid, is not subject to the arbitration procedure which may be invoked in case of disagreement in the Joint Committee. If the Joint Committee cannot come to an agreement, parties may impose measures to counter the effects of the subsidy in question. Secondly, the Joint Committee may refer a question to the ECJ, but any decision of the ECJ on the reference will be binding on the Committee.[115]

Evaluation

The EEA is the largest trading bloc in the world: with 380 million consumers, it encompasses about 46 per cent of the world trade.[116] The significance of the EEA, however, goes beyond mere size. First, institutionally, it is a unique hybrid that mixes conventional principles with modern institutions; it pays homage to traditional territorial autonomy (mainly of the two supranational bodies, the EU and EFTA) while reducing the national sovereignty of its signatories. Secondly, by establishing the EFTA Surveillance Authority and the EFTA Court it creates the second truly supranational institution in the world, modelled largely after the EU itself. Third, it is the first international agreement between two *supranational* institutions. In this part, I will discuss what I have termed the 'hybrid' nature of the EEA, that is, modern institutions based on conventional principles.

In many ways, there appears to be little difference between the EEA Joint Committee and the joint committee system employed in the EC–EFTA FTAs, or in any other free trade agreement of this nature. The only major significance seems to be that the scope of the EEA Agreement is much wider than most other international trade agreements, and that as a result the nature of the issues that the Joint Committee will have to resolve 'politically' will be much different from those faced by other institutions. However, this is not the only important point.

As noted above, in the area of state aid (Article 23 of the FTAs) the FTA Joint Committees dealt with disputes arising out of individual acts of subsidisation (practice-oriented dispute resolution). If there were questions of interpretation, they were secondary issues arising out of specific disputes. The task of the Joint Committees was not to harmonise interpretive practices of domestic courts (jurisprudence-oriented dispute resolution), but to force a political change of will through political and economic mechanisms. Were that change not to materialise, the parties could impose sanctions to bring about the change through penal measures. The EFTA Council operates on the same principle.

The EEA Joint Committee, on the other hand, does not have a penal or disciplining function. That function is exercised by the relevant courts in the two jurisdictions, and by the Contracting Parties themselves in case of an unresolved dispute. Instead, the Joint Committee will have the task of politically harmonising differences in legal interpretation and approach by the two courts.

A politically oriented dispute resolution mechanism could have disastrous consequences for the weaker party or parties. First, individual cases of concern to the weaker party may never find their way to the Joint Committee. Secondly, disputes that do get discussed by the Joint Committee are likely to be resolved in favour of the stronger party.[117] Third, even if the Committee resolves the issue in favour of the weaker party, enforcement through economic sanctions against the stronger party are not likely to lead to a change in political or economic practices. As a result, the compatibility of practices in issue with the provisions of the trade agreement will be largely determined by the stronger party. The smelters case in EFTA and the experience of the EC–EFTA FTAs point to the difficulty of maintaining harmonious trade relations governed by an asymmetrical political DRM.

The EEA Joint Committee is novel in the sense that the DRM will concern itself with interpretive inconsistencies between judicial organs, rather than specific practices at hand. In a sense, the Joint Committee is not a DRM at all. The Committee's task is not to settle disputes or investigate complaints. In fact, after the EU dropped its requirement for total legal homogeneity in the EEA,[118] the Joint Committee is not under an obligation to harmonise the interpretations, but to do so only 'if necessary'.[119] Since EFTA countries will be adopting most EU legislation, and given the mandate of the EFTA Court to give particular attention to the decisions of the ECJ, it is likely that the EEA Joint Committee will not have a difficult task of harmonisation.

This mechanism may not work under all conditions. The trade partners must be satisfied that the decisions by domestic courts will not be as politicised as bureaucratic decisions, and that the qualifications to the prohibition will be applied appropriately by domestic courts. They must also be cognisant of and willing to respect differences in national political, social and economic objectives that could and often do give rise to different interpretations by domestic courts; that is, there must be an understanding that fairness does not require adopting the socio-economic ideology of the stronger party. Finally, the trade partners must know what is the purpose of a prohibition of 'subsidies' within a trade agreement. In the case of the EEA, and in most trade agreement, the prohibition is an attempt to reduce trade barriers to allow greater movement of goods across the border. It is manifestly not intended to harmonise socio-economic programmes or national objectives, nor is it to reduce government involvement in the economy to some abstract theoretical minimum. The EEA Agreement seems to have addressed this problem.

MULTI/BILATERALISM: AND THEY NEGOTIATED HAPPILY EVER AFTER?

It is academically safe to suggest that the jury is still out on multilateralism. Practically speaking, however, such a tentative assessment is patently inaccurate. Multilateralism as a method of dispute settlement is dead; and even if not dead already, it is terminal. This is so despite laudable attempts by smaller countries to retain outdated conceptions of national sovereignty and their understandable desire to pursue their own national economic and social objectives. The cause of its 'illness' is the very nature of the disputes arising out of subsidies, and the difficulty of coming to terms with the conflicting demands placed on international institutions by the intensity of those disputes.

Subsidies are potent tools for advancement of national socio-economic objectives. Whether and how they affect trade among nations is questionable, but there is no question that they are *perceived* to have harmful effects on a nation's trading partners. As tariffs come down, and as the international economy becomes increasingly integrated, the impact of purely 'national' policies and instruments on 'foreign' economies becomes ever more obvious. Trading partners can no longer justify the 'harm' to their own economies on the basis of their partners' national sovereignty, and so the seeds of dispute are sown.

Multilateralism requires parties to negotiate; to do so effectively, it is often necessary for each party to understand the other's point of view. This may be possible if the parties share similar socio-economic objectives and approaches, but becomes more difficult as the divergence between national objectives of the parties increases. The larger the difference, the more intractable the parties may seem to one another, the more unreasonable their demands may appear, the more difficult it becomes to arrive at a solution. And then there will be a breakdown in the process.

The seriousness of a breakdown in trade negotiations over the issue of subsidies depends entirely on the scope of the problem and the relative power of the negotiating parties. It is obvious that given a gross asymmetry of economic or political power between the parties, a breakdown in negotiations and the possibility of disciplinary measures could have much more devastating consequences for the smaller party than for the bigger power. It is not surprising, then, that larger countries generally prefer multilateral systems to adjudicative models. The parties maintain their sovereignty, but the bigger parties remain invariably more sovereign than the smaller ones.

The following conclusions may be drawn. First, multilateralism involves the clash of politics and political choices between two nominal equals; but the parties are rarely equal. It requires an understanding of the rules and agreement thereto; but the parties rarely have the same understanding of the principles governing their disputes. In short, the current make-up of multilateral institutions makes bullying or breakdown almost inevitable. Therein lies the danger, for in the context of the politics of international trade, multilateralism all too often has made conditions ripe for heated trade wars that threaten the health of the international trading order.

Second, the potential for trade war increases with the level of generality of the rules governing the regulatory regime. In the GATT, where the rules are so general as to be devoid of substance, the potential is greater than, for example, EFTA, where repeated interpretations have narrowed the definition to a large extent. Similarly, the EEA is likely to prove more successful than either because of the vast subsidies jurisprudence of the EU Commission and the ECJ. In the EU–EFTA relationship prior to the EEA, the singular asymmetry between the parties and the potential for future membership of EFTA countries in the EU saved the FTAs from breakdown; war between EFTA and EU was a moot point. But such conditions do not duplicate themselves readily.

Third, lamenting the failure of multilateralism should not be taken as a vote of confidence in the adjudicative model. On the contrary, if the adjudicative model is adopted only to be abused by litigious countries, as the GATT process has been abused by the US, then it poses a greater danger to trade harmony than the multilateral process. It is even more troubling when litigation is coupled with traditional diplomatic pressures, thus subverting the very notion of adjudication. Such abuse threatens the integrity of the system, and encourages lawlessness among countries subjected to the abuse of process. Rather, a healthy dispute resolution mechanism is one which incorporates some of the best features of multilateralism, namely, the respect for national socio-economic objectives, and the understanding that dispute resolution does not have to result in harmonisation.

Fourth, multilateralism has been unable to resolve the paradox of subsidies. This is not to suggest that the paradox is resolvable, but that the approach taken by multilateral institutions, that is, negotiation among unequal trading partners, may not lend itself to workable solutions. Other regimes, it is true, have been even less successful, and they will be discussed later in this part, but as has been noted, the weakness of multilateralism lies in its lack of the elements that would make a resolution possible.

Finally, the success or failure of a regime depends to a great extent on its functional approach. While on the surface the above institutions have a similar *basic* objective, that is, curbing the use of harmful subsidies, they have used different arguments (instruments) to persuade their members to adhere to the regime. EFTA, for example, relies on 'competitiveness', while the EEA argues for equal conditions of competition. The GATT's failure lies in the fact that it has not been able to embody a coherent view as to why and how subsidies can be harmful. This has had serious consequences, for the US views all subsidies as necessarily deleterious to its interests, while the EU has a more pragmatic approach to state aid. It has been easier to convince EFTA countries of the damage to their own economies caused by subsidisation, than it has been for the US to convince its partners in the GATT that they engage in illegal and unfair trade practices, especially when they do not follow American market models. The failure of the GATT is not surprising in this context.

4

SUPRANATIONAL REGULATION OF SUBSIDIES

INTRODUCTION

Elements of supranationalism have already been discussed in the section dealing with the EFTA Surveillance Authority and the EFTA Court. The most important feature of supranational regimes is the existence of an autonomous body to supervise the operation of the regime, and to regulate and discipline the parties' behaviour in the areas in question. Dispute settlement is done through arbitration and binding authority, rather than through multilateral suspension of benefits. Its purpose is mainly to resolve disputes between the regulatory agency and the party in default, rather than disputes between contracting parties. The consequences of such arrangements are far reaching. Members to the treaty or treaties establishing the regimes transfer sovereign power in selected areas to a Court or a bureaucratic body with decision-making capacities independent of the parties themselves. Members will then be bound not only to decisions in whose making, through the operation of a Council, they have had a part, but also decisions by those bodies that do not normally take instructions from the Members. The regulatory agency may mix adjudicative powers with an investigatory or even executive authority.

In the following parts two systems will be examined. First, I will discuss the first (and ultimately abortive) EEA Agreement, which saw the creation of an EEA Court to govern and interpret the EEA Agreement. Since very little has been written on the topic, I will rely principally on the decision of the ECJ in *Opinion Regarding the Draft Agreement between the European Communities and the European Free Trade Association Relating to the Creation of the European Economic Area*[1] ('the EEA Decision') to analyse the structure of the EEA. Secondly, I will examine the EU state aid regime. As with the GATT, much has been written about the EU, and I do not propose to repeat this work. Instead, the section on the EU will assess the success or failure of the regime based on its stated, though evolving, objectives. It will be argued that the success of the EU regime lay in its ability to mix its bureaucratic/adjudicative functions with a dose of political realism (or cynicism). Therefore, although it has not been able to eradicate state aid in the EU, the Commission has managed to keep the issue of subsidies relatively under control.

THE EUROPEAN ECONOMIC AREA: THE FALSE START[2]

The principal surveillance bodies under the first EEA Agreement, as with the second Agreement, were the EU Commission and the EFTA Surveillance Authority. The EU Commission will be discussed in the next section. The EFTA Surveillance Authority has already been examined, and the reader's attention is once again directed to the supranational features of the EFTA Surveillance Authority: if the new EEA Agreement is ratified, the ESA is to be an independent body, it will take its decision by majority voting, and its decisions in the area of competition rules, especially state aid, are binding on Member States. Under the second Agreement, if the interpretations of the EFTA Surveillance Authority and the EU Commission differ on a matter of interpretation, or if the Courts of the two regimes do not agree, then the matter is to be referred to the EEA Joint Committee for a political resolution.

The first Agreement created an EEA Court and an EEA Court of First Instance, which had the task of settling disputes between the parties, creating a homogeneous legal order for the EEA, and functioning as an EFTA court for appeals from the Surveillance Authority. The Dispute Settlement provisions of the EEA Agreement were set out in Article 117. The Article stated that

> 1) The EEA Joint Committee or a Contracting Party may bring a matter under dispute which concerns the application of this Agreement before the EEA Court in accordance with the following provisions. . . .
>
> 3) A Contracting Party may bring a matter under dispute before the EEA Court. In doing so it shall, however, first

> submit the matter to the EEA Joint Committee. If it is not resolved after two consecutive meetings of the Committee, either the Committee shall, unless otherwise decided, or a Contracting Party may, bring the matter before the EEA Court.

The authority of the Court was to be binding not only on states, but also on 'persons other than States'.[3] This is important: one of the strongest tools of the EU Commission and a key reform to the present EFTA system in regulating state aid has been their power to order the repayment of illegally granted subsidies.

The ECJ suggested that the

> EEA is to be established on the basis of an international treaty which, essentially, merely creates rights and obligations as between the Contracting Parties and provides for no transfer of sovereign rights to the intergovernmental institutions which it sets up.[4]

On the other hand, as the Court pointed out, the Community forms a legal order in which the Members have limited their sovereign rights. In giving right of action to and binding not only the states but also private actors, the EEA Agreement was different from normal international treaties. Moreover, in the opinion of the ECJ, binding arbitration on such sensitive matters as competition policy (especially state aid) went beyond mere 'dispute settlement'. An EEA Court that could take advantage of the ECJ jurisprudence and develop its own jurisdiction in passing judgement on issues such as regional aid, social policy, and Research and Development expenditure, was hardly similar to other international fora. Therefore, while the EEA Agreement relied on the surveillance mechanism of its own Contracting Parties for the enforcement of its provisions, and while the objective of full 'integration' was not spelled out in the Agreement, the proposed EEA Court structure had strong supranational elements.

The EU, the subject of the next section, did not leave the task of 'surveillance' to the domestic courts of its Member States. The EU Commission, a Contracting Party to the EEA Agreement, has in the EU the function of devising rules, investigating complaints, disciplining wrongdoers, and maintaining the integrity of the single market. However, it will be argued in the next section that the EU Commission has used its powers in the area of state aid to further ends not envisaged by its constituent treaty. The significance of this point will become apparent when discussing the effectiveness of supranational institutions in carrying out their mandate versus the success of multilateral mechanisms.

THE EUROPEAN UNION

The rules governing state aid in the European Union are set out in the section of the Treaty of Rome dealing with rules of competition. The Directorate-General for Competition Policy of the Commission of the European Union is ultimately responsible for carrying out the terms of the Treaty in this area.[5] This is not an accident. The objective of the Treaty was to create an internal market without borders in which goods, services, capital and persons moved freely and competed on a 'level playing field'. The competition rules were designed to help remove all distortions of trade among Member States and thus improve competition in the internal market. It was believed that state aid could distort competition by diverting allocation of resources from their most efficient uses and also by giving unfair advantage to certain firms. Economic integration, in fact, required more than just the establishment of common rules and regulations of competition. It also required 'the progressive harmonization of social policies that can create artificial differences in costs. . . . One can allow the free play of prices internationally only if prices are established in different countries in an analogous manner'.[6]

Thus, 'any state aid that distorts competition by favouring certain enterprises or outputs is forbidden' by the Treaty of Rome,[7] except for certain derogations granted by the Commission. In the following I will discuss the conceptual considerations underlying the state aid policy of the Treaty of Rome. Then, I will examine the institutional arrangements of the Treaty in dealing with the question of state aid to industry. In the third part, the exemptions to the policy will be discussed to enable us to arrive at a clearer picture of the type of practices banned by the Treaty.

Conceptual considerations

The Commission defines subsidies broadly as

> all forms of specific transfers from the government sector which directly or indirectly benefit enterprises, for which the

government receives no equivalent compensation in return and which are granted with the purpose of changing market outcomes... State aids are basically those subsidies which distort intra-Community competition.[8]

Thus, for an aid scheme to be considered a state aid within the meaning of Article 92, it must 1) be granted by a public body, 2) involve cost to the public urse, 3) benefit enterprises, 4) be specific to certain sectors, regions or firms, and 5) affect competition with other Member States.[9] The last consideration is of key importance when assessing the work of the Commission in this area.

Two general concerns are operative here. First, as the ECJ held in *Philip Morris*, 'when state financial aid strengthens the position of an undertaking compared with other undertakings competing in intra-Community trade the latter must be regarded as affected by that aid'.[10] To the extent that subsidies from one state to its undertakings may negatively affect intra-Community trade, the Commission has the responsibility of regulating the granting of those subsidies.

Second, it was argued by the Commission of the EU that

> an optimum allocation of resources will not take place if undertakings consider that, in the market place, they are fighting competition not only from their true competitors but also from the finance ministries of the Member States in which they seek to advance.[11]

Therefore, unlike most anti-subsidy measures in the international arena, which are at best contingent protection instruments, the aim of the EU state aid policy is to protect the competitive health of the Community economy, and not to protect industrial competitors from injury. That is, it is the subsidy and not the trade remedy that is seen as a form of contingent protection. Indeed, the Commission suggested that state aids may be used illegitimately to 'defend companies or industries coming under pressure from...increased competition,... [and] that industrial structures will become ossified'.[12]

There is no indication that there is in the EU a particularly strong moral aversion (as witnessed in the USA) to government involvement in the enconomy.[13] The legitimacy of the goals advanced (or attempted to be advanced) by government practices is (generally) not denied; the chief concern is that advancing these interests by one government may increase the costs of maintaining the same interests in another country.[14] In balancing these interests, more than a simple denunciation of all subsidies is required. Thus, the Commission enjoys the power 'to take into account economic, social and political considerations' in determining the compatibility of state aids to the common market.[15]

The state aid policy is a key component of the Competition Policy of the Community, which in theory is driven by the imperatives of economic growth and integration of the economies of its Member States,[16] and it is in this context that it should be understood. As European economies are increasingly integrated and competition becomes more intense, the pressure on national governments to protect their own industries also increases. In the absence of duties (even – perhaps especially – countervailing duties) a favoured method of protection is state aid schemes. The Commission has reacted to this trend by 'strengthening the effectiveness of Community state aid control and identifying types of aid which merit particularly close attention'.[17] As a result, a number of surveys have been completed to increase the transparency of state aids in the Community.[18] Also, there have been detailed studies of ways of identifying the state aid element in areas where government involvement in the market place or government aid to industry may be otherwise justified.[19]

The difficulty is not just in areas where government expenditures (direct or indirect) affect the market. There are also concerns about 'distinguishing the grant of state aid from the operation of ordinary fiscal measures, social security measures, infrastructure improvements' and other instruments of social policy.[20] Or there may even be 'regulatory subsidies' when 'government regulations impose direct transfers from consumers to producers by fixing prices above market prices. . .'.[21] Developing jurisprudence looks to the effects of a measure to determine the existence of state aid.[22] Once aid is identified, there is a presumption that the interests of the Union are being affected adversely.[23]

Institutional framework

The Commission has the authority to regulate state aid to industry under Articles 92 and 93 of the Treaty of Rome. This authority has been further clarified and strengthened by a number of Council and Commission Regulations, Decisions, and Directives over the years. This section will examine the institutional framework in which state aid to industry is regulated by the Commission of the European Union.

Article 92.1 imposes a qualified ban on

> any aid granted by Member States or through State resources in any form whatsoever which distorts or threatens to distort competition by favouring certain undertakings or the production of certain goods . . . in so far as it affects trade between Member States.[24]

The qualifications, set out in 92.2 and 92.3, are aids

a) 'having a social character, granted to individual consumers',[25]
b) to assist with damage caused by natural disasters,[26]
c) to regions of the Federal Republic of Germany disadvantaged by the division, for 'abnormally' underdeveloped areas,[27]
d) for 'an important project of common European interest',[28]
e) 'to facilitate the development of certain economic activities or of certain economic areas' (but not shipbuilding),[29]
f) to 'promote culture and heritage conservation where such aid does not affect trading conditions and competition in the Community to an extent that is contrary to the common interest',[30]
g) to other areas as designated by the Council on the proposal of the Commission.[31]

The Commission is mandated under Article 93.1 to 'keep under constant review all systems of aid existing' in Member States. Under Article 93.2 the Commission may find that a state aid is incompatible with the common market and 'decide' that the state must abolish or alter the scheme. The Commission may take Member States to the ECJ if they do not comply with its decisions.[32] Member States are under an obligation under Article 93.3 to inform the Commission of any plans to 'grant or alter aid'. If the Commission finds such grants or alteration incompatible with the common market, it may initiate an investigation under Article 93.2.[33] The offending Member State is under an obligation not to implement the scheme until there is a final decision by the Commission.

In order to strengthen the notification rules of Article 93.3, the Commission may even require Member States to 'recover aid granted illegally from recipients',[34] including applicable interest charges,[35] or to suspend payment of unnotified aid should a Member State fail to reply 'satisfactorily' to the Commission's request for information.[36] The obligation to notify is without exception, so is the requirement under Article 93.3 for the suspension of benefits. In fact, in 1987 the Commission pointedly warned potential recipients of state aid 'of the risk attaching to any aid granted them illegally', in that absent a final decision by the Commission, the recipient may have to refund the full amount plus applicable interest charges.[37]

State aid covered by Article 92 must be sector- or region-specific. General measures that may distort competition are covered by Articles 101–2. This is a crucial difference, for as the Commission noted in its *Second Survey of State Aids*, the aim of the competition policy is not to remove fundamental differences in tax or cost structures among nations.[38] General measures that may distort 'conditions of competition' among Member States are to be considered by the Council, and the initial directives on the topic must be issued by unanimous vote.[39] However, the distinction may be artificial in certain circumstances. For example, 'general investment schemes which are not directed at a specific industry or region and do not pursue a specific community objective' were considered by the Commission to be state aid 'schemes most likely to distort competition and trade in the community'.[40] In the *Nineteenth Report on Competition Policy* the Commission reiterated its belief that general investment aids are 'generally lacking in any regional or sectoral impact', but promised that it 'will in future take an increasingly negative attitude to this type of aid. . .'.[41] Therefore, such schemes are governed by the provisions of Article 92, even though they may be general and widely available, or offered through 'ordinary fiscal measures'. The Commission, it seems, is casting as wide a net as possible to bring matters under Article 92, rather than leaving them to the Council under Article 101. It is not clear, however, who decides whether to pursue matters under Articles 92–3 or through the Articles 101–2 mechanism. If the decision involves the Member State under investigation, then it could throw the matter into the Council where the Member State may have more input in decisions made than if the Commission alone made a decision on the matter.

Derogations

The substance of the state aid regime in the European Community may best be understood by examining the exceptions to the prohibition. There are two broad categories of exceptions: 1) regional and sectoral aid schemes, and 2) 'matters of Community interest', which, broadly interpreted, include Research and Development expenditure, aid to the Airbus Consortium, and other aid schemes determined by the Commission to be of importance to the Community. Also known as 'horizontal policies', such schemes 'take as their starting point the desirability of aid to accomplish certain goals'.[42] The determination of the value of the goals to the Union is the responsibility of the Commission.

Many of the policies relating to these derogations have been developed in directives issued by a Commission trying to 'make the completion of the internal market politically acceptable'.[43] This is especially true in matters of regional aid and in countries such as Italy with extreme disparities of wealth among regions, or Portugal, which is a poor region in its entirety. In this way, the Commission reassures the poorer regions that 'Competition policy and cohesion[44] are . . . complements and not contradictory',[45] by ensuring that 'the benefits produced by [the economic] union are distributed in a way that is perceived as fair'.[46]

Regional aid schemes

The Commission has three basic concerns with regional aid schemes. First, such aid is generally aimed at keeping companies within the granting country. This is a form of regressive regional development, for if such aids are allowed, richer countries will be able to dissuade industries from relocating to and developing poorer countries. Secondly, regional aid may improve the returns of the recipient on its investment and thus distort competition. Third, the Commission is concerned with a Union-wide level of development, whereas granting countries have only their own national development levels in mind. This is problematic, because in the Union the poorest regions of the richest country are substantially better off than the richest parts of the poorest country, and nationally determined aid could further exacerbate the regional disparities among the Member States of the EU.

The first and third concerns were somewhat alleviated as a result of the growing acceptance by the Member States of a Union-wide understanding of regional development aid. Finding a solution was further aided by the development of a proportionality test for the provision of aid by national governments to sectors or industries located in disadvantaged regions.[47] For example, in a case dealing with the Shorts Brothers Plc. plant in Northern Ireland, the Commission determined that the aid was 'commensurate with the problems it was intended to resolve'.[48] There was also a shift in emphasis with the development of Union-wide programmes such as Structural Funds.[49] The objective is to make regional development an EU, rather than a national matter.

Aside from proportionality of aid to problem, the Commission also examines whether the region to which the aid scheme is directed is clearly identifiable (though larger than a single location; for example, Luxembourg as a whole is considered a region), the aid is open, and prior notification is given to the Commission, and whether the scheme fits within a co-ordinated EU regional aid programme.[50]

The second concern was more difficult to resolve. It arose out of the Members' propensity to provide operating grants, production aid, and investment aid to any firm in trouble. Operating grants, however, are considered to be particularly objectionable by the Commission; these are opposed even if the result of a remission or cancellation of an aid scheme is the closure of the prospective recipient.[51] Production aid schemes are viewed equally unfavourably.[52] However, in the context of the EU's rules on regional aid, both types of schemes, as well as employment maintenance schemes, may be acceptable.[53] This is partly the result of the clarification of the policy on regional aid, but other considerations may also have been operative.

One such reasonable justification is presented by Romoli with respect to the extensive operating grants by the Italian government to companies relocating in the poorest parts of Italy. The relocation of many companies to these underdeveloped and disadvantaged areas is not altogether voluntary. The imposition of such 'improper social and environmental burdens' on Italian companies by the Italian government[54] necessarily causes massive losses, which are covered by operating grants, forgiveness of loans, and other aid schemes. Therefore, the objective of the aid is not to make Italian companies more profitable, or to advance Italian export interests, but rather 'to promote such basic goals as the country's economic development, the alignment of the standard of life in southern regions, . . . [and] the increase of employment particularly in the country's underdeveloped regions. . .'.[55] In determining the nature of the aid and its impact on trade among EU Members, it is not relevant whether development of these regions would be better or more efficiently achieved through other means, as long as the measures are proportionate to the scale of the problem the aids in question purport to address. Whether for political or economic reasons, the Commission seems to have adopted Romoli's analysis.

'Matters of interest to the community'

This has become the most significant of the exceptions allowed under Article 92. The principal area in which derogation are granted by the Commission is in Research and Development (R&D) spending. Evans and Martin observe that underlying 'this policy is an evident belief in market failure, as regards technological advance. State aid is seen as a device for improving on the performance of the unaided market'.[56] A study prepared for the Commission also notes the 'favourable view of state aid to R&D' by the Commission and posits two reasons for this. First, the high financing requirements of R&D spending and the risks involved might result in a less than optimal investment by private actors in the market. Second, acceptable R&D spending is sufficiently distant from the marketplace so as to distort competition or trade within the EU minimally.[57]

However, the difficulty with this reasoning is that in determining the validity of an R&D scheme, the Commission makes no attempt to verify whether the research *could have been* undertaken by a commercial enterprise, or that competition or trade is not affected by the scheme. The study notes a number of ways in which even the most innocuous scheme could have an aid element[58] but does not arrive at a satisfactory solution. The *Second Survey* pointed out that 'certain aids having primarily horizontal objectives [R&D] may be used as instruments of industrial policy and have more in common with sectoral aids'.[59] Targeted R&D spending may go as far as 'aiding investment in the sector.'[60] There is more than a slight chance that R&D spending may distort competition or trade within the EU.

The Commission's view of aid to the European aviation industry highlights the true nature of the 'Community interest' exception to state aids. In assessing the compatibility of a German exchange rate guarantee to Messerschmidt–Bölkow–Blohm (MBB), the German arm of the Airbus Consortium (which scheme, incidentally, continues to be a major irritant in EU–US trade relations) the Commission considered the co-operation among several Member States in developing and manufacturing Airbus and agreed that 'the proposed measure would strengthen the overall competitiveness of the sector. . .'.[61] The scheme qualified for derogation under Article 92.3(b). Obviously the concern was with the international, and not the internal, competitiveness of the sector. It is difficult to determine where 'Community interest' ends and 'Community-wide industrial policy' begins.

Evaluation: Regulation or channelling of state aid?

The twelve countries of the European Union spent ECU89 b. on state aid schemes in 1990. This represented an overall decline from previous years.[62] The aid is heavily concentrated: 60 per cent of the total aid goes to three sectors: transport, the coal industry, and agriculture/fisheries. The remaining 40 per cent goes to manufacturing, with cars, electronics and aviation receiving 18 per cent of the total aid.[63] The absolute amount of aid can be staggering in some instances. For example, the government-owned Electricité de France has been allowed to run up a FFr240 b. debt load, with minimal repayments, to the French government. In Germany, coal subsidies run to about DM88 a tonne, compared with DM6 for Britain. In Britain, ECU14 b. was poured into the coal industry between 1980 and 1989.[64] Italy spends over ECU27 b. a year on industrial subsidies.[65] The Commission was optimistic that improvement of transparency, repayment of illegal aid, rules for steel and shipbuilding aid, and the establishment of clear priorities will help it in curbing distortive state aids.[66]

Indeed, the Commission has been diligent in initiating investigations of Member States' state aid practices.[67] However, the experience of the Commission in granting derogations to various types of state aid points to two interesting developments. First, especially in the case of regional aid but also in 'Community interest' derogations, the Commission has not been above the political fray, and its decisions point to a keen recognition of the difficulty of pursuing a strictly economic logic in assessing the legality of state aid schemes. There seem to be two considerations operating here:

a) Evans and Martin suggest that there appears to be a willingness on part of the Commission 'to permit the use of state aid as a device to resolve political problems,' especially those associated with the completion of the single market.[68] It may be said that the supreme interest of the EU, that is, the completion of the market, may override specific concerns over (possibly) distortive state aid in certain circumstances. It is, however, questionable whether a supranational bureaucratic body should be involved in such political decision-making practices.

b) The French paper and pulp subsidies case showed that the Council may avail itself of its power to intervene in state aid cases. There, the Council allowed France to retain its subsidies.[69] While such interventions are few, they add another layer of political considerations to the exercise. Thus, the Commission may not only be mindful of political difficulties in the EU at large, but may exercise its powers under Articles 92–3 with a diligent eye toward the Council.

Secondly, the 'Community interest' derogations point to an interesting trend. The Commission has expanded the meaning of Article 92 to cover most governmental industrial measures, but does not object to state aid that advances an EU-wide 'interest'. This is an important point, for it puts into question the sincerity of the Commission's vociferous and perennial criticism of state aid as 'a threat to social and economic cohesion'.[70] It appears that the Commission's powers are being used to replace national industrial policy with an EU industrial policy; state aid schemes are particularly suited to advance this objective. This seems to be the only explanation for the incongruity between Brittan's warning that 'governments [use] aids as a means of protecting national champions in key sectors'[71] (implying that such protection is not sound economic policy) and the Commission's practice, for example in its tolerance of German, English, French and Spanish state aid for the protection of an EU champion (Airbus) in a key sector (aviation).

This does not mean that Articles 92–3 are the only tools used by the Commission for the advancement of an EU industrial policy. As already noted, the Commission does not have a deep seated aversion to government involvement in the marketplace. Aside from the Structural Funds, which are regional development programmes administered by the Commission (and which, incidentally, are quietly but progressively replacing national regional aid programmes), the Commission intervenes in the market through subsidies in such areas as Research and Development, the coal and steel industries, and shipbuilding. The Commission justifies the exclusion of these programmes from the competition section of the Treaty on the ground that 'their resources are allocated according to Community criteria with the specific intention of avoiding any advantage to particular Member States which is not in conformity with Community policy'.[72] The Commission is of the view that 'the integration of competition policy with other Community policies is, in general, adequate and that there is no reason to fear the occurrence of serious anomalies'.[73]

If the concern over state aid to industry is healthy competition and efficient resource allocation, as the Commission emphasises time and again, this cannot be an adequate response. Avoiding advantage to

Member States says nothing about the allocative efficiency of the aid scheme, for example aid to shipbuilding, or even the more neutral and ambitious EU R&D programmes.

However, if regulation of state aid by the Commission is seen as an arm of its industrial policy development, then the many contradictions and exceptions begin to make more sense. The integration is 'adequate' and no 'anomalies' are expected, because the competition policy itself is driven by 'other Community policies'. Indeed, the Commission admits that although it has been strict in its monitoring of state aid,

> account must ... be taken of the common interest when determining the compatibility of aid with the common market. ... [the] derogations are necessary if competition policy is to play its role fully, without thwarting other Community policies provided for in the Treaty with a view to promoting the harmonious development of the Community as a whole. ... the Commission continue[s] to take a favourable view not only of regional development aid but also of *certain other types of aid that may be accepted where they are needed in order to encourage activities which are in the interests of the Community as a whole but which market forces alone might generate too slowly or in insufficient numbers.*[74]

Thus, whether by chance or by design, the mechanism set out in Articles 92–3 of the Treaty of Rome for imposing a discipline on state aid to industry now seems to advance the primary objective of developing an EU industrial policy and channelling state aid to serve that policy.

A secondary objective is to avoid the perverse redistributive effects of allowing richer areas to entice industries away from the poorer regions by providing generous aid, which is beyond the ability of those regions. As the Commission notes,

> the uncontrolled proliferation of state aids could vitiate the structural change necessary to achieve and underpin the single market and, given the volume of resources available to the richer central states, would threaten the efficient contribution of the Commission's Structural Funds to greater convergence and economic and social cohesion of the Member States.[75]

Eradicating state aid as an inherently market distortive practice comes in a poor third.

This discussion should be reevaluated, however, if the present trends continue in the Union. The Commission is increasingly dealing with cases on state aids to banking and insurance, the audiovisual sector, the entertainment and leisure industries and other service sectors.[76] This may be of significance given the newly added derogation for cultural industries. If this trend continues, and as traditional forms of subsidies are discarded in favour of more innovative policies due to ever increasing budgetary pressures, the focus of the Commission may change. The lack of a strictly doctrinaire approach to subsidies and their regulation enables the Commission not only to keep the Member states satisfied by judicious use of the derogations, as we have seen, but also to examine, pursue and discipline new methods of state aid in order to maintain the integrity of the single market.

SUPRANATIONALISM: POLITICS BY BUREAUCRATIC FIAT

The first EEA Agreement did not survive a judicial challenge and the EFTA Surveillance Authority has not come into being yet. The EU Commission is the only supranational institution charged with regulating and disciplining domestic industrial subsidies. Its success, and the success of other supranational institutions as they come into being, should be gauged against more than publicly stated objectives and conceptual arguments: the survival, health, and growth of the system itself is an objective, though usually ignored in academic studies.

A supranational institution is in a precarious position. It has no army and no police force to enforce its decisions. Instead, it relies entirely upon the goodwill of the Members it supervises to carry out its decisions, however unfavourable, however politically unpalatable. In fact, it is always in danger of issuing decisions that are too unpalatable, and this is where the task of the supranational body becomes difficult. Courts and bureaucracies are not, by nature, disposed or even equipped to be cognisant of, or responsive to, political considerations.

This is particularly true in Europe. In the EU and EFTA, supranational bodies are removed by geography and often by language and culture from populations who are affected by their every decision: Brussels will not feel the pressures a Greek government faces when European decisions harm Greek interests; a Geneva (or Brussels) based EFTA Surveillance Authority will hardly ever see the Icelandic fisheries workers or Finnish shipbuilders it will put out of work through its anti-subsidy decisions.

To a great extent, in the field of state aid the EU Commission seems to have recognised its inherent institutional weaknesses. The lack of a doctrinaire approach to subsidies in Europe has allowed the Commission to concentrate on reducing the negative trade effects of the most harmful subsidies programmes, while preserving, or even judiciously rechanelling, the most sensitive European state aid schemes. Because of the great powers it can exercise and because the exercise of those powers can come to nought if done rashly or dogmatically, the EU Commission has incorporated the paradox of subsidies in its investigative process. It can be expected that the EFTA Surveillance Authority and the EEA will follow the example of the EU, and even achieve its moderate success.

Another lesson to be learned from the EEA and the EU is that supranationalism cannot work without two basic elements; too basic, perhaps. The first is trust, and the second, goodwill. The EEA could not have come about, either as a supranational institution or as a multilateral one, if the Parties had not placed trust in the surveillance authorities to carry out their functions fairly and according to agreed upon rules. Each party, moreover, was able to set aside the beggar-thy-neighbour policies of mercantilism and attempted to make the shared institutions work. This is the element of goodwill. It involves avoiding the use of litigation for its own sake, accepting in principle different government policies and social objectives, generally being willing to compromise to ensure the proper working of the system, and not attempting to rig it for unilateral gain.

This is not to stay that the EU Commission has not faced major difficulties in establishing its authority. National governments, courts and undertakings have challenged the Commission at every turn. The Commission has had its share of success, but it has suffered setbacks as well. However, despite the ongoing challenge of identifying state aids, gathering information about them, and finally regulating them, the Commission has been moderately successful in exercising a measure of regulatory control of state aids in the EU, and has enjoyed a great deal of success in establishing its authority in this area.

5

UNILATERAL REGULATION OF SUBSIDIES

"I'll be judge, I'll be jury", said cunning old Fury;
"I'll try the whole cause, and condemn you to death".[1]

INTRODUCTION

The international institutions discussed so far have at least one thing in common: the definition of subsidies and the determination of whether certain practices constitute a subsidy are left to international bodies. In the case of GATT Track II, or even EFTA in the late 1960s, this led to definitional chaos and ultimately the breakdown of the process. However, the one constant was that no country judged the government practices of its trading partners unilaterally. Even in bilateral contexts, the emphasis was on negotiation and compromise through international institutions, rather than accusation and confrontation, practices which characterise unilateralism.

Any regime that regulates subsidies must have at least three components: definition, investigation and discipline. Unilateralism is characterised by the fact that all three components of the regulatory regime are established by the complainant country within a broad and generally unhelpful international framework. In this context, each country may decide for itself what it will determine to be a subsidy, how it will verify the existence of a subsidy, and which subsidies it will consider punishable.

The instrument of choice in unilateral regimes for the regulation of subsidies is the countervailing duty (CVD). CVDs are imposed pursuant to a successful allegation of subsidisation by a foreign government and the showing of injury to domestic interests before a domestic tribunal. The tribunals base their analyses on definitions provided by domestic authorities and impose CVDs on the basis of domestic criteria. These definitions and criteria may, for the most part, be altered unilaterally and without reference to international agreements by legislative, adjudicative, or even bureaucratic decree. It is therefore not surprising that unilateralism has been viewed as a major threat to the health of the international trading order and that there have been many attempts to bring it under multilateral control. This effort has met with mixed success.

The following discussion will concentrate on the problem as well as the cure; on CVD laws and international attempts at curbing them. Two regimes that have attempted to bring CVDs under control will be examined: the GATT Subsidies Code Track I DRM, and the Canada–US Free Trade Agreement, and its extension to Mexico, the North American Free Trade Agreement. As well, the CVD laws of the US, Canada and the EU will be examined in order to highlight the difficulties inherent in unilateralism.

GATT SUBSIDIES CODE TRACK I

Countervailing duties are governed by Article VI of the GATT and Part I of the Subsidies Code. Article VI of the GATT imposes two broad limits on the imposition of CVDs. First, according to Subarticle VI.3, the countervailing duty should be no more than the amount of the estimated subsidy granted to the product in question. Second, under Clause VI.6(a) no countervailing duty may be imposed unless the subsidy causes or threatens to cause material injury to an established industry, or retards the development of a domestic industry.

Part I of the Subsidies Code clarifies the application of Article VI. Of interest for our purpose is Article 4, which sets out the criteria for the imposition of countervailing duties. Clause 4(1) states that

> the decision whether or not to impose a countervailing duty in cases where all requirements for the imposition have been fulfilled and the decision whether the amount of the countervailing duty to be imposed shall be the full amount of the subsidy or less are decisions to be made by the authorities of the importing signatory.

This is the essence of unilateralism. It must be borne in mind that the GATT does not have a concrete definition of 'subsidy'. Thus, the investigating authority is left to define what a subsidy is and also to establish a domestic countervailing procedure within the broad outlines of the Subsidies Code.

Disputes over the GATT-legality of CVDs may be taken to the GATT dispute resolution mechanism. The GATT DRM, like the Track II mechanism discussed above, works through the consultation/conciliation/dispute resolution process. The contracting parties may discipline the wrongdoer by multilateral suspension of benefits; however, since the contracting parties must agree on measures unanimously, the party against whom the action has been brought can block the recommendation of the panel or the adoption of disciplinary measures. As a result, GATT has been unable to develop a strong jurisprudence in this area. The GATT Subsidies Code Track I mechanism is a 'unilateral' instrument for the regulation of subsidies insofar as the specific definition of wrongful practices, initiation of an investigation, and the imposition of a discipline measure *against the subsidised imports* are not contingent upon discussion and agreement by an international institution.

Since the Tokyo Round many countries have availed themselves of the opportunity offered by the Subsidies Code for unilateral regulation of subsidies by enacting countervailing duty provisions. Even those countries with CVD regimes before the Tokyo Round have moved to take advantage of all the measures allowed by the Code. In this section I will discuss the CVD regulations of the European Union. The CVD laws of the US and Canada will be discussed in the context of the Canada–US Free Trade Agreement, another regime that relies primarily on CVDs for the regulation and discipline of domestic subsidies. The differences between the European and the North American approaches are significant. However, the EU has used its CVD laws sparingly. As a result, there is much less material on the EU CVD regime than, for example, on the US trade remedy laws.

CVD Regulations of the European Union

The approach of the European Union is that 'State intervention in the market is not considered unfair *per se* [as] it often promotes important social purposes'.[2] Government involvement in the market and aid to industry are not synonymous with state aids (or subsidies). The mere presence of the government in the market cannot be dispositive of anything, since there is an acknowledgement that 'intervention in the market by governments may pose no more problems or adverse effects on trade flows than intervention in the market by the largest multi-national corporations'.[3] Even when this involvement has taken the form of industrial subsidies the Commission has reacted with less rhetoric and aggressiveness than the US. This has partly to do with the general approach of the Commission to most trade disputes among nations. As Malmgren observes, the practice of the Commission has been to work the problems out through conciliation and negotiation.[4] It also has to do with the conceptual basis of the Union's CVD Regulations. Unlike the US, the concern of the Commission is not so much with the aggrieved producers or manufacturers as it is with the competitive health of the Union.[5] The 'Community interest' test, which as we have seen is an integral part of the EU's internal state aid regulatory regime, is also an important element of its CVD Regulations.[6] In this sense, at an abstract conceptual level the Commission does not seem to treat foreign subsidisers differently from its own Member states.

Regulatory and institutional framework

The Commission of the European Union is responsible for investigating allegations of subsidisation and imposing protective CVDs. The antidumping provisions have by far been the more popular trade remedy provision, and therefore more has been written about these than the CVD regimes. However, since the Community's antidumping and CVD procedure are identical institutionally the analysis is interchangeable.

Investigation and determination

Two points are worth discussing here. First, The Commission is responsible for examining both the facts surrounding the alleged subsidy and the alleged resulting Community injury.[7] As will be seen, this is in sharp contrast to both the Canadian and the US practice, where the task of determining the margin of subsidisation and the examination of injury is bifurcated. Secondly, while autonomous of its political master (as are Canadian and US authorities, nominally at least), the Commission is not above the political fray. Unlike the US[8] and Canadian[9] trade remedy administering agencies, the Commission has the task of developing and administering the EU's trade policy; as a result it tends to have a more global view of its actions. To the extent that the Commission has to ensure that the Union's trading partners and Member States accept its decisions, and given the EU's preference for arriving at negotiated settlements rather than unilateral imposition of punitive measures, its processes are clearly politicised, if to a different degree and in a different manner than the US system.[10]

Imposition of CVDs

A positive determination of subsidisation or even injury does not imply an automatic imposition of CVDs. The Commission takes the view that CVDs (and antidumping measures, which are much more widely used)

> are measures for exceptional protection, and their adoption appears to be required, in spite of significant damage to an industry, only when the public sphere of interest is finally affected.[11]

The Commission is under an obligation to take into account more than the interests of the injured industry alone; it must, in addition, take into account 'other industrial and trade policy interests' of the Union.[12] Moreover, the Regulations expressly mandate the Commission to impose a lower duty than the level of subsidisation if it 'would be sufficient to eliminate the injury'.[13]

Definition of subsidy

Article 23 of the Regulations states that 'every sum granted directly or indirectly on the manufacture, production, export or transport of goods in the country of origin or exportation is to be regarded as a bounty or subsidy'.[14] No direct grant is necessary; indirect measures of aid, domestic aid, or any measure that may reduce the cost of manufacturing is covered by this provision.[15] The key question seems to be whether an impugned measure imposes a charge on the public account.[16] In *Ballbearings from Thailand* the Commission compared interest rates of government loans to an industry to bonds and bills issued by the government and not to other commercial loans available to the industry. In this case, despite an obvious benefit to the company, no direct cost to government was shown, and no subsidy was determined to exist.[17] However, should a charge on the public account be identified, the Commission does not take a 'net–net' approach to subsidies.[18] The only deductions from identified subsidies by the Commission for the calculation of the countervailing duty are taxes 'specifically designed to offset the subsidy' and other relevant charges, such as subsidy application fees.[19]

The Commission has been reluctant to impose CVDs against subsidies not directly tied to export enhancement. The only example seems to be CVDs on Brazilian IPI tax exemptions for imported industrial machinery.[20] It is argued that the reluctance of the Commission is due to its own involvement in massive industrial and agricultural subsidisation.[21] Bourgeois, however, states that the reason for Union's less active use of its CVD Regulations is that they are applied in strict adherence to the provisions of Article VI of the GATT and other provisions of the Subsidies Code. This, he argues, is in direct contrast to the broad interpretation placed on these provisions by US authorities.[22]

The trade remedy regulations of the EU are interesting, however, for reasons other than the Commission's preference for political or negotiated solutions, its strict adherence to GATT principles, or its definitional approach. Possibly as a result of the Commission's experience in the internal state aid regime of the EU, the CVD Regulations set the stage for the first application of trade remedy principles to trade in services, specifically to trade in maritime shipping services. This requires closer scrutiny.

'Unfair pricing practices in maritime transport'

Strictly speaking, the EU's charges on unfair pricing practices are not CVDs. The significance of this regulation lies in the fact that for all practical purposes, it seeks to impose discipline on subsidy-like measures aimed at protecting maritime shipping; Yi and Choi characterise it as a combination of antidumping and anti-subsidy notions.[23] It is a form of *unilateral* discipline mechanism, as yet unregulated by international law and practice, and likely to find favour as trade in services increases its share of trade among nations.

The relevant regulation was enacted under the authority of the Council under Clause 84(2) of the Treaty of Rome, the first article in the Treaty's competition section. It targets unfair pricing practices 'made possible by non-commercial[24] advantages granted [to a concern] by a state which is not a member of the Community'.[25] As with the CVD regulation, there is a requirement for showing of material injury to the complainants,[26] while the Council is obliged to take 'due account' of external policy considerations, port interests, and shipping policy considerations of Member States concerned.[27] Again, as with the CVD regulations, the amount of the duty is not to exceed the difference in freight rates between the domestic and (unfairly competitive) foreign shippers, and should be 'less if less is enough to remove the injury'.[28] Article 15 imposes a 'sunset' limit of 5 years, after which time the duty will be removed unless a review determines otherwise. Unlike the CVD regulations, however, 'non-commercial advantages' (subsidy-like measures) are not defined, and the final decision as to whether or not to impose a duty is left to the Council, a political body.

The scope of a 'non-commercial advantage' in Union parlance is almost as wide as what the USITA[29] considers – or may consider, if the present trend continues – to be a 'subsidy'. Yi and Choi argue that it could include

> direct or indirect financial aid, special credit conditions, advantageous tax regimes, the employment of seamen on terms and conditions which do not conform to ILO standards and cargo reservation schemes which grant national fleets more favourable access to cargo trade and guarantee them an income thereby enabling them to undercut market rates.[30]

By not defining 'non-commercial advantages', the Commission and Council have allowed themselves a wide latitude to investigate and discipline practices in maritime transport which may be injurious to EU interests, regardless of the fact that the impugned activities may otherwise be considered legitimate by the international community.

The first effective action against trade in services was brought before the Council in 1988. In Council Regulation no. 15/89[31] the Council assessed a duty against Hyundai, the Korean multinational conglomerate. The case involved a cargo reservation scheme devised by the Korean government to benefit Korean shipping companies including Hyundai, by granting them exclusive rights on carrying cement, iron, and steel from Korea, and preferential rights to carry all other cargo. The Council was of the opinion that

> a cargo reservation scheme in international shipping [was] a unilateral impediment to the principle of free access to cargoes in ocean trades and thus a non-commercial advantage for the shipping companies benefiting from it.[32]

The Council argued that the 'guarantee of access to a substantial volume of business' to the Korean shippers secured them a base load and gave them 'valuable support in a world market still facing recession'.[33] The revenue and commercial flexibility which Hyundai gained as a result of this guarantied business were disadvantageous and uncompetitive for the European shipping companies.

The advantages to Hyundai did not end there. According to the Council, Hyundai benefited from a refinancing scheme which was an 'unusual commercial practice even in Korea'.[34] While the refinancing was not done by the Korean government itself, its encouragement of Korean bankers and other authorities granted 'Hyundai advantages which under normal commercial conditions were not available'.[35] As a result, and following the rejection of a 'Community interest' argument advanced by Hyundai,[36] a duty was imposed on all containerised cargo on board Hyundai ships.

Analysis

The lack of a definition in the GATT of what constitutes a subsidy has meant that national authorities have been free to define foreign practices which they consider to be 'subsidy' or state aid measures. The EU has not been active in this area, but it, too, has begun testing the waters of unilateralism. Not only did it enact, and subsequently use, CVD regulations (however limited the use may have been compared with the US), but it proceeded to extend anti-subsidy concepts to trade in services.

The enactment of the maritime transport regulations has probably more to do with the vacuum existing in GATT's definitional approach to subsidies than its silence on the issue of services. A key component in any viable international instrument must be a limitations clause: a clause that will foreclose the possibility of negative evolution – the extension of CVD concepts to trade in services, for example – within the system. Multilateral instruments protect against this by requiring unanimous consent for any change; there the danger is stagnation, not regression. The maritime transport regulation is a good example of negative evolution or regression in the international CVD regime.

GATT's difficulties do not end here. The failure of multilateral institutions to deal with long-standing trade disputes between the USA and Canada led the latter to 'sue for peace' and request the opening of bilateral trade talks. The Canada–US Free Trade Agreement was intended to address the issue of subsidies and perhaps even resolve it. It nearly broke down on the first and did not do the second. But it did create a mechanism that incorporated elements of unilateralism with pseudo-supranational arbitration panels. I will examine this mechanism in the next part. I will also examine the CVD laws of the US and Canada, in order to put the GATT and the FTA in a fuller perspective. It will be argued that some of the most fundamental flaws of the unilateral system of the GATT were not dealt with and that what promised to be a cure-all of sorts may yet end up being disastrous for Canada–US trade relations. It will be argued that the potential for regression is as strong as it was before the Canada–US FTA came into force.

THE CANADA–US FREE TRADE AGREEMENT

The FTA owes its survival to a literally last minute improvisation by the political masters of the trade negotiators for the two countries. Two significant points in the compromise on the question of subsidies/countervailing duties (and antidumping duties) made an agreement possible after the initial breakdown of the Canada–US free trade negotiations: first, the agreement 'does not alter the substance of existing antidumping and countervailing duty laws'.[37] Thus, the US retains its freedom of action in disciplining practices it considers 'pernicious'. Secondly, Canada has gained a limited right to 'have an influence on US trade law decisions'[38] through a binational judicial review process. The FTA does not have a subsidies code, nor does it have a commission or a panel that can define, investigate, or regulate the state aid practices of the parties; the agreement relies on a unilateral policing of each party's subsidies by the other party. To understand the regime by which subsidies are defined and regulated it is necessary, therefore, to study the national laws dealing with countervailing duties. In the following, I will examine the trade remedy laws of the US and Canada. Next, I will discuss the DRM outlined in Article 1904 to resolve disputes arising out of the imposition of unilateral measures to curb the use of harmful domestic industrial subsidies, and incidentally (at least from a Canadian perspective, as argued by Anderson and Rugman, *supra*), to give Canada a voice in the development of US trade law jurisprudence.

The United States Countervailing Duty Law

Much has been written about the historical development of CVDs, which are the most important instrument of contingent protectionism in the US. It is not necessary to retrace the entire history of the law. It suffices to point out the periodic review by Congress of the United States trade laws and the developing tendency of these laws toward unilateral action, removal of executive discretion in imposing duties, providing greater opportunity for private interests to initiate investigations, and the widening ambit of governmental actions that may be subject to a positive finding of subsidisation.[39] Based on historical trends, it is likely that Congress will in the future further limit the discretion of the Executive and administrative agencies in investigating cases, make it easier for US industry to file and win claims, and, as it has done in its anticircumvention measures,[40] make it more difficult for companies to avoid the effects of these duties by relocation or by devising even more elaborate methods of subsidisation.

The current law, amended by the 1988 Trade Act,[41] is codified in Subtitle IV, Title 19 of the US Code. In the following I will study the institutional framework within which CVD determinations are made. Then, I will discuss the substance of the US CVD law. But first, an examination of the conceptual basis of the law will be helpful for achieving a better understanding of the US law and practice in this area.

Conceptual considerations

It is difficult to determine with certainty the underlying rationale of the US CVD law. Broadly speaking, it aims to alleviate harm to US industries caused by foreign subsidisation practices. But some aspects of the law, and the developing practice, may bring that into question. Recently, there have been attempts by some academic commentators to fathom the rationale and perhaps even suggest better and more conceptually coherent approaches to subsidy and injury determinations.[42] However, the extent to which either the ITA or the United States International Trade Commission (ITC) is responsive to academic concerns is not clear. Nor is it at all clear that the various organs responsible for the making of trade policy in this area, including the White House and Congress, pursue or even intend to pursue a coherent philosophy in shaping CVD law and practice in the United States.[43] Understanding this fragmentation of policy-making foci is crucial in developing protection against CVD determinations.

The US Senate, in a Report on the Trade Agreements Act of 1979, said that subsidies are one of the 'most pernicious practices which distort international trade to the disadvantage of United States Commerce. . . . Countervailing duties are special duties imposed to offset the effects of the foreign subsidy'.[44] The House of Representatives noted with satisfaction the recognition by the GATT Subsidies Code that domestic subsidies used to promote important objectives of national policy can also have harmful trade effects. The United States merely sought greater discipline over 'subsidies that confer unfair competitive advantages upon the products of the subsidising country'.[45] De Kieffer argues that the purpose of the countervailing duty law in the United States is 'merely to equalize the conditions of competition in a capitalist economy'.[46] Brown, in discussing the famous *Zenith* case[47] suggests that 'since the US has emerged as a world leader in production and marketing techniques, domestic producers no longer require the security of protective tariffs.'[48] Therefore, he argues,

> countervailing duty policy has changed from a protective device to one designed to neutralise any unfair competitive advantage bestowed upon foreign producers, so as to maximize those benefits presumed to flow from fair and equal competition.[49]

Another Member of Congress, a Chair of the Subcommittee of Trade of the House of Representatives, believed that countervailing duties were normatively proper, since 'victimized firms had a right to offsets for foreign subsidies . . .'.[50]

Thus, two general justifications advanced for the use of countervailing duties against foreign government subsidy practices are 1) harm to domestic industry resulting from 'unfair' competitive advantage, and 2) distortions caused in international trade by the subsidies. However, the CVD law in the US does not seem rationally connected to either basis.

First, the US CVD regime does not have a strong causation test. That is, in making an injury determination, there is very little analysis done by the ITC to separate the operation of ordinary market forces from the effects of the subsidy practices and the subsidised imports on the injured industry.[51] As such, fair and unfair competitive advantage seem to be devoid of any real meaning.[52] Second, the requirement that the duty imposed be in the amount of the subsidy is problematic. As Diamond observes, such a duty 'may have no relationship whatsoever to the injury caused to the US producers'.[53]

Cass also observed that no analysis is undertaken to gauge the effect of subsidies on the competitive advantage of the recipients.[54] Third, no attempt is made to calculate the true market distortive effects of foreign subsidies, nor to assess the impact of US subsidisation practices on the distortive effects of foreign subsidies. This is especially problematic because the target of CVD actions has shifted away from export subsidies to encompass all subsidies, presumably in order to preserve some ideal state of international competition.[55]

This conceptual quagmire accounts for the scepticism with which the US CVD law is viewed by many observers. Hufbauer notes that the present US system of countervailing duties is regarded as 'a vast and complicated system of contingent protection, largely erected for the benefit of US business'.[56] Anderson and Rugman view the prolific use of the US trade remedy laws[57] as a type of non-tariff barrier and have coined the term 'administered' protection to highlight the nature of the practice.[58] It is then no surprise that, as Hufbauer observes, 'the US business community seems more anxious, on balance, to retain unfettered access to the US CVD laws than to acquire new international discipline over foreign subsidies'.[59] De Kieffer notes that due to the costs of legal action, merely filing a complaint is enough in most cases to cause a restriction of activities by foreign companies.[60] Indeed, the conceptual confusion, coupled with porous definitional analysis by the ITA and the ITC, has created a potent tool for the harassment of foreign competitors of US industries.

Institutional aspects

Two agencies are charged with the administration of the US CVD law: The International Trade Administration at the Department of Commerce determines whether a subsidy has been granted and the amount of the subsidy; the International Trade Commission, an independent quasi-judicial body, determines whether there is actual or potential material injury to the complainant US industry.[61] The determinations of either body may be appealed to the Court of International Trade. Neither the CIT nor the Supreme Court has shown a reluctance to overturn the decisions of the ITA or the ITC on grounds of administrative expertise. This may be important in assessing the efficacy of the FTA Chapter 19 mechanism.

An investigation may be initiated in two ways. First, the ITA may determine, 'from information available to it, that a formal investigation is warranted'.[62] Secondly, an interested party may file a complaint on behalf of an industry. If the complaint is accompanied by 'information reasonably available to the petitioner supporting those allegations' then the ITA must commence a CVD proceeding.[63] The GATT is generally suspicious of unilateral initiations of investigation,[64] but the threshold of 'information reasonably available' is quite low, thus making it relatively easy for interested parties (companies with foreign competition) to initiate an investigation. Another important element, required by the GATT Subsidies Code,[65] is whether a petition is being filed on behalf of an industry or for the benefit of the complainant alone. However, the requirements are relatively lax and the ITA does not rigorously verify the representativeness of the complaint.

The ITA does not have any discretion in the amount of duty imposed, nor is it permitted to examine any interest other than the complainants' in determining whether a duty is warranted. Therefore, unlike the Commission of the EU in administering trade remedy laws, neither the ITA nor the ITC may consider the broader economic or foreign policy interests of the United States when assessing whether or not to impose a countervailing duty, or the level at which the duty should be imposed.[66] Another interesting point is that the ITA is part of the Department of Commerce, which is the Department responsible for government relations with US business.[67] This may raise the question of whether the allegiance of the ITA is to the international trade and competition interests of the United States, or to the client industries of Commerce.

The substance of the US CVD law

The US concern with foreign subsidies is wide-ranging and all encompassing; unlike the state aid regime of the EU or even the Union's CVD Regulations, no significant derogations or exceptions are permitted by the US CVD law. The definition of 'subsidy' in *United States Code Annotated* (*USCA*) 19, §1677 covers all export subsidies as well as those domestic subsidies 'provided or required by government action to a specific enterprise or industry. . .'.[68] A special rule requires the ITA to determine whether a government programme is in fact, as well as in law, generally available.[69] The range of offsets that may be used by the ITA in determining the net subsidy in any instance is limited by the provisions of *USCA* 19, §1677(6). Only certain administrative charges or taxes intended to offset the effects of domestic subsidies may be used as offsets by the ITA, and concerns of the type raised by Romoli[70] may not be taken into account.

In 1989, the ITA proposed to codify its administrative practices and definitional analyses in *Code of Federal Regulations* (*CFR*) 19, 355 ('Rulemaking'). The Rulemaking proposals followed a number of appendices in which the ITA set out its methodology and also attempted to respond to the criticisms by the CIT of a number of its decisions in the early 1980s. The proposed Rulemaking summarises much of the ITA's definitional analysis over the past ten years, thus making a thorough case study unnecessary for the purposes of this work.

There are a number of important elements in the approach of the ITA to the question of subsidy definitions, three of which will be examined below. First, the ITA is mandated to investigate subsidies provided only to 'a specific enterprise or industry'.[71] However, the ITA's understanding of specificity is broader than theoretical analysis can sustain. For example, Rulemaking argues that regional aid subsidies are specific (to a region) and thus countervailable.[72] No analysis of regional disparities in wealth are deemed necessary to verify the actual market distortive elements of a regional subsidy.[73] Moreover, the ITA did not agree with the court in *Cabot Corp.* that 'the provision of a foreign government of infrastructure never can constitute a countervailable subsidy'.[74] Presumably, this refers to general infrastructure schemes that may be 'specific' to a region, or benefit predominantly an industry or sector (such as stumpage fees). Thus, the ITA leaves the door open for questioning the general socio-economic policy decisions of foreign governments.

Second, the ITA's basis for finding a subsidy is benefit to a firm, rather than cost to government.[75] For example, in assessing the aid element in the provision of goods or services by the government to a firm, the benchmark price used by the ITA is the commercial price of the goods or services, rather than the cost to government of providing those goods or services. Only if the goods are not commercially available, the ITA may look at the government's 'cost of producing the good or service'; it may also look at the 'external price' of the good or service.[76] This represents a significant change over the years. In *Softwood Lumber* I the ITA had argued that 'it is not the DOC's policy to use cross-border comparisons in establishing commercial benchmarks, because such comparisons fail to account for differences in comparative advantage between countries'.[77] However, in the aftermath of *Softwood Lumber* II and the codification of Rulemaking, in areas where the competitors of US industries have a comparative advantage any provision of a good or service by government may be suspect, because it will be automatically priced lower than what is available to US industries ('external cost') and may constitute a benefit to the foreign industry.[78]

Third, the secondary or tax consequences of a subsidy are not reviewed.[79] This should not be altogether surprising, since even the primary consequences of a subsidy are not analysed thoroughly. These are simply corporate decisions, marginal costs, and output data that are *assumed* by the investigative agency to be affected by the subsidy; data that are, however, rarely examined thoroughly. For example, a subsidy to a firm to relocate to an underdeveloped region may not have any effect whatever on the firm's output or marginal costs, but is countervailable. Or, a grant may be diverted to the shareholders and of no consequence in regard to the corporate strategy of the firm, and therefore of even less consequence to any distortions in the American market: While distortive in a macroeconomic or ethical sense (other firms or people were taxed to provide jobs or to enrich the shareholders of the recipient) the subsidy is not distortive of or injurious to American producers *per se*.[80] In any event, Rulemaking makes it clear that the ITA is not concerned with the extent to which the benefit to the firm is taxed back, or with other benefits the firms may have to forego as a result of the subsidy. This codifies the approach of the ITA in *Oil Country Tubular Goods From Canada*, where in a remarkable analytical lapse it argued that 'we do not consider the secondary effects of subsidy. Since [the recipient] did, in fact, accept the grant funds, the hypothesis it poses is speculative'.[81] The problem with this sort of thinking is that the concept of a market distortion is about counterfactuals, which are, of necessity, speculative.[82]

Analysis of US CVD practice

"Curiouser and curiouser!" cried Alice.[83]

Ideally, the codification of Rulemaking proposals should make it easier to predict the outcome of CVD proceedings initiated by the US industry. It should also make it easier, both politically and legally, for the ITA to dismiss frivolous or unfounded allegations. However, it has been shown that the conceptual basis for Rulemaking is, at best, confused, and the practice, flawed. This is to be expected. Though nominally independent, the ITA and the ITC have many different constituencies to serve, the most important of which is the United States Congress.[84] Congress, divided as it is between the House and the Senate, with staggered elections and different constituencies, has its own agenda and conflicts to manage. US trade remedy laws are the result of compromises among the many competing interests inside and outside Congress and the White House; conceptual confusion and flawed practice are endemic and not peculiar to American trade policy, such as it is.

While exasperating, the 'protectionist' attitude of the ITA and the ITC can be easily explained by the political imperatives of their masters. As Kalt notes in his analysis of *Softwood Lumber* II, the ITC was wrong in its injury determination, but Congress was moving to impose a tariff unilaterally.[85] It was necessary, he argues, to keep the final decision in the hands of the Executive branch, and this is what happened in the end. As well, in many ways the ITC and the ITA serve the purpose of deflecting pressure from Congress.[86] One must, in my judgement, recognise the political value and function of these institutions and the intensely political nature of US trade laws, before one argues for a solution or a mechanism aimed at resolving the contradictions inherent in the interplay between national trade laws and the economic imperatives of free trade. A legal or economic analysis untempered by a sound appreciation of the politics of US CVD determinations may fail to provide an accurate understanding of the best ways of approaching CVD investigations in the future, or developing a mechanism to counter their deleterious effects.

Trebilcock points out that the seven cases in which CVDs were imposed on Canadian products since between 1981 and 1990 'involved subsidies as to which there is no international consensus that their adverse trade effects necessarily outweigh a range of legitimate domestic policy objectives that the subsidies may be designed to further'.[87] The history of Canada–US trade difficulties extends further back. The first instance in which a domestic subsidy was countervailed was the Treasury decision in the *Michelin* case.[88] Guido points out that 'the Canadian practices countervailed against in *Michelin* [were] embarrassingly similar to US programs designed to achieve similar goals'.[89] This did not stop Treasury, and in a similar future case will likely not stop the ITA, from making a subsidy finding. Then, as now, CVD determinations were responses to internal political pressures, just as subsidies are in other countries. If subsidies are, for most countries, important tools of economic self-determination (regardless of actual or potential adverse economic and trade effects on other countries), so are CVDs for the United States. Understanding this point, far more than grasping the inefficiencies or irrationalities of the US CVD law, can help provide a basis for agreement on the best mechanism to reduce trade disputes between Canada and the United States.

Canada's Countervailing Duty Law

The Canadian CVD law is modelled, with two modifications, after the US law. However, the practice so far has been significantly different from the US approach. This may be due to three factors. First, the Canadian political system is not as fragmented politically as the US and therefore has fewer access points at which interest group pressure may be exerted. Second, the CVD law itself is more streamlined and allows the principal actors, the Canadian International Trade Tribunal (CITT) and Department of National Revenue (MNR), less room to manoeuvre politically. There has been very little written about the conceptual grounds upon which the Canadian CVD law is based. This is not surprising, as the *Special Import Measures Act* (SIMA), which contains the CVD provisions, was clearly drafted with the intention of taking advantage of all the protective devices allowed by the GATT Subsidies Code.[90] Third, subsidies jurisprudence is sparse in Canada and the MNR has not been exposed to the wide range of complaints and governmental practices with which the ITA and ITC have had to contend. Therefore, in the following I will forego discussing the conceptual background and the specific provisions of SIMA on CVDs, and concentrate instead on the distinguishing features of the Canadian CVD provisions.

Institutional aspects

The Deputy Minister of National Revenue (DMNR) is responsible for initiating an investigation either on his or her own initiative or following the filing of a 'properly documented' written complaint. Unlike the requirement for simultaneous filing of complaints with the ITA and the ITC, documentation filed with the MNR must include evidence of injury at the preliminary stage.[91] However, once the evidence is deemed to be sufficient, the system is bifurcated. The

DMNR determines whether subsidisation exists and to what degree; the CITT has the responsibility of determining whether there has been material injury to the production of a like good in Canada.

Asked about the possibility of political pressures to achieve desired legal outcomes, an official at the MNR argued that the degree of politicisation of the process is minimal. He cited the lack of any appreciable bureaucratic discretion resulting from the watertight language of the Act or the Regulation as the most important factor. Indeed, unlike US CVD law, 'subsidy' has been clearly defined in the Act and the Regulations; unlike in the US, where CVD regulations were developed in a number of 'methodology appendices', little *ad hoc* rulemaking discretion is left to the Canadian administering agency.[92] Moreover, the ITA has pointedly ignored certain CIT decisions which attempted to give direction to the haphazard development of the trade remedy law through administrative 'methodology' appendices; Revenue Canada has been noticeably reticent to challenge the Canadian judiciary to the same extent.

Whether the lack of discretion and clearer rules have led to less politicisation in Canada is open to question. The Canadian political system and trade policy structure is not as open and politicised as the American model. Therefore, the dirty laundry of political influence in decision making by the DMNR is not aired publicly as are the dramatic speeches made by Senators and Representatives for the benefit of their constituencies *and* the administering agencies. But a point that might lend support to the contention of the MNR official has to do with the difference in the governmental structure of the two countries. Most public political trade policy debates in Canada are contained in the daily parliamentary Question Period. In the best traditions of responsible government, the largely powerless Opposition may question the Minister but not the officials who actually make the decisions and who are not, by and large, political appointees. Moreover, trade policy-making is firmly in the hands of the Executive Branch and is not open to much influence by Parliament. In Washington, on the other hand, the politics of trade are at the centre of a triangular battleground in which the administering agencies, packed as they are with political appointees of an Executive (from a different party, for the most part, or at least with a conflicting political agenda or constituency), are seen as part of the problem by the warring arms of Congress. Therefore, while trade policy is a serious political issue in Canada, trade policy-making is not open to the same type or degree of political manipulation as in the US.

The substance of Canada's CVD law

Countervailing duties are imposed on subsidised imports pursuant to the provisions of SIMA and the relevant Regulations. The Act and the Regulations are very comprehensive in their coverage of the prohibited subsidies and are similar to the US legislation. What differences exist are mainly due to the fact that CVDs are not important tools of protectionism (or any other aspect of trade policy) in Canada, and therefore in their administration slightly different considerations are played out than in the US context. Some of these are outlined in the departmental manual of the MNR, but two important legal differences are in the Act, which will be discussed shortly.

Canadian and US differences in practice

The introductory paragraphs of the manual are instructive. The administrators are cautioned that subsidies are an area of 'great interest, and some controversy' to the GATT signatories. Therefore, it is suggested, it is 'important that any decision made by the Canadian administration in the course of a subsidy investigation should be consistent with positions adopted by Canada in the international forum'. In fact, the manual recommends that 'the Policy unit [of the Department] be contacted at an early stage in a subsidy proceeding, for advice and policy guidance'.[93] The nature of such advice and guidance cannot be determined from the development of case law in this matter, but the frank recognition that the law should be applied in accordance with the international trade policy objectives of Canada is worth noting. The manual has a detailed discussion of GATT rules in the section dealing with the determination of the amount of subsidies.

Another difference in approach has to do with the calculation of the aid element in the provision of government loans. Unlike the American approach[94] Regulation 28 provides that the aid element be determined on the basis of cost to government of providing the loan, rather than benefit to the recipient. This approach finds favour in the EU, but has not been incorporated in the Uruguay Round Agreement on Subsidies and Countervailing Measures. Case law in Canada, however, is not as developed as in the US, and further analysis of the differences between the two regimes is not possible.

Canadian and US differences in law

There are two differences in law that make the calculation and imposition of CVDs (but not the definition and calculation of subsidies) in Canada different from that in the US. The first is s.45 of SIMA, which is the 'public interest provision' also found in the CVD Regulation of the EU, but not in the US. Under this section, the CITT may refer a case to the Minister of Finance if it finds that the imposition of a duty in the full amount 'would not, or might not' be in the public interest. In at least one case,[95] the reference has resulted in a lowering of duties. Presumably, this allows for the representation of consumer or end user interests that might be hurt as a result of the imposition of a CVD. It has been used sparingly.[96]

Another legal difference, which may be of interest, is the sunset clause, under which a finding of subsidy automatically expires after five years unless reviewed by the CITT. A study found that in Canada's experience less than 50 per cent of findings in place for five years were deemed to be still necessary.[97] Few GATT signatories, including the US, have such a provision.

Case law in Canada

There have been very few CVD cases in Canada. Many of these have involved various export subsidies by Brazil. The domestic subsidies that have been reviewed have largely involved agricultural products. Therefore, no analysis of the present case law can provide a sound understanding of the approach the MNR would take with regard to domestic industrial subsidies in future cases. Moreover, case law analysis of regional subsidies, equity infusions, R&D schemes, and other borderline state aids is non-existent. Thus, while the substance of the law in the US and Canada is almost identical, the difference in guidelines, especially the GATT reminder in the manual, may result in the development of a unique analytical approach to the problems of specificity and government participation in business ventures.

Analysis of Canada's CVD law

Prior to 1984, an investigation of the subsidisation practices of a trading partner was launched after an allegation was issued by an Order-in-Council (a political act). Now CVD investigations are initiated by the Deputy Minister of National Revenue (a bureaucratic process) on the 'properly documented' allegation of private parties. Prior to 1984, the process was deliberately politicised; but, Tougas believes, 'whether it was a negative aspect of Canadian trade law is certainly arguable'.[98] The change reflected two developments. The first was the changing attitude in the GATT with respect to CVD actions which made unilateral initiation of CVD investigations by governmental bodies suspect and undesirable. This explains the reluctance of the Deputy Minister to initiate investigations absent private party allegations, even though an investigation may be justified.[99] The second was the move by Canada and other countries to take advantage of all the protection afforded by the CVD provisions of the Subsidies Code which had been conceded only as the price of US adherence to the meagre limits it required, such as 'material injury' requirements.

A related reason might be maintaining a façade of diplomatic amity. A positive political act to impose a CVD may be viewed as a hostile action by foreign governments, and the Canadian government may be put in an embarrassing position if asked to initiate an investigation by the private sector. However, an ostensibly objective bureaucratic mechanism that responds to 'legitimate grievances' of injured industries is likely to elicit a less unfriendly response from target countries. Thus, the move to a more 'structured' mechanism improved the chances of Canadian industries in having an investigation initiated, and perhaps in having a CVD imposed.

The cynic would predict a flood of harassing allegations and a torrent of countervailing duty determinations; the cynic would further see the lack of materialisation of such as proof that Canada's own reliance on industrial subsidies makes it naturally timid in questioning other countries' similar programmes. The cynic was, and would be, wrong. Canada's CVD laws are underused, but they are so for the most part not for any timidity on part of the Canadian government.[100] The reasons lie in the private sector, are strategically sound and economic in nature.

First, the vast bulk of Canada's trade is with the US, and many Canadian industries are highly dependent on imports from the US. Therefore, a CVD has the potential of harming many industries that are dependent on cheap imports from the US. As a result, there is no guarantee that hard-won CVDs will not be reduced by the Department of Finance on a s.45 application. Moreover, Finance is also responsible for the development of international trade policy. While stressing that s.45 of SIMA has been used very rarely, there is nothing to stop Finance from putting countervailing duties in the broader context of its trade policy, or even from taking a European approach (consumer- and market-centred) as opposed to a producer-oriented one in assessing the impugned CVDs. This added element of risk does not exist in the US system and may make costly and lengthy applications to the MNR less attractive.

Second, many industries that might be hurt by US subsidised imports into Canada are also industries with extensive trade with (read *export into*) the US. A CVD investigation against a US company (thus questioning the accepted dogma in Washington that the US does not subsidise) risks angering US trade officials and observers such as the US Congress, and quite possibly triggering a host of trade remedy actions against the complainant industry.[101] The arsenal of US trade remedy laws is well equipped to handle actions which a US industry might consider an 'unfair trade practice', (e.g. section 301, Super 301 and Special 301 of the US); accusing the US of engaging in a 'pernicious' practice such as subsidisation could potentially be considered an unfair trade practice. In short, regardless of US practice, in many instances it may be practically and politically unfeasible to engage Canada's CVD law against US subsidies. A unilateral mechanism for the definition and regulation of subsidy practices will not help Canada to discipline US subsidy practices. Therefore – and this is the key point that emerges from a study of the Canadian CVD law – a unilateral mechanism is not in the best interest of Canada.

The Canada–US Free Trade Agreement

Chapters 18 and 19 of the Canada–US FTA outline the procedure by which trade disputes between the two countries are to be resolved. Chapter 19 is strictly to govern disputes over antidumping and countervailing duty determinations; however, if a subsidies code is successfully negotiated,[102] then the Chapter 18 mechanism may become the operating DRM. In this part, I will primarily discuss the Chapter 19 DRM, although to the extent relevant some discussion of Chapter 18 will also be made.

The Chapter 19 procedure

The Chapter 19 procedure is designed to protect each party from the other's use of its trade remedy laws to frustrate the benefits expected from free(r) trade, namely, the lowering of trade barriers between the two countries. Given the vastly divergent interests at stake, the provisions of Chapter 19 are remarkable in that they satisfy, to some extent, the concerns of each party to the Agreement. For Canada, the existence of binational panel review may serve to curb the more blatantly political manipulations of the US trade remedy law by its administering agencies. The US, on the other hand, has reserved to itself the right to determine what constitutes a subsidy within its existing framework of trade law and practice, and the freedom to alter that framework after only 'notification and consultation' with Canadian authorities. In the following, I will first discuss the Chapter 19 panels; then I will briefly examine what I call (for lack of a better term) the '*per se* exclusion' rule of trade law amendment.

Binational panels

Under Article 1904(2) a binational panel composed of independent trade experts may be struck to review the final determinations of a trade remedy administering agency. This review procedure replaces judicial review of these determinations by the national courts of competent jurisdiction (the Court of International Trade in the United States and the Federal Court of Appeal in Canada). Moreover, the decisions of the panels are binding on the parties and may not be appealed or reviewed further (except by the Extraordinary Challenge Committee, to be discussed later). The Standards of Review, as set out in the FTA, are somewhat different as between Canada and the United States due to different domestic judicial review standards.[103] This may be of significance in protecting Canadian industry from legally untenable outcomes in US determinations; however, as will be shown later, it will be of little significance in protecting Canada from frivolous actions and trade remedy harassment, by far the greatest source of anxiety and market instability for Canadian exporters.[104]

Once a review by a panel is completed, decisions deemed inconsistent with national laws may be remanded to the administering agency, along with panel decisions to guide the agency in its redetermination of the matter. The redetermination itself may be subject to further review and remand. Also, the decisions of the panel may be referred to the Extraordinary Challenge Committee.

The right of application for review to an Extraordinary Challenge

Committee (ECC) is limited to three circumstances: where a member of the panel is guilty of gross misconduct, where the panel has 'seriously departed' from a fundamental rule of procedure, and where the panel has manifestly exceeded its powers, authority or jurisdiction. In the *Pork* decision, the ECC clarified its role *vis-à-vis* the panel. It stated that the process of a challenge is not to serve as a routine appeal. Rather, it argued, the decisions of a panel may be challenged and reviewed only in extraordinary circumstances.[105] Thus, for all practical purposes, binational panels are the final arbiters of whether or not each country has applied its own anti-dumping or countervailing laws properly.

Per se exclusion rule

This provision in the FTA serves to protect the parties from unilateral changes to national trade remedy laws. It provides that 1) amendments to trade remedy statutes will not apply to the other party unless it is specifically named, and 2) each party must be notified and consulted before any changes are made in trade remedy laws that may affect the interests of the other party to the FTA. A binational panel may be struck to review the proposed amendment and give a declaratory (non-binding) decision. Presumably, this is to make it politically more difficult for each party to amend its laws in such a way as to directly affect the interests of the other party. However, whether the US will risk offending domestic interests by not naming Canada in trade remedy law amendments in order to preserve some semblance of diplomatic amity is questionable. No new amendments are expected in the near future to provide an opportunity to gauge the effectiveness, or even the relevance, of the 'notification and consultation' and *per se* exclusion requirements of the FTA.

Perhaps more importantly, as Dearden and Palmeter have observed, the notification and consultation rights are restricted to an amendment to a party's antidumping or countervailing duty *statutes* as opposed to *laws*.[106] This is crucial because part of the problem in the US CVD practices has been a haphazard and inconsistent development of methodology by the ITA. Even with the codification of Rulemaking, the ITA will be under no obligation to notify or consult Canadian authorities when developing new rules or amending old ones in ways that might seriously prejudice Canadian interests. Nor will it be required to name Canada specifically in so doing. In most cases, therefore, even the expected political price of naming Canada specifically in a trade remedy law amendment may not have to be paid.

The Chapter 18 procedure

The Canada–US Trade Commission is charged with the resolution of disputes outside of the area of antidumping and countervailing duty determinations. Should a subsidies code be successfully negotiated between the parties, the Commission may be charged with the task of settling disputes in this area as well. While the success of the Working Group on subsidies is not at all guarantied, and although the Working Group may decide to develop a new DRM to govern an FTA subsidies code, it may be useful to examine this procedure. Moreover, since GATT disputes may also be referred to the FTA dispute resolution mechanism, the ratification of the Uruguay Round Agreement and its subsidies code may breathe new life in the Chapter 18 process. The Commission may be entirely unsuitable for the resolution of disputes of the type the current binational panels have to examine.

The Commission, unlike the binational panel, is not a novel idea. In its functions, it is very similar to the EFTA Council; it is, but for the range of issues it considers, identical to the EFTA–EC FTA Commissions.

The Commission

Under Article 1802 of the FTA, one of the functions of the Commission is to resolve disputes that may arise over the FTA's implementation and application. It is composed of the highest Trade Officials of the two countries, or their representatives, and is assisted in its work by a permanent Secretariat. The Commission is a reactive body in that the onus is on the parties to provide it with adequate information as to proposed or actual measures which may affect the working of the FTA. According to the FTA, the parties must make every attempt to arrive at a mutually satisfactory resolution of the matters brought forward for consultation. Should the Commission be unable to arrive at a satisfactory resolution of the problem through consultation, it may refer the matter to a Chapter 18 Panel of Experts. The decisions of these panels may be binding or non-binding.

Chapter 18 panels

A dispute may be referred to a binding arbitration panel, but this is different in operation from the Chapter 19 procedure. Under Chapter 19, a remanded decision of an administering agency does not have legal effect until finally approved by the reviewing panels. Chapter 18 panels have no power to affect the decisions of domestic administering agencies. The chief deterrence against ignoring a binding panel decision is the threat of sanctioned, or legal, retaliation. The decisions of non-binding panels are to be referred to the Commission, which may or may not adopt the decision.

Dearden and Palmeter believe that following a dispute, the resolution adopted by the Commission will closely follow the recommendation of the panel.[107] They note that 'the rate of compliance with GATT dispute panel reports is very high'. Nevertheless, the concern over non-compliance exists; the success of the FTA dispute settlement mechanism depends on the parties' willingness to 'preserve the integrity of the institutional provisions set out in Chapter 18 regardless of the domestic political consequences of doing so'.[108]

The North American Free Trade Agreement

There are three significant changes in the Chapter 19 review process under the North American Free Trade Agreement (NAFTA).[109]

First, and most significantly, NAFTA abolishes the Working Group on Subsidies established under Article 1907 of the FTA. This is significant in a number of ways, not all of which are positive. For one thing, making the binational panel review process permanent removes some of the uncertainties surrounding the whole institution. It is clear, and not surprising, that after nearly five years, the Working Group has not been successful in even proposing an outline for a subsidies code. The concern as to what to do when the seven-year term of the Group comes to an end, especially given the relative success of the entire process as far as Canada is concerned, must have weighed heavily on the minds of the negotiators of NAFTA.[110] However, the changes make permanent a system that was essentially an afterthought and designed as a stopgap measure. While it has proven more successful than perhaps its designers had expected, the Chapter 19 process is, as will be seen below, fundamentally flawed. Its continuation in a trilateral trade regime is an admission of defeat in the attempt to find a common ground in the definition and regulation of subsidies, rather than an accomplishment in finding a new procedural solution to the problems that plague trade relations among the parties.

Secondly, Article 1905 of the NAFTA contains provisions to safeguard the panel review system. Where a party alleges that another party's domestic law has a) prevented the establishment of a panel requested by the complaining party, b) prevented a panel from rendering a final decision, c) prevented the implementation of a panel or denied it binding force, or d) resulted in a failure to provide proper opportunity for review of a final determination by a panel, the complaining party may request consultations with the offending party or parties. If the matter has not been resolved within a specified period, the parties may strike a special committee. Should the special committee find the allegations substantiated, the complaining party may suspend the application of Article 1904 or other benefits under NAFTA to the party at fault. This appears to be similar to the panel review of proposed amendments to domestic trade remedy laws and, accordingly, suffers from the same problems: in an asymmetrical relationship, suspension of benefits (or in the case of panel review of amending legislation, revocation of the agreement) is a useless safeguard. The smaller party, or the party that is dependent on its trading partners, will not have a realistic option of suspending the benefits accrued to the larger party under the Agreement without at the same time hurting itself; even were a realistic option to exist, the threat of suspension of benefits by a smaller party is likely to have little impact on the behaviour of larger parties.[111]

Finally, Article 1907 of NAFTA contains guidelines for the administration of antidumping and countervailing duty laws. These include publication of notices of initiation of investigation, notices of times required for submission of information and the like. Since these provisions already exist in Canadian and US trade remedy laws, it can be assumed that this article was simply intended to bring Mexico's trade remedy laws in line with the regimes already in operation in the other two countries.

Evaluation: Does the FTA DRM work?

The prospects for the long-term success of the FTA DRM can perhaps be better assessed by comparing it with one of the institutions examined in a previous chapter, and the most fascinating institutional contrast exists between NAFTA (and the FTA, of course) and its European counterpart (of sorts), the EEA: In NAFTA, a single body has the responsibility of ensuring compliance with three different sets of trade remedy laws, whereas in the EEA, two different and apparently sovereign institutions are entrusted with applying a single system of laws across the entire territory of the Agreement. It is too soon to predict which of these instruments, each covering nearly entire continents and markets of over 350 million people, will be the more successful in the long run – both politically and economically. However, the fundamental difference in perspective, that is, the trust and goodwill that seems to permeate the EEA and the mistrust that lies at the core of NAFTA, should be obvious to all but the most optimistic North American free trade advocates: where the EEA strives to ensure 'fair' markets by establishing continent-wide rules, the US continues to insist on retaining its sovereignty in disciplining 'unfair' market players.

The key that could open the trade deadlock that threatens to undermine Canada–US relations is, in fact, a truism: for the Canada–US FTA to work, whether in the political dispute settlement mechanism of a Chapter 18 Commission,[112] or in the quasi-judicial binational panels of Chapter 19, there must be a commitment on part of the parties to opening the trade borders. Absent such goodwill, or absent a *mechanism* to impose such goodwill on the parties, the deal may yet unravel, in spirit if not in letter. Part of the problem lies in the beggar-thy-neighbour mentality of the remnants of mercantilism in Washington and Toronto (significantly, not Ottawa). This is a subtle influence, however, and impossible to prove or even to trace.

The largest part of the problem lies in the 'domestic political consequences' of pursuing an activist free trade policy. The fruits of freer trade (if any, of course) take a long time to ripen, and when they do, they are generally too broadly distributed to affect the political fortunes of the advocates of freer trade. The ravages of an efficiency driven market, however, are concentrated and immediate. While this may be a good argument for strengthening labour adjustment policies,[113] denouncing freer trade or impeding its progress may be more useful politically. This is what a trade deal between the two countries must be able to counter, and this is precisely what at least half of the dispute resolution mechanism in the Canada–US FTA, the Chapter 18 DRM, is manifestly unfit to do: in a war of political wills (and survival) neither side is legitimately to be expected to sacrifice domestic political interests, however 'unfair' or 'unjust,' for the sake of a trade agreement. In such a match of wills, the bargaining power of the United States and Canada's dependence on the US market make for an unfavourable balance of power for Canada.

Chapter 19 panels are more promising; but optimism about their proper functioning must be guarded. The Chapter 19 mechanism is indeed an improvement over the previous system; but almost anything would be. In assessing the value of a Chapter 19 mechanism, attention must be paid as much to what it does not do as to what it in fact does. Therein lies the problem.

Potential for harassment

One of the most important irritants in the US law is the potential for harassment in its private-sector driven trade remedy process. Aside from plunging Canadian industry into often frivolous and costly actions, repeated trade remedy applications reduce market stability for Canadian exports, thus increasing the risk premium and making Canadian products more costly, uncompetitive, and unattractive in the US market. Panels may remand an unsupported determination, but this is cold comfort to industries whose business has been disrupted by multiple and often ill-supported trade remedy applications.

Canadian imports into the US can be subjected to two classes of harassment: horizontal and vertical. Horizontally, all imports into the US are subject to multiple actions under the panoply of trade remedy laws in the US, and the actions under each of the trade remedy provisions may be recommenced annually at the instigation of either the industry concerned or the ITA. Vertically, because of the lack of finality in review applications before the binational panels, Canadian imports may be subjected to a multiplicity of review/remand applications. Either of these concerns could increase costs and market uncertainty associated with exporting to the United States. *Softwood Lumber* (I through VI) highlights the concern with both horizontal and vertical harassment.

First, Anderson and Rugman were optimistic that with an independent binational panel of experts looking over their shoulders, the US trade remedy administering agencies may resort less to legal fiction in protecting US industry. These hopes may prove to have been overly optimistic. Although the ITA purports to be sharper in its analysis of alleged subsidies than it was in the past, for example in *Softwood Lumber* II, legal fiction is still fiction, however deftly composed. Regardless of the discipline received by the culprits, for example in *Pork* or in the latest decision of the binational panel in the *Softwood Lumber* saga,[114] the sequelled harassment of imports through the trade remedy complaint process will continue to leave its scars on the economies of both countries.

Secondly, and more importantly, not only has the ITA not been chastened, it appears to have been invigorated by the challenges posed by the binational panel process. Arguably, the first signs of the vertical harassment were visible in the repeated remands by the panels in the *Pork* case, which was ultimately brought before the Extraordinary Challenge Committee and resolved in favour of the panels. In *Softwood Lumber* V (the decision of the ITA on remand following *Softwood Lumber* IV),[115] however, the ITA has gone much further, as it proceeded to lecture the panel on its methodology and analysis, even asserting that the Federal Court of Appeal case law on which the panel had relied and by which, in the ordinary course of events, *both the ITA and the panel should have been bound*, had been wrongly decided and should not have been followed. Thus, the ITA argued, 'However well intentioned, the Panel's reliance on the quoted statement simply perpetuates the Federal Circuit's original error'.[116]

This virtual rebellion by an administrative tribunal against its reviewing agency would be amusing were not the very integrity of the binational review process at stake. The response of the panels to this direct challenge is not yet clear. It is certain, however, that *Softwood Lumber* V raises serious questions about the efficacy of the process in *settling* disputes, as opposed to merely recycling them – either in a cat-and-mouse game of remand and countermand, or in the inevitable annual resurfacing of complaints before the ITA.

Settlement of disputes over subsidies, entrusted by the FTA to the binational panels, requires finality. It is not clear, however, how this can be achieved when the administrative tribunals subject to judicial review by the panels take it upon themselves on remand to lecture the panels, and not just to argue before them, on what is the law. The lack of finality in the dispute settlement process in turn reduces market certainty – the *sine qua non* of growth in trade and investment and the *raison d'être* of most free trade agreements.

Potential for judicial abuse

Much of the difficulty in the application of the US trade remedy laws lies in the administering agencies and not the judiciary. It was curious, then, that the appeal route and not the administering agency was replaced by the Chapter 19 mechanism. While the potential for abuse has thus been reduced, optimism about the long-term effectiveness of the Chapter 19 panels must be guarded. The decisions of the ITA and the ITC in *Softwood Lumber* II and III are instructive. *Softwood Lumber* II was the focal point at which a number of developments since 1983 converged, not all of which were political. Indeed, the ITA relied heavily on the decision of the Court of International Trade in *Cabot Corp.* to sustain its reasoning for the change in direction since *Softwood Lumber* I. Whatever the merits of the ITA's reasoning, it is unquestionably true that the CIT had sharply rebuked the ITA in *Cabot*, as it had been doing in a number of earlier decisions. *Cabot*, of course, involved Mexico and not Canada. As well, as noted by Weiler and Dearden's dissent in *Softwood Lumber* IV[117] *Softwood Lumber* III was based on an analysis that had had no precedent until the decision of the ITA in *Leather from Argentina*.[118] It was in that case that, for the first time, a border measure was determined to be a countervailable subsidy. The dissent argued that 'the administrative authors of that ruling did not seem to realize the fundamental change in statutory direction they were taking'.[119] Nevertheless, the dissenting panellists were not able to convince their colleagues that the log export restraint policy of the British Columbia government, which policy was not even considered in *Softwood Lumber* II was not a subsidy and that the ITA had erred in so holding. The profound change in the hundred-year-old administrative practice of the US trade remedy regime thus came in a way that seriously affected Canadian interests without Canada's being afforded any chance to respond to or question the change.

Under the FTA Canada can only apply for review of those decisions of the ITA in which it is involved directly and not cases that, through precedent setting, may affect its legal interests in trade issues. ITA rulings in cases that do not involve Canada are reviewed by the Court of International Trade. Thus, the ITA may argue before the CIT for a change in the interpretation of trade laws or regulations in order to circumvent unfavourable decisions of the Chapter 19 panels. There is no restriction on the ability of the CIT, or any other American court, to change the law to Canada's detriment: It was a judicial reinterpretation that smoothed the way for *Softwood Lumber* II. Whether and to what extent the CIT will be sympathetic to the ITA is uncertain, but Canada has no protection against judicial lawmaking and reinterpretations of trade remedy laws that arise out of third country litigation.

Potential for legislative abuse

While binational panels may reduce the possibilities of judicial or administrative abuse in the application of US trade remedy laws, there is little to protect Canadian industry from *legislative* abuse of trade remedy procedures. The Notification and Consultation procedure is devised to reduce this possibility, but the potential exists for the US Congress to continue to harass Canadian exporters with threats of one kind or another. Inserting the word 'Canada' in US trade law amendments is not difficult; any of the 535 Senators and Representative is capable of being persuaded to insist that trade law amendments be applicable to Canada. The lack of a line-item veto means that a President sympathetic to freer trade with Canada may be in danger of scuttling trade remedy legislation by insisting that Canada be removed, or not be included, as a target. Depending on the circumstances, this may not be a politically attractive or plausible proposition. In any event, Notification and Consultation will take place between the Executives in both countries and will be of little help to Canada where it really matters: in Congress. Moreover, the problem with the ITA and the ITC is not that they are inherently incapable of applying US trade legislation correctly; rather, the difficulty is the close supervision of a Congress ready to override administrative discretion to advance its own trade or political agenda.

The addition of Mexico to the panel review process is not likely to reduce the problems outlined above. The binational panel process has worked well so far; the jurisprudence of the panel does not indicate a national bias on the part of its membership. Therefore, the addition of Mexican panellists – assuming of course that they, too, will follow the precedent set by American and Canadian panellists – should not affect the balance of the process one way or another. NAFTA, in short, will not improve upon the FTA insofar as American litigiousness in trade remedy law is concerned.

The question of subsidies (and countervailing duties) goes to the very core of domestic political conflicts as few other trade issues do. To ask politicians to ignore their political interests in favour of such abstract goods as freer trade or economic efficiency is unrealistic. The half-hearted attempt to depoliticise the issue by the invention of Chapter 19 panels may bear fruit in the short term, but it does little to increase market stability and certainty for Canadian products in the longer term. On the other hand, should bilateral negotiations for a subsidies code be successful, the Commission may be given the responsibility of supervising its implementation. Given the vast difference in ideology and perspective, and the immense divergence of interests between the two countries, a political mechanism has the potential of leaving disputes between the two countries unresolved; unresolved (and, in many respect, unresolvable) trade disputes could develop into trade wars. War is not just politics by other means, it is an inevitable outcome of the breakdown of politics.

UNILATERALISM: SPEAK LOUDLY AND SWING A BIG STICK

If the weaknesses of multilateral institutions may cause a breakdown in trade relations and ripen the atmosphere for a trade war, unilateralism is war in stasis – at least between equals. Between and among unequals, the GATT subsidies regimes and the FTAs modelled after the Canada–US example serve as little protection for the smaller party(ies). Dispute resolution once a CVD has been imposed is but too little and too late a protection for countries subjected to the caprice of 'Fair Trade' advocates in Washington and Brussels.

The principal difficulty seems to be the lack of a definition for the term 'subsidy'. The accusing country now has the liberty of defining the crime, naming the accused, investigating the circumstances, trying the accused, and imposing a penalty. This does not bode well for a 'fair' system, or one conducive to better and more harmonious relations among nations. If, as Hudec observes, the GATT Track II systems suffers because the accused appoints the jury and may hang the judge, here the pendulum has swung too far in favour of the accusing country – only if, of course, it is strong enough to actually affect the interests of its partners. Lest I be accused of cynicism, it must be said that this work has not even concerned itself with the new breed of 'fair trade' legislation in the US such as ss. 301 and Super 301. Unilateralism may yet be taken to heights undreamed of since the heyday of protectionism in the 1930s.

What then? The participants in the Uruguay Round of Multilateral Trade Negotiations (the Uruguay Round) have attempted to deal with some of these problems. It goes without saying that there is little chance that supranational institutions such as the Commission of the

European Union will be created to oversee the problems created by subsidisation and indiscriminate countervail. On the other hand, a strong attempt has been made to try to strengthen the multilateral aspects of the GATT, strengthen the definitional weaknesses (by far the weakest point of the GATT) and also to widen the scope of the GATT to cover services. In the next chapter, I will review the result of these negotiations.

Part III

THE OUTLOOK

6

THE URUGUAY ROUND

INTRODUCTION

Coming to an agreement on a 'new and improved' Subsidies Code has not been an easy task; it has taken nearly eight years for the 117 members of the GATT to reach a final agreement on some of the most contentious trade issues of our time. Throughout the tumultuous process, the breakdowns, and the walkouts, part of the difficulty was the divergent expectations and objectives with which the participants entered into the negotiations. Aside from issues such as agricultural subsidies and the civil aircraft problem that threatened to derail the entire process, the key participants in the negotiations over the subsidies code could not agree on why a subsidies code was even needed.

The US ostensibly sought strict controls on subsidies, although its commitment to a subsidies code was less than apparent. Canada and the EU's primary objective was to contain the US use of CVDs,[1] while neither was willing to admit that the US use of countervailing duties is, in essence, no different from their own use of subsidies. The US and Canada pursued a more judicial approach to subsidies regulation, while the EU argued that 'the dispute settlement procedure cannot be used to create new obligations or to replace the process of negotiation',[2] even though the highly judicialised internal dispute resolution mechanism of the EU has, in many ways, fostered negotiation rather than stifled it.

The Agreement[3] attempts to bridge these widely divergent, and even contradictory, approaches. It does so first by adopting what the literature has termed the 'traffic light' approach to subsidies. Second, it remains faithful to the principle of multilateralism enshrined in the GATT and the Subsidies Code. Third, while retaining the principal CVD provisions of the Code, the Agreement places new controls on their use and new avenues to challenge the unilateral imposition of CVDs to regulate subsidies. Finally, the dispute resolution process has been strengthened by the creation of a World Trade Organization.

NEGOTIATING FRAMEWORK

A new agreement had to address a number of concerns. First, it had to define 'subsidy'. Second, it had to address the paradox of subsidies in a more coherent and detailed way than the Subsidies Code had done. Third, the notification, surveillance and dispute resolution mechanisms of the Code had to be refined and strengthened. Fourth, greater controls had to be devised for countervailing duties, and fifth, the new mechanisms and measures had to be able to respond not only to direct harm caused by subsidies, but also to import displacement and third country effects.

Communication from Canada

The framework established by the Subsidies Group set out a 'traffic light' approach to subsidies by dividing them into three groups: prohibited, non-prohibited and countervailable.[4] Canada's Communication followed this approach. With respect to prohibited subsidies (mostly export subsidies) Canada argued that 'the appropriate remedy for any violation of a prohibition should be recourse to GATT dispute settlement procedures and multilaterally sanctioned remedies'.[5] The nature of the available remedy should be 'restricted to the imposition of increased duties, equivalent to countervailing duties, applied against exports from the subsidizing country'.[6] The Communication highlighted the lack of precision in the GATT and the Code on 'what subsidy practices should be subject to [unilaterally imposed] countermeasures'.[7] It argued for strengthened rules to enhance stability and predictability, and also to reduce the possibility of 'procedural harassment'.[8] In discussing the conditions for countervailability, the Communication from Canada adopted the European view that financial contribution by the government – either direct or indirect – should be a basic condition before a 'subsidy' is identified or countervailed.[9] It also argued for greater clarification of methods of calculating subsidies, both in total amounts and in the per unit assessment for the purposes of countervailing.[10]

One of the most important problems identified by Canada and the EU in dealing with the US has been countervail actions brought by enterprises that are being subsidised themselves. In *Michelin* this was particularly problematic because that case set the stage for a general attack on foreign domestic subsidies by the US trade bureaucracy. Canada argued, therefore, that

> the determination of the *amount of the subsidy should be based on the difference between the subsidy on imports and the subsidy on domestic production of the like products*.[11]

Finally, Canada argued that the failure of the existing process to resolve disputes was due to the 'absence of clarity in the obligations and rights associated with the existing rules'.[12] Another difficulty identified by Canada was the adoption and implementation of panel reports; however, Canada did not elaborate on this concern.

The European Union

In a report prepared for the Economic and Social Committee of the Commission of the European Union, Romoli and Pelletier argue that

> the EC view is that the banning of subsidies should hinge on distortion of international trade. Consequently, subsidies which intrinsically do not influence foreign trade as they are dictated by domestic policy (e.g. subsidies for research and innovation, regional development, structural [and] environmental protection, etc.) should be permitted. . . .[13]

This is not satisfactory. Such an argument is as insupportable as suggesting that a necessary link exists between all 'subsidies' and foreign trade. The question is not 'intrinsic' effects on foreign trade, but rather the types of foreign trade effects nations of the world are willing to suffer in order to preserve international comity and a semblance of respect for national domestic policy-making. If, for example, regional development programmes are to be protected, it is because they are considered to be a subset of domestic policies that merit protection regardless of certain effects on foreign trade; the benefits of regional development programmes and research and development expenditure outweigh, for many countries, possible or even probable foreign trade detriments. For this reason an

EU Ministerial Conference concluded that 'the possibility of an agreement on subsidies and countervailing measures hinges on whether the US is prepared to accept a meaningful green list or not'.[14] The 'green list' refers to the 'traffic light' approach advocated by Canada and the EU, and opposed by the US, which view prevailed in the final agreement.

Another basic objective of the negotiations, it was argued, should be to 'scrap unilateral protectionism and retaliatory measures'.[15] However, the EU was convinced that US negotiators were ready to live without an agreement at all if it meant compromising the ability of the US to countervail.[16] For its part, the EU argued for strengthening the dispute resolution mechanism, while acknowledging the lack of consensus among industrial countries 'on how to make the dispute settlement procedure more effective in tackling the more politically charged disputes'.[17] As noted previously, the EU was not prepared to adopt an adjudicative model of dispute settlement, as such a mechanism, the EU argued, would foreclose further avenues of negotiation.

The Subsidies Group of the Uruguay Round MTN identified several objectives. They aimed to: 1) identify and *define* three classes of subsidies: prohibited (red; *prima facie* subject to countermeasures), non-prohibited but actionable (amber; subject to countermeasures following investigation and showing of material injury), and non-prohibited and non-actionable (green); 2) retain countervailing duties as an avenue of remedies; 3) strengthen the provisions dealing with dispute settlement; and 4) narrow the conditions under which countervailing duties could be imposed.[18] The Agreement follows the original framework.

REGULATORY AND INSTITUTIONAL FRAMEWORK

Unlike its predecessor, the Agreement starts by defining 'subsidy'. It goes on to define concepts such as 'specificity' and 'domestic industry' that have been a major source of international acrimony over trade remedy actions and the regulation of subsidies. The Agreement then identifies a class of non-actionable subsidies. The Countervailing Duty provisions of the GATT are further interpreted and elaborated in Part V, and the Notification and Surveillance procedure of the Subsidies Committee is strengthened in Part VII.

The substantive framework

'Subsidy'

The Agreement identifies three classes of subsidies: non-actionable, prohibited, and non-prohibited but actionable.

A subsidy arises when two factors are present: 1) a financial contribution by 'a government or any public body within the territory of a signatory', and 2) a conferral of a benefit. The contribution by the government may be direct (in the form of grants, special loans, equity infusions, or loan guarantees), or indirect, such as foregone revenues (in the form of tax expenditure) and government provision of goods and services other than 'general infrastructure', or through directing private bodies to confer the benefits. Only 'specific' subsidies are prohibited by the Agreement.[19]

'Specificity'

The 'specificity' requirement is a crucial one, for otherwise any government action or expenditure may be caught by the prohibition on subsidies. It arises from the argument that a country's general expenditures are not trade-distortive and do not enhance its comparative advantage, or that they are offset through exchange rate adjustments. While these assumptions are questionable to a degree, the test of specificity seems, for the moment at least, to be the most workable test for distinguishing a government's general infrastructure spending from targeted subsidisation of its industries.

The principal criterion for determining whether a subsidy is 'specific' is the extent of its availability to enterprises.[20] If a subsidy is limited to certain enterprises, it is specific. If, however, 'objective criteria or conditions' govern the grant of a subsidy and payment is automatically made pursuant to eligibility, then the subsidy is not specific. Where there is an 'appearance of non-specificity' but 'there may be reasons to believe that the subsidy may in fact be specific', other factors such as

> use of a subsidy programme by a limited number of certain enterprises, predominant use by certain enterprises, the granting of disproportionately large amounts of subsidy to certain enterprises, and the manner in which discretion has been exercised by the granting authority in the decision to grant a subsidy[21]

may be considered to prove specificity.

The regional development provisions correct a serious anomaly in the GATT. Under the Subsidies Code, national governments are prohibited from granting subsidies 'specific' to a region. However, a regional government may initiate a similar programme, even funded by the national government, and yet it will be considered a 'general' programme within that region. The Agreement now considers all regional subsidies, whether granted by the national government or regional governments, to be specific.[22]

There are at least two problems with this approach. First, although regional governments may continue to have differential tax rates and dissimilar social programmes, the freedom of provincial, state or Land governments in domestic economic and industrial policy-making is being curtailed by an international agreement, and it is not clear to what extent those regional governments were consulted or involved in agreeing to these provisions. Secondly, the new requirements are conceptually problematic. For example, a small country such as Luxembourg or Estonia could provide a 'general' subsidy that would not be considered 'specific', while a subsidy programme designed to assist a 'region' such as Western Canada would be caught by this provision. The economic logic of this provision is, at best, suspect.

Finally, a showing of specificity must be substantiated on the basis of positive evidence.[23]

The specificity requirement is not clear on a number of issues. Most important, it does not address the case where a programme is general in nature and in application, but because of performance requirements only a few enterprises are able or willing to take advantage of it. Few subsidies have no conditions; in the rest these conditions may be so onerous as to make them unattractive to but a few enterprises, based on prevailing commercial considerations. In the *Softwood Lumber* and the *Pork* cases, for example, certain programmes were being used by only a handful of enterprises. The question was whether the limited use by a small number of companies was intended by the government, or whether business decisions and 'objective' criteria had led to the limited use of those programmes. The definition in the Agreement seems to adopt the American view of specificity based on use rather than on government intention.

Benefit to industry

The provision of government services, loans or capital to domestic industries is not considered to be a subsidy unless a benefit is thereby conferred to the industry. The Agreement clarifies what it means by 'benefit' – or, at least, what it does not mean – in Article 14. Government provision of capital must not be considered a benefit unless the investment decision 'can be regarded as inconsistent with the usual investment practice of private investors in the territory of that Member'.[24] A loan by a government is a benefit only to the extent that 'there is a difference between the amount that the firm receiving the loan pays on the government loan and a comparable commercial loan which the firm could actually obtain on the market'.[25] A loan guarantee is a benefit to the extent that the cost of borrowing is thereby reduced for the firm receiving the guarantee.[26] Finally, the provision of government services is a benefit to the extent that the purchase of the goods or services from the government is made for more than adequate remuneration, determined in relation to prevailing market conditions for the good or service in question in the country of provision or purchase.[27]

Non-actionable subsidies

Subsidies that are not 'specific' are *prima facie* non-actionable, that is, they may neither be countervailed nor be subject of a GATT complaint.[28] However, certain 'specific' subsidies are also on the green list. These are precompetitive research and development expenditures[29] and 'assistance to disadvantaged regions within the territory of a signatory given pursuant to a general framework of regional development and non-specific . . . within eligible regions'.[30] Other suggested exceptions such as environmental protection expenditures[31] also found their way to the Agreement.

Actionable subsidies

Subsidies that a) cause material injury to the domestic industry of another signatory, b) nullify or impair benefits accruing to a signatory under the GATT, or c) cause serious prejudice to the interests of another signatory, are actionable under the Agreement.[32] Serious prejudice is *deemed* to exist (unless otherwise proven by the subsidising country) where subsidies a) exceed 5 per cent of value of the product, b) cover operating losses sustained by an industry or an enterprise, except for one-time only worker adjustment assistance programmes, or c) are in the form of direct forgiveness of debt.[33] Serious prejudice may also arise, according to the Agreement, in cases of import displacement, third country export displacement, or an increase in world market share of the subsidising country.[34] Unless also covered by Article VI of the GATT, actionable subsidies are only subject to the multilateral track of the Agreement.

Prohibited subsidies

Two classes of subsidies are absolutely prohibited: subsidies contingent upon export performance, and subsidies contingent upon use of domestic over imported goods. No showing of material injury or nullification and impairment is necessary for action to be taken in reaction to these forms of subsidy.[35]

The institutional framework

As with the Subsidies Code, there are two tracks of remedies available to aggrieved signatories. One track is unilateral action through the countervailing duty procedure, still governed by Article VI of the GATT. Improvements include provision of definitions for subsidies and greater evidentiary requirements for initiating investigations or showing injury. The second track is the multilateral route, which has also been strengthened. The remedies sections of the Agreement signal three significant changes to the multilateral dispute resolution mechanism of the Subsidies Code. First, the grievance procedure is telescoped, so that it will be more difficult to use the GATT as a delaying tactic. Secondly, a Permanent Group of Experts is created. Third, it has become more difficult for an offending country to block the adoption of reports by the relevant institutions.[36] Remedies available to aggrieved parties depend upon the nature of the offending subsidy.

Elements of dispute settlement

Consultations

'Consultation' is the first stage of dispute settlement. Whenever a Member believes that a subsidy is being granted or maintained by another Member contrary to the GATT, it may request consultations with the alleged subsidising state. The request must be accompanied by evidence of such subsidisation, and the alleged subsidising state is required to enter into consultations 'in good faith'[37] in order to 'clarify the facts of the situation and to arrive at a mutually acceptable solution'.[38] If within thirty days of the request for consultations the Members have not arrived at a mutually satisfactory solution, the matter may be referred to the Dispute Settlement Body ('DSB') for the 'immediate establishment of a panel,' unless the DSB unanimously decides not to establish a panel.[39]

The Dispute Settlement Body

The Dispute Settlement Body (DSB), established pursuant to Sub-article IV.3 of the Agreement Establishing the Multilateral Trade Organization, is composed of the representatives of all the Members and is governed by the Understanding on Rules and Procedures Governing the Settlement of Disputes. The DSB has the task of administering the consultation and dispute settlement provisions of the Agreement on Subsidies. Accordingly, it has the authority to 'establish panels, adopt panel and Appellate Body reports, maintain surveillance of implementation of rulings and recommendations, and authorize suspension of concessions and other obligations under the covered agreements'.[40] The DSB may, upon the request of a Member party to a dispute, appoint a panel to investigate and report on an alleged infringement of the GATT.[41]

Panels

Members of panels must be experts in the field of international trade law or policy with a proven track record in the practice or teaching of international trade law, or with a governmental or GATT background in the field. They should be selected 'with a view to ensuring the independence of the members, a sufficiently diverse background and a wide spectrum of experience'.[42] Panels may be composed of three or five members, and may not include citizens of disputing countries, or countries belonging to the same common market agreement as the disputing countries. Panellists must serve in their individual capacities and may not accept instructions from or be influenced by governments.[43]

The function of a panel is to 'assist the DSB in discharging its responsibilities under [the Understanding] and the covered agreements'. Therefore, a panel 'should make an objective assessment of the matter before it, including an objective assessment of the facts of the case and the applicability of and conformity with the relevant covered agreement'.[44] In making its assessment, a panel may 'seek information and technical advice from any individual or body it deems appropriate', or 'consult experts to obtain their opinion on certain aspects of the matter'.[45] The report of a panel must be adopted by the DSB unless one of the parties to the dispute seeks an appeal to the Appellate Body, or the DSB unanimously refuses to adopt the report.[46]

The Appellate Body

The Appellate Body is responsible for hearing appeals from panel cases. It is to be composed of seven persons appointed for a maximum of two four-year terms, of whom three serve on any one case. The members of the Appellate Body must be persons of 'recognized authority, with demonstrated expertise in law, international trade and the subject matter of the covered agreements generally';[47] they must also be broadly representative of membership in the WTO.

Panel decisions may be appealed only by the parties to the dispute and not third parties. However, third parties that have notified the DSB of a substantial interest in the matter may make submissions before the Appellate Body. The appeal is restricted to 'issues of law covered in the panel report and legal interpretation developed by the panel'.[48] As a general rule, the proceedings must not exceed sixty days from the day the notice of appeal is issued by a party to a dispute. The report of the Appellate Body must be adopted by the DSB unless it refuses to do so by consensus.

Recommendations and rulings

Where a measure is found to be inconsistent with a covered agreement, a panel or the Appellate Body must recommend that 'the Member concerned bring the measure into conformity with that Agreement'. In addition, the panel or the Body may suggest ways in which the recommendations can be implemented.[49] Within thirty days of the adoption of the recommendations, the Member concerned must 'inform the DSB of its intentions in respect of implementation of the recommendations and rulings of the DSB'.[50] The Member may propose a time frame that may be approved by the DSB, or, within forty-five days, it may come to an agreement with the other parties to the dispute. In the absence of an approval or agreement, the matter may be put to arbitration.[51] The DSB has an on-going obligation to supervise the implementation of its rulings and recommendations.

Dispute settlement and the agreement on subsidies

Bodies specific to the agreement on subsidies

The Committee on Subsidies and Countervailing Measures, composed of representatives from each of the Members, is responsible for establishing a Permanent Group of Experts ('PGE').[52] The PGE will be composed of 'five independent persons, highly qualified in the fields of subsidies and trade relations'.[53] The Committee may send a matter to the PGE and request an advisory opinion on the existence and nature of a subsidy; the PGE may also be consulted for a non-binding and confidential advisory opinion by signatories intending to initiate a subsidy. The PGE is different from the current Panel of Experts in that it is permanent; currently, the *ad hoc* panels take a long time to come together.

Prohibited subsidies

The dispute settlement mechanism for prohibited subsidies is composed of two bodies, a panel and the PGE, and two steps, consultation and adjudication. If no satisfactory solution to the dispute is found within thirty days of the request for consultations, a panel may be established upon the request of a party to the dispute. The panel may, in turn, seek the assistance of the PGE 'with regard to whether the measure is a prohibited subsidy'. The PGE must, in such a case, 'review the evidence with regard to the existence and nature of the measure in question and shall . . . report its conclusions to the Panel within a time limit determined by the Panel'.[54] The panel must accept the PGE's conclusions on the issue of whether or not the measure in question is a prohibited subsidy. The report of the panel, or the Appellate Body if there is an appeal from the report of the panel, must be adopted by the DSB unless it refuses to do so by consensus. If the recommendations of the DSB pursuant to the report of the panel are not followed within the specified time period, the DSB must authorize the complaining Member to 'take appropriate countermeasures' unless it refuses to do so unanimously. Significantly, all time tables applicable under the Understanding are halved for the purposes of Article 4 of the Agreement.[55]

Actionable subsidies

Where consultations fail to result in a satisfactory solution to a dispute, parties may request that the DSB establish a panel. The panel so struck shall review the matter and submit its report to the DSB, which must adopt the report (or the report of the Appellate Body, if there has been an appeal) unless it decides not to do so by consensus. Where a report determines that 'a subsidy has resulted in adverse effects to the interests of another Member within the meaning of Article 5 of this Agreement, the Member granting or maintaining such subsidy shall take appropriate steps to remove the adverse effects or shall withdraw the subsidy.'[56] Unless appropriate steps are taken within six months to remove the effects of the subsidy or to compensate the complaining Members, the DSB must authorise the complaining Members to take countermeasures, 'commensurate with the degree and nature of the adverse effects determined to exist'.

Non-actionable subsidies

If a Member believes that another Member's subsidies, even though consistent with the criteria laid down in Article 8 of the Agreement, have resulted in 'serious adverse effects to the domestic industry of that Member, such as to cause damage which would be difficult to repair', the injured Member may request consultations. If consultations are not successful, the matter may be referred to the Committee on Subsidies and Countervailing Measures. In such a case, the Committee shall review the matter and the evidence of the injurious effects. If the Committee determines that such effects exist, it may recommend to the subsidising Member to modify its programmes in such a way as to remove the effects. If the Committee's recommendations are not followed within six months, 'the Committee shall authorize the requesting Member to take appropriate countermeasures commensurate with the nature and degree of the effects determined to exist.'[57]

Countervailing duties

Countervailing duties must continue to conform to the requirements of Article VI of the GATT. The Agreement contains additional procedural safeguards against abusive use of CVDs.

A request for an investigation into the existence and extent of a subsidy programme by national trade remedy law administering authorities must satisfy three conditions. It should include sufficient evidence of the existence of 1) a subsidy, 2) material injury, and 3) a causal link between the subsidised import and the alleged injury, that is, that 'the alleged material injury to a domestic industry is caused by subsidized imports through the effects of subsidies'.[58] The evidence of both subsidy and injury must be considered simultaneously, both in the decision whether or not to initiate an investigation and during the course of the investigation. The administering authorities should satisfy themselves, based on positive evidence, that the allegation and the investigation have the support of the domestic industry before initiating an investigation.[59] No investigation may be initiated if the domestic producers expressly supporting the application account for less than 25 per cent of total production of the like product by the domestic industry.

Amount of the subsidy

For the purposes of a Countervailing Duty assessment, as noted above the amount of the subsidy is to be determined on the basis of 'benefit to the recipient'. The guidelines have adopted the 'commercial considerations' test common to both the EU and the USITA.[60] According to this approach, government provision of equity and loans must be consonant with prevailing commercial considerations. For example, a loan guarantee that reduces the interest rate paid by an enterprise may be considered a countervailable subsidy to the extent that the enterprise's interest payments are reduced by the guarantee, regardless of the actual or potential costs to the guarantor. Finally, provision of goods or services by a government for less than 'adequate remuneration' may be countervailed to the extent of the 'benefit'.

While from an economic point of view these qualifications seem to make sense,[61] a global view of what governments do in an economy and the motivations behind most government activities undermine the force of the 'commercial consideration' test. The key question of 'why' a government may be providing loan guarantees or equity infusions is not asked. The 'why' could supplement or even supplant the commercial consideration criterion. Besides, a commercial consideration for a state is, or at least may be, quite different from a commercial consideration by private market actors. For example, market actors do not benefit from increased tax revenues, or decreased crime and poverty, or any other benefits of increased employment. A commercial enterprise may lay workers off for commercial reasons where a government may not be able to do so for legitimate socio-political reasons.

Moreover, what services are provided by governments as a general service to trade and industry is not uniform across the globe. Some countries, for example, take the 'user pays' view to cover the cost of building bridges, tunnels and most national highways (and even some regional roads). Others may conceptualise 'government services' differently, to the point of almost completely relieving the private sector from the responsibility of providing such services as personnel health care coverage. The Countervailing Duty provisions of the Agreement do not adequately address these concerns.

Imposition of the duty

The Agreement reaffirms Article VI of the GATT to the effect that

> the decision whether or not to impose a countervailing duty in cases where all requirements for the imposition have been fulfilled and the decision whether the amount of the countervailing duty to be imposed shall be the full amount of the subsidy or less are decisions to be made by the authorities of the importing country.[62]

This 'unilateralism' is tempered by the provision of definitions set out above. However, the Agreement loses its vigour at this point. It states that it is 'desirable' that the imposition of CVDs be permissive,[63] that it be less than the amount of the subsidy if the lesser duty would be enough to remove the injury, and that authorities be allowed to consider other domestic interests than those of the injured industry when imposing a CVD.[64] These are essentially EU (and Canadian) positions which the US Congress (despite pressure from the Administration) has been particularly unwilling to adopt. A further requirement that CVDs be provided with a five-year sunset clause may prove to be unacceptable in the US.

Notification and surveillance

Members are obligated to notify most subsidies, as defined in the Agreement, *granted or maintained* within their territory.[65] In order to allay the understandable fears of the notification process, the Agreement recognises that

> notification of a measure does not prejudge either its legal status under the General Agreement and this Agreement, the effects under this Agreement, or the nature of the measure itself.[66]

The Committee will examine notifications under Article 25, and submit reports semi-annually.

ANALYSIS

In discussing the existing regulatory framework, two major problems have been identified. First, no definition of subsidy is provided in the GATT or the Subsidies Code. Secondly, the institutional arrangement of the Code is not conducive to speedy dispute resolution. These weaknesses have fostered unilateralism, aggravated trade disputes, and generally increased instability in world trading relations. The Agreement overcomes these weaknesses to a large extent. It does so through three developments: the 'traffic light' approach, stronger discipline on countervailing duties, and improvements to the institutional arrangements.

The definitions provided in the Agreement potentially introduce much needed discipline on unilateral action by domestic legislatures and trade remedy agencies. However, whether these definitions are *conceptually* sound is another matter. First, the rejection of the 'net–net' approach proposed by Canada signifies a sacrifice of logic for political expediency. Few enterprises in the world, especially those involved in international trade, are untainted by some form of government assistance, or subsidisation; there is no question, either economically or even from a point of view of fairness, that heavily subsidised enterprises should not be allowed to complain about other countries' subsidies, which may be more modest than the complainant country's. Secondly, the Agreement does not, in either its definition of subsidies or the section dealing with the method of calculation of subsidies, seek to identify and calculate the costs to enterprises associated with accepting certain subsidies.[67] This treatment of subsidies in the abstract makes little economic sense. Third, given this conceptual incoherence, it is not clear what is meant by 'countermeasures commensurate with the degree and nature of the adverse effects determined to exist'. Does the Agreement sanction the use of countermeasures only so far as is needed to remove the injury, or does it permit measures aimed at the subsidy itself? Is there an attempt to alleviate harm, or is the countermeasure to be used as punishment? The nature and scale of the countermeasure depend, to a large degree, on the view one takes of the objectives to be gained by the imposition of countermeasures.

These conceptual shortcomings are not surprising. In the negotiations leading up to the Agreement, the institutional limitations and political requirements of the countries involved dictated a departure from conceptual coherence. There was, it appears, an element of common sense in adopting the more straightforward approach. Expecting already overtaxed and strained trade remedy administering agencies – which are established to protect domestic industries and not necessarily domestic economic or trading interests – to explore their own governments' subsidies (or other industrial and economic policies) in determining the net amount of a foreign subsidy would, perhaps, be asking the impossible. In fact, even carrying out the simple obligations imposed by the Agreement, such as establishing a causal relation between foreign subsidies and domestic injury, may prove to be unduly burdensome.

For example, Subclause 11.2(e) requires that in imposing countervailing duties, there should be 'evidence that any alleged material injury to a domestic industry is caused by subsidized imports *through* the effects of subsidies . . .'.(emphasis added) The attempt is to link the injury to the subsidy and not, as is normal practice, to the subsidised import. This is, however, inconsistent with the 'subsidies per unit' approach adopted elsewhere in the Agreement – at least, the approach is irrelevant to the requirement. As I have already noted, in Chapter 2, the exact effect of domestic subsidies on the manufactured product or the market of the importing country cannot be determined by a simple subsidy per unit linear equation.[68] An analysis of the effects within the importing country requires the construction of two counterfactuals: a foreign (production without subsidies) counterfactual and a domestic (import of non-subsidy-related products) one. Export-contingent subsidies are considered *per se* distortive primarily because the link between manufacture or export and subsidisation is direct. Domestic subsidies are, however, different.[69] Nevertheless, the approach adopted by the Agreement may be more practical than a theoretically sound methodology. If subsidies are to be internationally regulated and in the absence of a supranational harmonisation of domestic industrial and social policy, the international community must be content with the imperfect, and largely illogical, counterfactuals that link the subsidy to domestic injury through the subsidised imports, or that permit subsidised industries to take their foreign competitors to task for being subsidised.

The institutional changes envisioned in the Agreement should be cause for some optimism. The requirement for the adoption of the reports of the panels or the Appellate Body by the DSB unless there is unanimous consent not to do so means that the subsidising country cannot single-handedly block the adoption of the report – one of the most frustrating inadequacies of the present system. Moreover, the DSB must recommend the imposition of countermeasures upon the required adoption of the reports. This is much closer to an adjudicative model (albeit one without much enforcement power) than the institutions of the Subsidies Code.

However, the difficulty with the present GATT Subsidies Code DRM is not simply institutional ineffectiveness. It was noted above that even under the present GATT system, which affords the subsidising country many opportunities to consult, conciliate and finally to block the adoption of the report of the experts, a request for consultations is invariably interpreted as a hostile act. Even the EU, long an advocate of negotiation over adjudication, did not fail to become indignant when the US finally requested consultations in the Airbus matter before the GATT. The question is the extent to which a request for consultations under the proposed system will be interpreted as a friendly – or even neutral – gesture. Otherwise, consultation will have little chance of working.

Moreover, while the notification procedure of the Agreement is an improvement over the Subsidies Code, its effectiveness is questionable. The notification procedure of the EU is effective (to the degree that it is so) because of the power of the Commission to order the repayment or suspend the payment of undisclosed (illegal) subsidies by the subsidised enterprise. Even with such a power and the Commission's resources for investigation and enforcement many state aid measures are not notified by the Member States.[70] In EFTA the situation is even more critical; statistics are provided only sporadically and hardly ever completely, and proposed state aid measures are almost never cleared with the EFTA Secretariat or Council before implementation. Whether the proposed GATT Committee on Subsidies will have greater success in encouraging disclosure is doubtful.

Finally, the success or failure of the Agreement will depend almost entirely on the degree to which Members of the new subsidies code will want it to succeed; to a great extent the responsibility for maintaining the integrity of the new code will rest on the shoulders of the EU and the US as the two largest trading powers in the world. However, two major stumbling blocks exist. The first is the Agreement's singularly tentative move toward an adjudicative model of dispute resolution. The second is the inability of the Agreement to resolve the fundamental tension between the objectives of the EU and the US: the disciplines on subsidies are as weak as the restraints on the imposition of countervailing duties. Albeit an interesting compromise and a laudable achievement, the Agreement does not appear to satisfy either the EU requirements or the long-standing US concerns, as stressed by Congress. If both trading blocs accept the Agreement as a workable compromise, there may yet be hope for a functioning international dispute resolution mechanism for subsidies. If, on the other hand, the Contracting Parties abuse or ignore the new code as they have done the existing GATT system, the improvements may be of little help in saving the new institutions from irrelevance.

7

CONCLUSION

With far the greatest part of [hu]mankind, interest is the governing principle. . . . It is vain to exclaim against the depravity of human nature on this account. . . . No institution, not built on the presumptive truth of these maxims can succeed.
George Washington[1]

As a matter of moral analysis this statement may be of dubious validity. However, it aptly describes the environment within which international law, including trade law, and institutions are developed and the framework within which an analysis of these laws and institutions must be conducted. And while recognition of the importance of 'interest' in the development of trade policy may seem elementary, defining 'interest' is not easy. Does it mean economic interest, military interest, or diplomatic interest? How do these 'interests' interact with one another? Is it at all accurate or helpful to pigeonhole the different aspects of a country's 'national interest'?

As noted in Chapter 2, one of the most potent critiques of classical free trade theory is that it ignores the political or cultural objectives of nations in assessing the success of their international trade policy; trade theory does not seem at all interested in determining the 'interests', broadly defined, of participants in international trade. If anything, there is a tendency in classical free trade theory circles to deride the operation of 'interest' (whether in domestic policy making or in international trading relations).[2] However, less theoretically pure circles are now beginning to question the wisdom of this approach. Johns' and Porter's critiques signal the development of a greater sensitivity to and tolerance of the influence of non-economic factors in shaping domestic and international trade policy. The recognition of the legitimacy of non-economic interests should mark the end of the untenable distinction between trade policy and trade politics.

This development should not indicate a defection to the nihilism of the school of 'all-is-politics-why-bother-with-theory-or-consistency', nor should it herald the advent of a golden age of interest group politics. The point is not to abandon principle or rationality altogether; rather, we must reconceptualise them in the context of international trade. Expanding the definition of 'interest' in the analysis of international trading relations to include political and strategic objectives will enable us to have a better appreciation of hitherto 'cynical' or 'irrational' behaviour. For example, in this context, in regard to the massive subsidisation of Airbus by European governments, the question is not 'why would European taxpayers subsidise Canadian air travel?'. The only viable answers to such a question are 1) the Europeans are insane, or 2) the EU is trying to destroy the Canadian aircraft industry. Instead, the more globally (politically, socially and economically) sensitive question is the one asked by the EU Commission: Does the development of a thriving European Aircraft industry serve the long-term interests (strategic as well as economic and political) of the European Union? Subsidies to the European civil aircraft industry, although still problematic, may seem less irrational in this light.

A reconceptualisation of the basis of our understanding of 'interest' is necessary for the development of viable international trade institutions. For one thing, the theory of free trade has been unable to provide a realistic framework for understanding the true socio-economic and trade effects of domestic industrial subsidisation. More important, though, the inextricable link between domestic subsidies and a state's socio-political objectives make a thorough understanding of these objectives – national and international – a *sine qua non* of a sound analysis of subsidies and their regulation. Whether and which subsidies are rational, and what the responses of the international community ought to be thereto, therefore, should not depend on an abstract economic analysis, nor will an ethical analysis abstracted from political and military considerations be adequate.[3] Of course, as I stated in Part I, the point of this study is not to determine whether subsidies are good or bad; rather, it is to determine what are the elements of a successful regulatory approach to subsidies.

International trade is governed by 'interest'. Trade, in fact, is an important and powerful instrument of international relations.[4]

Regardless of this bald reality, most international trade institutions, and specifically institutions for the regulation of subsidies, have not been cognisant of the importance, or responsive to the question, of 'interest' as defined in this chapter. The one leads to paralysis, and the other to trade war: Multilateral institutions, consumed by ever-present but unacknowledged 'interest', have not been able to function properly, while unilateral instruments have not only not been able to bring subsidies under control, but, by advancing the interests of the complaining country regardless of the legitimate interests of the subsidisers, they have caused great friction in trading relations among nations.

The only relatively successful mechanism, the EU, has the balance of 'interests' indelibly etched into its regulatory consciousness.[5] Although its success in curbing the most market-distortive effects of subsidies cannot be described as anything but modest, the EU has been able to have a more balanced conception of 'interest' than other mechanisms. This is partly due to the relative homogeneity of the Union (as compared with GATT) and hence the relative ease of convergence of interest:[6] It is not surprising that the EU has had more success in obtaining state aid concessions from Scandinavian and central European countries than, for example, from Greece. It is also due to the fact that the state aid policy of the EU advances the cause of greater integration of European economies and does not further national protectionist objectives.

But if the successes of international regulatory mechanisms are modest, the failures have been spectacular. That the GATT has not been successful in resolving the problem of subsidies is not surprising. Like its counterpart in the world of politics (the United Nations) the GATT has become a battleground for the superpowers of trade; the successful conclusion of the Uruguay Round is causing a thaw in the international cold war in trade, an event as miraculous as the end of the other cold war. Whether in the form of agricultural subsidies, R&D spending, or defence expenditure, the trade and industrial policies of trade superpowers have so far threatened international economic security, as the deterrence of MAD had held the security of the planet hostage to its insane logic. Latter day cold warriors in the US – the unions, the extreme isolationist right and the environmentalists – have now abandoned the banner of free market and picked up that of 'fair trade' to fan the fires of protectionism.

The GATT, like the UN before the 'new world order', has been unable to provide a solution to problem of superpower 'interest'. The institutional arrangement of the GATT is not entirely to blame. There is little question, however, that despite its successes in reducing tariffs, the GATT has failed to reduce international trade tensions. The successes have been badly overshadowed, in the past decade or so, by the failure to discipline egregious uses of non-tariff barriers such as 'voluntary' export restraints, quotas, antidumping and CVD actions, and certain subsidies – and the list goes on.

Under the present circumstances and speaking strictly ideally, a bureaucratic or adjudicative model along the lines of the Commission of the EU would probably provide more stability in international trade than has existed since the breakdown of the post-war economic *Pax Americana*. Such an institution does not have to exercise the wide-ranging and intrusive powers of the Commission. As the ECJ also observed in a different context

> the fact that the provisions of the [EEA] agreement and the corresponding Community provisions are identically worded does not mean that they must necessarily be interpreted identically. An international treaty is to be interpreted not only on the basis of its wording, but also in the light of its objectives.[7]

The point, of course, is not to eliminate the role of politics, but to subsume it under the rubric of administrative policy-making or judicial interpretation. Such an institution may be – indeed it will have to be – as aware of the importance of the politics of trade as the Commission has been. Its value would lie in appearing to depoliticise trade issues and defuse the intense political sentiments that trade matters can generate. Politicians often resort to thinly veiled administrative organs to advance their domestic political agenda; there is no reason why an international administrative body cannot be trusted with the preservation of national trade interests in an international context. If the nations of the world are committed to stronger trading relations and a more stable international marketplace, such an institution may provide a useful framework without unduly affecting national policy-making powers, or national identities.

Such a scenario, however, is unlikely. Whatever measures that might be conceived to make a European Commission-like institution function well will ultimately drown in the cauldron of the international cold war in trade. In any event, the fear of losing sovereignty, of political reprisals at home, of losing the ability to manage the domestic economy – whether rational or not, these concerns exist and they must be addressed when one is proposing a new international order. An administrative or adjudicative tribunal is not likely to be able to survive deep seated hostilities toward supranationalism.

What, then, is the answer? To begin with, it must be stressed again that to argue that 'interest' must be given its due recognition by international trade institutions is not to say that all 'interests' are necessarily legitimate; not all conduct of politics is rational. Examples of irrational conduct in international relations abound: *Ex post*, it is clear that the US foreign policy in Vietnam, Cuba and the Republic of Iraq, or to a lesser extent the red scare of the 1950s and the early 1980s, were costly mistakes born largely of an 'irrational' understanding of the politics of international relations. The point is the need for a more expansive understanding of 'rational' behaviour in international trade – more expansive than allowed by traditional free trade theory, on which the existing international institutions are based – and not a total abandonment of it.

In the context of trade, for example, the stable trading relations between the EU and EFTA can be considered a model of 'rational' trading relations. On the other hand, trading relations between the US and EU have been marked by numerous costly and disruptive trade lawsuits in domestic and international fora, and may be considered an example of 'irrational' conduct of trading relations, insofar as the market uncertainty created by the lawsuits and the political disharmony between the partners have reduced investment, trade, and growth in both markets and lessened the chances of greater economic integration and expanded trade.[8]

The pursuit of 'interest' through international institutions must be informed by two corollaries: 1) the validity of other nations' 'interests', and 2) the fragility of rational political behaviour. This does not imply disinterested bargaining or unilateral compromise. Schelling observes in the context of international relations (I argue it is equally applicable to trade negotiations) that bargaining among nations over questions of interest may '[be] polite or rude, entail threats as well as offers, . . . [be] respectful or vicious . . . [but] there must be some common interest'.[9] The problem is that it has been all of those without any attempt at locating the 'common interest'; hence my argument for an administrative or an adjudicative dispute resolution or regulatory mechanism along the lines of the EU Commission.

For the moment, however, before we can attain the largely illusory goal of a world supranational regulatory agency (in spite of the promise of the World Trade Organization), the primary objective of trade theoreticians and practitioners must be to come to a common understanding of the terms of the argument. As I noted in Part I, there is little use decrying the cynicism of politics if the underlying theory of international trade is incapable of providing guidance. Evidence of trade institutions in action clearly indicates that where 'interest' is not accepted as a valid component of international trade policy-making, the chances of coming to a lasting and working agreement are very low. That is when 'fair trade' and unilateralism become instruments of trade policy, and that is when the international trading order breaks down.

I submit my prognosis. If the prescription is lacking in potency, it is due to the fragility of the terminal patient, the international trading order. The shot in the arm provided by the success of the Uruguay Round may in the end prove to have been a temporary fix.

NOTES

1 INTRODUCTION

1 Vernon, Raymond, and Debora Spar, *Beyond Globalism: Remaking American Foreign Economic Policy*, (New York: The Free Press, 1989), at 171.

2 DOMESTIC INDUSTRIAL SUBSIDIES IN INTERNATIONAL TRADE TRADE THEORY

1 Cantin, Frederic P., and Andreas Lowenfeld, 'Rules of Origin, the Canada–US FTA, and the *Honda* case', *American Journal of International Law* (1993), 87, 375 at 387.
2 See generally Leamer, Edward, *Sources of International Comparative Advantage – Theory and Evidence*, (Cambridge: MIT Press, 1984); Johns, R.A., *International Trade Theories and the Evolving International Economy*, (London: Frances Pinter, 1985); Balassa, Bela, *Competitive Advantage: Trade Policy and Economic Development*, (London: Harvester Wheatsheaf, 1989); Baldwin, Robert, *Trade Policy Issues and Empirical Analysis*, (Chicago: The University of Chicago Press, 1988).
3 Leamer, ibid., at xii.
4 Ibid., at 31.
5 Manchester, William, *The Last Lion – Visions of Glory*, (New York: Dell Publishing Inc., 1983), at 351–5. Reynolds is sceptical of the importance of ideas. He quotes an article by Gary Anderson and Robert Tollison, in which it is argued that repeal of the corn laws had more to do with the textile lobby's efforts to repeal duties on cotton than it did to the zeal of free traders. See Reynolds, Alan, *The Political Economy of a North American Free Trade Agreement*, (Vancouver: The Hudson Institute and The Fraser Institute) at 22. However, a closer look at the political players and the ideological environment of the period reveals a more fundamental shift in national ideology – with its attendant political and economic ramifications – than is allowed by a lobby-driven repeal of protective tariffs on foodstuffs. See for example,

Morris, James, *Heaven's Command*, (London: Penguin, 1973), particularly at 164–5.

6 Johns, op. cit., at 149.

7 Quoted in Baldwin, op. cit., at 1.

8 Rivers, Richard, and John Greenwald, 'The Negotiation of a Code on Subsidies and Countervailing Measures: Bridging Fundamental Policy Differences', *Law and Policy in International Business* (1979), 11, 1447 at 1449.

9 See European Free Trade Association, Economic Committee, Working Party on Government Aids, *Final Report*, (Geneva: EFTA, 1986), or Commission of the European Communities, Directorate General for Economic and Financial Affairs, *European Economy* no. 48: *Fair Competition in the Internal Market: State Aid Policy*, (Luxembourg: Office of Official Publications of the European Communities, 1989).

10 Hudec, Robert, 'Regulation of Domestic Subsidies Under the MTN Subsidies Code', in Wallace, Don Jr., Frank Loftus, and Van Krikorian, eds, *Interface Three: Legal Treatment of Domestic Subsidies*, (Washington, DC: The International Law Institute, 1984), at 4.

11 See for example Goetz, Charles J., Lloyd Granet, and Warren Schwartz, 'The Meaning of "Subsidy" and "Injury" in the Countervailing Duty Law', *International Review of Law and Economics* (1986) 6, 17; Schwartz, Warren, and Eugene Harper, 'The Regulation of Subsidies Affecting International Trade', *Michigan Law Review* (1972), 70, 831; EFTA, *Final Report*, op. cit.; *European Economy*, op. cit.; Hudec, Robert, '"Mirror, Mirror, on the Wall" The Concept of Fairness in the United States Trade Policy', paper presented at the 1990 annual meeting of the Canadian Council of International Law, in Ottawa on 19 October 1990; Bhagwati, Jagdish, 'Fair Trade, Reciprocity and Harmonization: The Novel Challenge to the Theory and Policy of Free Trade', (mimeo, Columbia University, August 1991).

12 It is acknowledged that many of these distinctions are artificial. For example, it is difficult to differentiate between cultural activities and activities of 'cultural' industries; it is not clear why commercial activity by 'cultural' industries should benefit from more protection than other industries. Similarly, the difference between certain social programmes and industrial assistance programmes is at best negligible.

13 Thomas, Jeffrey, *Subsidies and Countervailing Duties in the Canada–US Free Trade Agreement: Trends, Critiques and Proposals for Rational Reform*, (Toronto: Faculty of Law, University of Toronto, 1989), at 1/16.

14 Jackson, John H., *The World Trading System*, (Cambridge: MIT Press, 1989), at 265.

15 Barceló, John J. III, 'Subsidies, Countervailing Duties and Antidumping after the Tokyo Round', *Cornell International Law Journal* (1980), 13, 257 at 282–3.

16 Johns, op. cit., at 37.

17 Baldwin, op. cit., at 96.

18 Hufbauer, Gary Clyde, and Joanna Shelton Erb, *Subsidies in International Trade*, (Cambridge: MIT Press, 1984), at 8.

19 Baldwin, op. cit., at 1. This is problematic. For one thing, foreign

treasuries are not bottomless. Despite the apparent willingness of many governments to fund losing propositions, the day of reckoning will come for their treasuries. More important, to talk of 'foreign treasuries' gives a more majestic aura to these 'treasuries' than is warranted. A single US corporation such as GE, GM or IBM is larger and richer than three quarters of the treasuries of the world. Most multinationals that have the funds to tie up their competitors in endless lawsuits in Washington can outcompete most foreign treasuries without much difficulty.

20 Hudec, 'Mirror', op. cit., at 18.

21 Sykes, Alan O., 'Countervailing Duty Law: An Economic Perspective', paper presented at the Law and Economics Workshop Series at the Faculty of Law, University of Toronto, (1989), at 67.

22 Ibid.

23 Jackson, *World Trading System*, op. cit., at 254.

24 Hudec, 'Mirror', op. cit., at 1.

25 Jackson, *World Trading System*, op. cit., at 254.

26 Hudec, 'Mirror', op. cit., at 5.

27 This is not a novel observation, but Fallows outlines his argument against unfettered free trade by pointing to the expansion of US industrial capacity throughout the nineteenth century that came about essentially as a result of high tariffs and well-planned industrial spending by the US government, or the fact that the British Industrial Revolution was fed by protective tariffs in the eighteenth century. He argues that 'while American industry was developing, the country had no time for *laissez-faire*. After it had grown strong, the United States began preaching *laissez-faire* to the rest of the world – and began to kid itself about its own history'. Fallows, James, 'How the World Works', *The Atlantic Monthly* (December 1993), 60 at 79.

28 Ibid., at 62 and 73.

29 Hindley, Brian, 'Subsidies, Politics and Economics', in *Interface Three*, op. cit., at 31.

30 Ibid.

31 Ibid., at 12.

32 See ibid.; Bhagwati, op. cit.

33 Johns, op. cit., at 149.

34 Ibid., at 143.

35 Ibid., at 135.

36 I highly recommend Robert Cullen's article 'The True Cost of Coal', in the December 1993 issue of *The Atlantic Monthly*, at 38. He points out that coal accounts for more than half of America's electricity because it is so cheap, and it is so cheap because no one other than society at large and probably not even this generation pays the high environmental price of its mining and burning.

37 Ibid., at 142.

38 Baldwin, op. cit., at 1.

39 Naidin, L.C., from the Ministry of Finance of Brazil, 'Comment' on Depayre, G., and R. Petriccione, 'Definition of Subsidy', in Bourgeois, Jacques H.J., ed., *Subsidies and International Trade: A European*

Lawyers' Perspective, (Deventer: Kluwer Law and Taxation Publishers, 1991), at 77.

40 *European Economy*, op. cit., at 21.

41 Malmgren, Harald, 'Session One', in Wallace, Don, George C. Spina, Richard M. Rawson, and Brian McGill, eds, *Interface One*, (Washington, DC: The Institute for International and Foreign Trade Law, 1980), at 58. See also Trebilcock, Michael, J., 'Throwing Deep: Trade Remedy Laws in a First Best World', in Trebilcock, Michael J., and Robert C. York, *Fair Exchange: Reforming Trade Remedy Laws*, (Toronto: C.D. Howe Institute, 1990), at 244: '. . .the exchange rate is increasingly determined by capital flows and not goods flows'. Market inefficiencies may not be reflected in the exchange rate and may require an extra-market intervention for correction.

42 Barceló, John J. III, 'Subsidies and Countervailing Duties – Analysis and a Proposal', *Law and Policy in International Business* (1977), 9, 779 at 792.

43 Porter, Michael E., *The Competitive Advantage of Nations*, (New York: The Free Press, 1990), at 305.

44 Ibid., at 29.

45 Ibid., at 1.

46 Ibid., at 67.

47 Ibid., at 77.

48 Ibid., at 73.

49 Emphasis added. *The Natural System of Political Economy*, quoted in Fallows, op. cit., at 66.

50 Porter, op. cit., at 29.

51 The numbers in this particular sector are mind-boggling. In France, for example, government support for shipbuilding constitutes some 57 per cent of the sectoral GDP, compared with only 3.6 per cent for the rest of the French manufacturing sector. See Ford, Robert , and Wim Suyker, *Industrial Subsidies in the OECD Economies*, Working Paper no. 74, (Paris: OECD, Dept. of Economics and Statistics). This is a marked decline from the 118 per cent level of subsidies to French shipbuilders in 1986. In Italy and Portugal, subsidies continue to constitute 84.8 per cent and 78.6 per cent, respectively, of value added in the shipbuilding sector. See Commission of the European Community, *Third Survey on State Aids in the European Community in the Manufacturing and Certain Other Sectors*, (Luxembourg: Office of the Official Publications of the European Community, 1992), at 14. In Norway in 1984, subsidies per person employed in the shipbuilding sector were 135 per cent of average wages of industrial workers. In Sweden in 1982 the figure was 217 per cent. See Wieser, Thomas, 'Government Aids to Industry in EFTA', *EFTA Bulletin* (1987), 28 (2), 13 at 14.

52 Porter, op. cit., at 39.

53 See Porter for a more detailed elaboration and analysis.

54 Nyerges, Janos, 'Session Two', in *Interface One*, op. cit., at 103.

55 Ibid. Bence and Smith found that the USA uses traditional methods of subsidisation to a lesser extent than other countries. However, subsidies do exist, and quite substantially in some cases. For example, the subsidy

rate for the forestry industry in the USA is close to 12 per cent; the subsidy rate for the same industry in Canada is less than 1 per cent. See Bence, J.-F., and Murray Smith, 'Subsidies and Trade Laws: the Canada–US Dimension', *International Economic Issues*, (April 1989), 1 at 28–9, tables 8 and 9.

56 Diaz-Alejandro argues that 'market rules of the game, and the determination of which markets are allowed to operate, are essentially political decisions'. Quoted in Leamer, op. cit., at 25. He also suggests that 'some would argue that markets must be viewed as creatures of social and political systems, not as mechanisms, arising spontaneously and inevitably out of economic necessity, [for the latter shows a] naive disregard of socio-political realities and of vested interests'. Quoted in ibid., at 139. Phelps Brown argues that 'if there is another great synthetic statement to cover economics . . . then that new statement of theory will not be a general theory of economics alone, it will instead be a general theory of social affairs'. Quoted in ibid., at 147.

57 Quoted in Johns, op. cit., at 139.

58 Ibid., at 137.

59 Mundheim, Robert, and Peter Ehrenraft, 'What is a "Subsidy"? A Discussion Paper', in *Interface Three*, op. cit., at 96–7.

60 Johns, op. cit., at 143.

61 See Barceló, 'Analysis', op. cit., at 836; Gaisford, James D., and Donald McLachlan, 'Domestic Subsidies and Countervail: The Treacherous Ground of the Level Playing Field', 24 *Journal of World Trade* (1990), 24 (4), 55 at 61.

62 Trebilcock, op. cit., at 243.

63 Ibid.

64 Fed Reg 49, 19374 at 19375.

65 Sykes, Alan O., 'Second-best Countervailing Duty Policy: A Critique of the Entitlement Approach', *Law and Policy in International Business* (1990), 21, 699 at 699. See also Baldwin, Robert, 'Trade Policies in Developed Countries', in Jones, Ronald W., and Peter B. Kenen, eds , *Handbook of International Economics*, (Amsterdam: North Holland, 1984). Baldwin states that 'there is still widespread disagreement within and among nations concerning the effects and legitimacy of various forms of subsidies', (at 604)

66 Nyerges, op. cit., at 101.

67 See Barceló, 'Analysis', op. cit., at 822.

68 Schwartz and Harper, op. cit., at 841.

69 Ibid., at 833. Alessandrini notes that 'in the presence of market failure or of aggressive behaviour of foreign enterprises that distort the domestic market, there are some offsetting policies that have some adverse "indirect effects", but would still bring about an improvement and maximise the national output'. See Alessandrini, S., 'Subsidies, Strategic Trade Policies and the GATT', in Bourgeois, op. cit., at 7.

70 See *European Economy*, op. cit., at 21.

71 Hudec, Robert, 'Regulation. . .', op. cit., at 31.

72 Thomas argues that 'only if the market cannot be depended upon to provide the optimal amount [of a good] – there exists an efficiency or

public goods rationale – can there be considered to be an adequate justification for public subsidization. As a country, we must direct our resources to those activities with the greatest return. In the absence of positive externalities, the market can be depended upon to make the proper and efficient determination as to where those activities should take place'. Thomas, op. cit., at 5/79. This type of argument is truistic, circular, and ultimately irrelevant. It is a truism that we want the best value for our money; it is circular because the market is already defined as the only mechanism that can deliver the best value; it is irrelevant because it is not at all clear why an economist's conception of the economically rational return is or should be the only way the social value of an activity can be determined. As I have already noted, most socio-economic issues do not lend themselves to a strict and narrow economic analysis of the type undertaken by most economists.

73 Guido, Robert, and Michael Monone, 'The Michelin Decision: A Possible New Direction for U.S. Countervailing Duty Law', *Law and Policy in International Business* (1974), 6, 237 at 255.

74 Mauer, Laurence, Jay, and A.J.W. van de Gevel, 'Non-tariff Distortions in International Trade: A Methodological Review', in Scaperlanda, Anthony, ed., *Prospects for Eliminating Non-tariff Distortions*, (Leiden: A.W. Sijthoff, 1973), at 40.

75 Ibid., at 48. See also Jackson, *World Trading System*, op. cit., at 263; Thomas, op. cit., at 5/76. Barceló argues that '. . .government intervention may be aimed at an objective which would not ordinarily be governed by the efficiency considerations of the marketplace. . .'. Barcelló, 'Analysis', op. cit., at 782. Rivers and Greenwald point out that when 'the Italian, Canadian or Israeli government decides to encourage business to locate in a depressed region, the effects of such regional development programmes on international trade are not likely to dictate government policy'; op. cit., at 1470. Lowenfeld suggests that 'so long as we are not willing to legislate world-wide uniformity in wage-scales, exchange rates, environmental controls, . . . interest rates, and accounting techniques, and indeed comparable relations between government and industry, what is fair and what is unfair is in large part coincidence'. Lowenfeld, Andreas, 'Fair or Unfair Trade: Does it Matter?', *Cornell International Law Journal* (1980), 13, 205 at 219.

76 Barceló, 'Tokyo Round', op. cit., at 264. Diamond argues that government action may be necessary for the 'efficient attainment of public goals'. Diamond, Richard, 'A Search for Economic and Financial Principles in the Administration of United States Countervailing Duty Law', *Law and Policy in International Business* (1990), 21, 507 at 524. Barceló suggests that 'in practice we can never know clearly which foreign subsidies are efficient and which are not. Indeed, the very concept of efficiency is fraught with difficulty when applied to the many subsidy programs designed to achieve a goal . . . desired collectively by a society . . . but which a free market would not provide'. Barceló, John J., 'An 'Injury-Only' Regime For Imports and Actionable Subsidies', in *Interface Three*, op. cit., at 21.

77 There is, clearly, a moral difference between different causes – dying of

natural causes is morally distinguishable from being murdered. The argument is, however, that in matters of national trade policy the morality of the cause is of less importance than the consequence. The question is what are we trying to do: protect domestic interests or police international trade morality? If the objective is to protect the injured domestic industry, then it matters not whence the injury came. If, on the other hand, there are moral choices to be made – fair versus unfair trade practices, level playing fields, and the like – then we are back to the problem that plagues the entire issue: the lack of international consensus as to the precise nature and detriments of 'subsidies'.

78 See, for example, Hindley, op. cit., at 33. Also see *infra* the section on the political economy of subsidisation. This observation is axiomatic with respect to domestic subsidies.

79 For a comprehensive analysis of the ethical considerations of subsidisation see Trebilcock, M.J., R. Howse, and M. Chandler, *Trade and Transition*, (London: Routledge, 1990).

80 Hindley, op. cit., at 33–4.

81 Steenbergen, Jacques, Guido De Clerq, and René Fogué, *Change and Adjustment*, (Deventer: Kluwer Law and Taxation Publishers, 1983), at 148–9.

82 Pelkmans, Jacques, 'Government Aid to Industry in the Benelux Countries', in Scaperlanda, op. cit., at 107.

83 Ibid.

84 Trebilcock, Howse, and Chandler, op. cit., at 110.

85 For the latest arguments in favour of strategic subsidisation, see Kuttner, Robert, 'Clinton Is Wrong to Launch His Missiles at Airbus', the *International Herald Tribune*, (26 February 1993), at 4.

86 Hufbauer and Erb, op. cit., at 119. As Canada's experiments with the aerospace industry demonstrated, attempted strategic subsidisation can also entangle governments in costly and futile enterprises.

87 Ibid.

88 Porter, op. cit., at 78.

89 Katz, Lawrence, and Lawrence Summers, 'Can Interindustry Wage Differentials Justify Strategic Trade Policy?' in Feenstra, Robert, ed., *Trade Policies for International Competitiveness*, (Chicago: The University of Chicago Press, 1989), at 86.

90 Ibid., at 105.

91 Ibid., at 101.

92 Porter, op. cit., at 6.

93 Earl, Victor, 'Who Needs It?' in *Eurobusiness* (September 1990), at 31–3.

94 In fact, Walther argues that strategic subsidies can have serious adverse effects. He observes that 'subsidies as a means of strategic trade policy provoke a general change in industrial management which has severe performance and welfare reducing consequences'. See Walther, R., 'Comment', in Bourgeois, op. cit., at 18. Whether, in fact, 'strategic subsidies' are truly aimed at improving the country's strategic trade performance is also open to question. See the section on the political economy of subsidisation, *infra*.

95 Baldwin, Robert, and Paul Krugman, 'Industrial Policy and Inter-

national Competition in Wide-bodied Jet Aircraft', in Baldwin, op. cit., at 45–6. See also International Trade Administration, US Department of Commerce, *A Competitive Assessment of the US General Aviation Aircraft Industry*, (June 1986).

96 Ibid., at 50.

97 Harris, Richard, 'Comment', on Baldwin and Krugman, ibid., at 74.

98 United States International Trade Commission, *Global Competitiveness of US Advanced-Technology Manufacturing Industries: Large Civil Aircraft*, Publication 2667, (Washington, DC: USITC, 1993) at 7–1. This is not to say that support has been restricted to 'indirect and incidental' programmes. In late 1960s and in early 1970s, both Lockheed and McDonnell Douglas averted bankruptcy only following generous loan guaranties by the US government, at 2–2, 3. According to an OECD study, in 1989 the US Government funded nearly three-quarters of the $24 billion spent on aerospace R&D, at 5–2; see also OECD, *Internationalisation of Industrial Activities: Case Study of the Aerospace Industry*, (Paris: 10 January 1990), at 17. As well, 'cutbacks in military spending' in the USA was among the reasons cited by the ITC for the lack of future prospects for a new American wide-bodied aircraft manufacturer, at 2–3.

99 Ibid., at 7–1, 2.

100 Baldwin and Krugman, op. cit., at 53.

101 For further discussion see Barnes, Christopher, 'New and Improved Awards without Discussions or Foreign Competition', *Public Contract Law Journal* (1991), 20, 532.

102 Morgens Carl, an official at the Commission of the European Communities remarked that 'the level of indirect aid [to the aircraft industry] that has been identified is greater, in the United States, than any other industrial sector in the world (with the exception of the East European Countries). . . . [at a qualitative level] this is *de facto* a true industrial policy'. Agence Europe, (7 December 1991) no. 5625. See also Kuttner, op. cit.

103 USITC, op. cit., at 2–1.

104 Commission of the European Communities, 'European Community 1989 Report on US Trade Barriers', in Simmonds, Kenneth, and Brian Hill, *Law and Practice under the GATT*, (New York: Oceana Publications, 1991), at III.B.9(23). See also Mann, Catherine, 'Comment' on Baldwin and Krugman, op. cit., at 77.

105 USITC, op. cit., at 5–3; see also Eberstadt, George, 'Government Support of the Large Commercial Aircraft Industries of Japan, Europe, and the United States', prepared for the Office of Technology Assessment, *Competing Economies; America, Europe, and the Pacific Rim* (Washington, DC: Congress of the United States, 1991).

106 Harris, op. cit., at 74. The US and the EU have reached an agreement on the level of aid to their aircraft manufacturing industry. The agreement limits direct subsidies to 33 per cent of the development costs, and indirect subsidies to 4 per cent of company sales, and 3 per cent of annual aircraft industry sales in the US or the EU. Both US competitors of Airbus support the deal. The US had initially wanted a higher cap on

indirect subsidisation – 5 per cent of company revenue, and 4 per cent of industry income – because of 'its high military spending'. This seems to counter the argument advanced by Baldwin and Krugman that the US aircraft industry is not being subsidised. See 'US, EC Finalize Controversial Accord limiting Aircraft Subsidies, Official Says', *International Trade Reporter* 9, 826. In a speech to Boeing workers, President Clinton argued that he will 'try to change the rules of the game'. This was interpreted by some observers to mean that the US intended to renegotiate its agreement with the EC. The Administration softened Clinton's remarks a day later. In his speech and later in the week, Clinton promised billions of dollars in additional R&D expenditure in high-tech industries. See Malkin, Lawrence, 'Airbus Flap: Washington Says What It Wants', the *International Herald Tribune* (24 February 1993), at 1; see also Kuttner, op. cit.

In most cases, the American proselytising on the question of subsidies must be taken with a grain of salt. A letter written by US legislators to President Clinton just before the deadline for the GATT negotiations termed the limits on research and development subsidies in the subsidies code 'extremely detrimental to US interests'. It argued that the transfer of technology from federal laboratories to US industry represented a legitimate effort to capture the economic benefits of federal research for US companies over the past few years. See 'Lawmakers call for shift in US position on research subsidies in GATT trade talks' International Trade Reporter (1993), 10, 1957. The US and the EU did not, in the end, agree on a civil aricraft subsidies code in the Uruguay Round.

107 *European Economy*, op. cit., at 25.

108 Anthony Downs, quoted in Reynolds, op. cit., at 8.

109 As defined by Macey, 'The theory of the firm and the theory of market exchange', *Cornell Law Review* (1988), 74, 43, rent-seeking is an 'attempt to obtain economic rents (i.e., payments for the use of an economic asset in excess of the market price) through government intervention in the market'. Quoted in Farber, Daniel, and Philip Frickey, *Law and Public Choice: A Critical Introduction*, (Chicago: The University of Chicago Press, 1991), at 15n10.

110 Which costs may even exceed the expected benefits of the sought-after rent. See Reynolds, op. cit.

111 *European Economy*, op. cit., at 26.

112 Thomas, op. cit., at 2/3. See also Farber and Frickey, op. cit., at 22.

113 Becker, quoted in Farber and Frickey, ibid., at 14–15.

114 Quoted in Reynolds, op. cit., at 3.

115 Mueller, Dennis, *Public Choice II*, (Cambridge: Cambridge University Press, 1989), at 243.

116 *European Economy*, op. cit., at 26.

117 Farber and Frickey, op. cit., at 15; also at 23, quoting Mancur Olson's seminal work, *The Logic of Collective Action: Public Goods and the Theory of Groups* (1965).

118 Krueger, Anne O., 'The Political Economy of the Rent-Seeking Society', *The American Economic Review* (1974), 64, 291 at 292.

119 For the impact of labour unions in the shaping of the Labour Party Manifesto of 1983 see McLean, Iain, *Public Choice: An Introduction* (Oxford: Basil Blackwell Ltd, 1987), at 77–8.

120 Krueger, op. cit., at 293. This type of behaviour can, depending on the circumstance, be quite pronounced. See, for example, Krueger's own examples: India and Turkey. See also Mueller, op. cit., at 230, for a more detailed discussion of wasteful behaviour by potential recipients of rents, in whichever form.

121 Mueller, ibid., at 231.

122 Farber and Frickey, op. cit., at 22.

123 Trebilcock, Chandler and Howse, op. cit. While this may appear cynical, it may be closer to the truth than one would expect. In *The March of Folly*, Tuchman defines 'folly' as pursuit of policies detrimental to national interest in total disregard of all evidence and argument to the contrary. Her chronicle of one of the most disturbing episodes in recent history, the US involvement in Vietnam, illustrates how electoral politics were partly to blame for the disastrous widening of the war (New York: Ballantine Books, 1984), at 234 *et seq*. Recent speculation on the assassination of President Kennedy blames the 'military-industrial' complex for the deed (the movie *JFK* was only the most publicised version of the various conspiracy theories on Kennedy's death); if true, this would be the ultimate form of rent-seeking behaviour. If a policy so clearly detrimental to the national interest can be pursued by 'the best and the brightest' in several administrations and in the course of two decades, why not subsidies? See also Halberstam, David, *The Best and the Brightest*, (New York: Penguin, 1969).

124 The high cost of informing him/herself substantially exceeds the returns, as each voter knows that his/her vote is only marginal to elections and therefore of no influence in their outcome.

125 Posner and Landes argue that 'legislation is supplied to groups or coalitions that outbid rival seekers of favourable legislation. The price that the winning group bids is determined both by the value of legislative protection to the group's members and the group's ability to overcome the free-rider problems that plague coalitions. . . . In short, legislation is "sold" by the legislature and "bought" by the beneficiaries of the legislation'. See Posner, R., and William Landes, 'The Independent Judiciary in an Interest-Group Perspective', *Journal of Law and Economics* (1975), 18, 371 at 371.

126 Otherwise it will be worthwhile for the consumers to organise and outbid the interested pressure group. The ability of an interest group to advance its claims and obtain its rent is directly proportional to the inability of the group on which the costs of the rent falls to overcome free-riderism and rational apathy.

127 McLean, op. cit., at 70.

128 For greater elaboration see Trebilcock, Michael J., Douglas Hartle, Robert Prichard, and Donald Dewees, *The Choice of Governing Instrument*, (Ottawa: Economic Council of Canada, 1982).

129 The striking imbalance between rural and urban representation in many Commonwealth jurisdictions could explain the panoply of protective

measures (marketing boards, import and production quotas, subsidies and other relief programmes, and tariffs, to name a few) devised for the enjoyment of farmers to the detriment of consumers. In one of the most extreme cases, until recent reforms to its electoral laws, 35 per cent of the population of the state of Queensland in Australia (mostly rural) controlled over 65 per cent of the seats in the Queensland legislature. See for example Patience, Allan, *The Bjelke–Petersen Premiership* (Malaysia: Longman Cheshire, 1985).

130 Schlozman, K.L., and John T. Tierney, *Organized Interests and American Democracy* (1986), quoted in Farber and Frickey, op. cit., at 19.

131 Ibid.

132 A view that more sophisticated economists would reject as well. A government that can put its legislation for a bid is hardly in the 'control' of interest groups.

133 Reynolds, op. cit., at 14.

134 Ibid., at 24.

135 Trebilcock, Chandler and Howse, op. cit., at 173.

136 Reynolds, in fact, makes an interesting but ultimately, in my view, implausible argument about possible reasons for the conclusion of free trade agreements. Noting the ruinously expensive costs of competitive lobbying and rent-seeking behaviour, Reynolds believes that 'such broad, multi-industry treaties can provide a "truce" in the rent-seeking battles, together with the prospect of effective enforcement. Once such an agreement is enacted, specific industries cannot effectively lobby for special treatment, because such treatment becomes impossible without violating the whole treaty. Indeed, . . . free trade agreements may be thought of as a device for allowing rent-seeking interests to collude in order to avoid the prisoner's dilemma'. While ingenious, this proposition suffers from over-analysis. The history of every free trade agreement shows that what they do not do is to dampen the zeal of trade lawyers and special interests for finding ways of circumventing such treaties, not to mention the push for special protection at the negotiation stages. Both the Canada–US Free Trade Agreement and NAFTA are riddled with so many loopholes and protective clauses as to make suspect the notion that the parties intended to open up their borders at all, except in certain select sectors. In fact, as will be argued in later chapters and as the evidence suggests, neither agreement is likely to reduce administered protection; thus, even if a truce has been declared, it is just that, and not an everlasting peace.

137 Perhaps one of the more striking problems with these lines of argument can be found in Reynolds' analysis of administered protection. He suggests that the confluence of interest between Congress and the bureaucracy could explain 'why legislators prefer methods of protection that allow for administrative discretion, rather than specific, legislated tariffs, since that allows politicians to provide special favors to constituents'. However, at least in the trade area, this is patently inaccurate. The history of US legislation shows an increasing tendency by Congress to *reduce* administrative discretion, and to have legislated rules for the imposition of trade remedy tariffs. While the outcome is still the

extraction of rents by protected (complaining/injured) industries, the methodology of protection is not in line with Reynolds' analysis.

138 Farber and Frickey, op. cit., at 26.

139 McLean, op. cit., at 70.

140 Reynolds, op. cit., at 21.

141 Ibid.

142 McLean, op. cit., at 70.

143 Farber and Frickey, op. cit., at 27.

144 Ibid., at 28.

145 Ibid., at 29 *et seq*. The social and political attitudes of two California counties pose an interesting contrast. Orange County near Los Angeles and Marin County near San Francisco have a similar economic (and significantly, racial) make-up, nevertheless, in the past thirty years they have consistently voted differently in US Congressional and Presidential elections. The states of New Hampshire and Vermont share the same geography and economic basis, but they, too , have consistently voted along different ideological lines in Congressional elections; see Wilson, James Q., *American Government*, (Lexington: D.C. Heath and Company, 1983), at 111. For the influence of ideology on policy-making, see also Trebilcock, Chandler and Howse, op. cit., at 111.

146 Or, as McLean puts it, at least have the intention of advancing the public interest. He cites the *Sherman Anti-Trust Act* and the *Clean Air Act* of 1970 in the US; op. cit., at 70. We may also cite the Canada–US FTA, and perhaps even the Treaty of Rome.

147 Ibid., at 32. McLean is sceptical on this point; ibid. An example best illustrates the difficulty of viewing the influence of interest groups on public issues in strictly economic terms. In the 1992 Referendum on amendments to the Canadian constitution, financial contributions to the 'Yes' side outstripped contributions to the 'No' side by a margin of ten to one. Contributions by *business* groups to the 'Yes' side were almost 800 times the contributions made by companies to the 'No' side. The 'Yes' forces purchased eleven times more advertising than the 'No' side. Nevertheless, the 'Yes' side lost in most provinces and also nationally. (*The Globe and Mail*, 23 July 1993, at 1).

148 *Supra* note 32 and accompanying text.

149 Farber and Frickey, op. cit., at 34.

150 Ibid. It is suggested by some economists that the regulation of logging is inefficient: whoever wants to stop the logging can attempt to pay for it. If no one does, it is because company profits are higher than harm to the environmentalists. What if, Farber and Frickey argue, *environmentalists* had an *ex ante* right to prevent logging? They may demand a much higher price to sell that right to lumber companies than they were willing to pay themselves. The new cost-benefit analysis may now show that logging is inefficient. It can be observed that this type of analysis is highly indeterminate. Other factors must be weighed to determine whether and to what extent trees may be permitted to be cut.

151 Carroll, Lewis, *The Complete Works of Lewis Carroll*, (London: Penguin Books, 1986), at 61.

152 Trebilcock, Chandler and Howse, op. cit., at 174.

153 Lewis, op. cit., at 196.

154 See Barceló, 'Analysis', op. cit., at 807.

155 Ibid., at 809; Barceló says they are acceptable.

156 These tax adjustments are the only domestic subsidies countervailed by the EC and one of the few non-agricultural domestic subsidies countervailed by Canada.

157 See Barceló, 'Analysis', op. cit., especially at 822–3. Mundheim and Ehrenraft do not agree, see Mundheim and Ehrenraft, op. cit. Komoroski believes that there is a minimum acceptable level of international environmental controls. Lack of adherence by a country to these standards could constitute, he argues, assistance to industry. For further elaboration see Komoroski, Kenneth, 'The Failure of Governments to Regulate Industry: A Subsidy under the GATT?', *Houston Journal of International Law* (1988), 10, 189. Steve Schrybman, Counsel to Greenpeace, argues that low environmental regulation should be considered as subsidies. However, this is driven by environmental concerns and is not supported by a cogent economic rationale. Conference on NAFTA, Toronto, (23–25 June 1993).

158 Mundheim and Ehrenraft, op. cit., at 95.

159 Malmgren, Harald, *International Order for Public Subsidies*, (London: Trade Policy Research Centre, 1977), at 25.

160 Especially when the industry is of regional, social or strategic importance and is not run with profit as the main objective. Passenger transport, oil and gas, and the aircraft industry are good examples of industries where profit may not be the only reason for government ownership or management.

161 *Certain Softwood Lumber Products from Canada*, Fed Reg 57, 22570, (28 May 1992), reaffirmed by the United States International Trade Administration after remand by the Chapter 19 binational panel on 18 October 1993, but remanded once again by the Chapter 19 binational panel (17 December 1993).

162 Malmgren, op. cit., at 24.

3 MULTILATERAL REGULATION OF SUBSIDIES

1 For further elaboration see Thomas, Jeffrey, *Subsidies and Countervailing Duties in the Canada–US Free Trade Agreement: Trends, Critiques and Proposals for Rational Reform*, (Toronto: Faculty of Law, University of Toronto, 1989).

2 *Agreement on the Interpretation and Application of Articles VI, XVI and XXIII of the General Agreement on Tariffs and Trade*, 1189 United Nations Treaty Series 204, GATT BISD 26th Supp. 56 (1978–9) ('Subsidies Code').

3 Although reference is made throughout to the European Union, the FTAs were concluded before the EU came into existence, hence the continued use of EC.

4 As among three countries of A, B and C, if both A and B export to C, and A starts a subsidies programme, exports of B to C will drop. B is

harmed absolutely, because the consumers of C will reap the benefits of subsidisation by A and the workers of A will benefit from the growth in exports. B's only recourse will be to the GATT Track II process, since it cannot impose any trade remedy measures to counteract A's subsidies.

5 This is valid at least until the Uruguay Round Subsidies Code comes into effect, expected by the middle of 1994.

6 Simmonds, Kenneth, and Brian Hill, *Law and Practice under the GATT*, (New York: Oceana Publications, 1991), at II.c.1.

7 Ibid.

8 Ibid.

9 Subsidies Code, op. cit.,, Article 8.3.

10 Simmonds, op. cit., at 16.

11 Ibid., at 17.

12 Thomas, op. cit., at 2/50.

13 Pescatore, Pierre, William Davey, and Andreas Lowenfeld, *Handbook of GATT Dispute Settlement*, (Ardsley-on-Hudson: Transnational Juris Publications, Inc., 1991), at 57.

14 Emphasis added. Völker, E.M., *Protectionism and the European Community*, (Deventer: Kluwer Law and Taxation Publishers, 1987), at 196.

15 GATT, Article XVI.A.1.

16 Subsidies Code, op. cit., Article 7.1.

17 The Article uses the imperative 'shall'. In practice, given the nature of the GATT and the unenforceability of its sanctions, this cannot be anything other than an exhortation.

18 Subsidies Code, op. cit., Article 18.5.

19 Ibid. Articles 18.9, 13.4.

20 Pescatore, op. cit., at 68.

21 Koteen, Lisa, 'GATT Dispute Settlement of Antidumping and Countervailing Duty Cases: A Primer', in Willkie, Wendell II, *The Commerce Department Speaks 1990: The Legal Aspects of International Trade*, (Washington, DC: Practising Law Institute, 1990), at 412.

22 Hudec, Robert, 'Legal Issues in US–EC Trade Policy: GATT Litigation 1960–1985', in Baldwin, Robert, Carl B. Hamilton, and André Sapir, eds, *Issues in US–EC Trade Relations*, (Chicago: The University of Chicago Press, 1988), at 24–5.

23 Ibid., at 39.

24 Ibid., at 44. Whether the US will actually follow a 'judicial' decision with which it disagrees is another question altogether.

25 Koteen, op. cit., at 412.

26 Hudec, 'Legal Issues', op. cit., at 42.

27 Hayes, J.P., 'Comment' on Hudec, 'Legal Issues', op. cit., at 63.

28 Hudec, 'Regulation. . .', op. cit., at 2.

29 Trebilcock, M.J., 'Is the Game Worth the Candle?', *Law and Policy in International Business* (1990), 21, 723 at 730.

30 Hudec, 'Legal Issues', op. cit., at 29. He argues that the timing of US actions coincides with events in Congress, either just before a major vote on a trade law, or seemingly in response to Congressional demands. The EC, on the other hand, launched its first major GATT action against the US DISCs and only after a whole series of US actions against its own

domestic practices. See also Hudec, Robert, 'GATT Dispute Settlement After the Tokyo Round: An Unfinished Business', *Cornell International Law Journal* (1980), 13, 145.

31 Völker, op. cit., note at 196.

32 Middleton, Robert, *Negotiating on Non-tariff Distortions of Trade: The EFTA Precedent*, (London: The Macmillan Press Ltd., 1975), at 9.

33 Curzon Price, Victoria, *Free Trade Areas: The European Experience*, (Toronto: C.D. Howe Institute, 1987), at 6.

34 Middleton, op. cit., at 10. EFTA was originally composed of Britain, Switzerland, Iceland, Norway, Sweden, Denmark, and Portugal. Britain, Denmark and Portugal later joined the EC, while Finland and Liechtenstein joined EFTA in the 1980s.

35 Middleton, op. cit., at 45. See also European Free Trade Association, 'EFTA Agreement on Government Aid', *EFTA Bulletin* (October 1968), 9 (7), 17; European Free Trade Association, Economic Committee, Working Party on Government Aids, *Final Report*, (Geneva: EFTA, 1986), at 7.

36 EFTA, 'EFTA Agreement', ibid., at 17.

37 Paragraph iii of the Agreement, ibid.

38 *Treaty Establishing the European Free Trade Association* ('The Stockholm Convention'), (1960), *United Nations Treaty Series* 1 at 22.

39 Rekola, Esko, 'Subsidies as a Barrier to Foreign Trade', *EFTA Bulletin* (December-March 1982), 23 (1), 17 at 17.

40 Ibid.

41 EFTA, *Final Report*, op. cit., at 7.

42 Ibid., at 13.

43 See Rekola, op. cit.

44 Pono, Giuseppe, 'Government Aids: The Rules in EFTA, the EC and GATT', *EFTA Bulletin* (October-December 1982), 23 (4), 13.

45 Lanner, James, 'Aspects of Regional Policy in EFTA', *EFTA Bulletin* (April-June 1984), 25 (2), 13.

46 Ibid., at 13.

47 See Trebilcock, Michael J., Robert Howse and Marsha Chandler, *Trade and Transition*, (London: Routledge, 1990).

48 Chapter 2, note 60 and accompanying text.

49 For further elaboration see EFTA, 'EFTA Agreement', op. cit.; *Annual EFTA Reports 1984–1989*; Rekola, op. cit.; Pono, op. cit.; Lanner, op. cit.; and Wieser, Thomas, 'Government Aids to Industry in EFTA' *EFTA Bulletin* (April-June 1987), 28 (2), 13.

50 The Stockholm Convention, op. cit., at 14.

51 And not, significantly, the benefit bestowed on the corporation.

52 EFTA, *Final Report*, op. cit., at 3.

53 EFTA, 'EFTA Agreement', op. cit., at 17; see also Curzon Price, op. cit., at 28.

54 Weiss, Friedl, 'EC–EFTA Relations: Towards a Treaty Creating a European Economic Space', *Yearbook of European Law* (1989), 9, 329 at 344.

55 Ibid.

56 Ibid. See also EFTA, *Final Report*, op. cit.; EFTA, *Government Aid in 1988: Annual Report by Secretariat*, (Geneva: EFTA, 1989); EFTA, *State Aid in EFTA in 1990: Fifth Annual Report by the Secretariat*, (Geneva: EFTA, 28 January 1992).
57 Curzon Price, op. cit., at 28.
58 Curzon, Victoria, *The Essentials of Economic Integration: Lessons of EFTA Experience*, (London: Macmillan, 1974), at 98.
59 Ibid., at 101.
60 Middleton, op. cit., at 53.
61 Ibid., at 91.
62 Curzon Price, op. cit., at 12.
63 Middleton, op. cit., at 4.
64 Hufbauer, Gary, 'Procedures for Monitoring and Disciplining Government Aids', EFTA Economic Affairs Dept. Occasional Paper no. 30 (Geneva: EFTA, 1990), at 13.
65 EFTA, *Final Report*, op. cit., at 9–13.
66 Hufbauer, op. cit., at 13–4.
67 *The Stockholm Convention*, op. cit., at 22.
68 Ibid., at Article 32.1.
69 Ibid., at Article 32.5.
70 Ibid., at 22.
71 Ibid., Article 31.
72 Ibid.
73 Hufbauer, op. cit.
74 Curzon Price, op. cit., at 6.
75 Ibid., at 12.
76 Hufbauer, op. cit., at 14.
77 See Middleton, op. cit., at 49.
78 Ibid.
79 The success of the free trade arrangement has been so great, in fact, that most EFTA countries are now expanding the scope of their arrangement with the EC. See the discussion on the EEA, *infra*.
80 Weiss, 'EC–EFTA Relations', op. cit., at 344.
81 Curzon Price, op. cit., at 30.
82 European Free Trade Association, *Regional Development Policies in EFTA*, (Geneva: EFTA, 1968), at 5.
83 Norway applied for membership of the EC in December of 1992.
84 Formal negotiations for a treaty of accession between Austria, Sweden and Finland were successfully concluded on 2 March 1994, only two days behind schedule; the date of accession has been set for 1 January 1995. The terms of the Act of Accession are to be based on the comprehensive framework negotiated in the EEA Agreement. Norway also came to an agreement with the EU, but its accession seems increasingly doubtful. All countries accept the basic legal framework of the EU (*European Law Review* August 1993, 18, 269).
85 In its 6 December 1992 referendum Switzerland rejected, by just 24,000 votes, the EEA Treaty. A week later, Liechtenstein ratified the Treaty in its referendum (Note BIO(93) Aux Bureaux Nationaux, 21 January 1993, 10). As a result of the Swiss vote separate protocols were drafted

to remove the name of Switzerland from the text of the Treaty and also to re-examine EFTA's contribution to the EC's Cohesion Fund (Agence Internationale D'Information Pour La Presse – 'Europe' (new series, 'Agence Europe'), nos 5895, 5904, 5911, 5921, 5924, 5936). The Protocol on Enforcement of EEA without Switzerland was signed on 17 March 1993 (Agence Europe, no. 5938) Despite the negative vote, Switzerland allocated nearly SwF500 m to the Community's research and education programmes over four years (Press Release, Commission of the European Communities, 24 December 1993). As of the time of writing this book, the other EFTA countries have already ratified the EEA Treaty. Switzerland will continue to seek EC membership (Agence Europe, nos 5898, 5907, 5915).

86 As indeed will be the case for Switzerland.

87 The Members of the EC are France, Germany, Italy, Belgium, the Netherlands, Luxembourg, Portugal, Spain, Greece, Britain, Ireland and Denmark. The Members of EFTA are Sweden, Switzerland, Norway, Iceland, Austria, Finland and Liechtenstein. See the above note re Switzerland and Liechtenstein. For the purposes of analysing the EEA, any reference to EFTA should be read as referring to the six EFTA states that have ratified the EEA Treaty (the Norwegian Cabinet determined that the EEA Treaty need not be ratified by a referendum).

88 *Austria–EC Free Trade Agreement*, (1972), OJ L300; *Finland–EC Free Trade Agreement*, (1973), OJ L328; *Iceland–EC Free Trade Agreement*, (1972), OJ L301; *Norway–EC Free Trade Agreement*, (1972), OJ L171; *Sweden–EC Free Trade Agreement*, (1972), OJ L300; *Switzerland–EC Free Trade Agreement*, (1972), OJ L300.

89 Curzon Price, op. cit., at 1.

90 Ibid., at 3.

91 Weiss, Friedl, 'The Legal Issues', in Wallace, Helen, ed., *The Wider Western Europe: Reshaping the EC/EFTA Relationship*, (London: Frances Pinter Publishers, 1991), at 249.

92 Although the FTAs were concluded individually between each EFTA country and the EC, they are substantially similar in content. The competition section is the same in all FTAs.

93 Wahl, Nils, *The Free Trade Agreements between the EC and EFTA Countries*, (Stockholm: Institute for Intellectual Property and Market Law, 1988) at 101. The case involved subclause 23(1)(i), which involves undertakings. But the analysis deals with the wording of the opening part of the section itself, and is, therefore, applicable to 23(1)(iii), the state aid provision.

94 This is significant, especially in light of the Decision of the Court of Justice of the European Communities (ECJ) in *Kupferberg*. In this 1982 decision, the ECJ argued that those provisions of the FTAs that have the character of being directly applicable are part of the Community's legal order. Based on the arguments advanced in the *Adams* case, it may be argued that the State Aid provisions of the FTAs do not have such a character; thus, EFTA countries do not have standing to challenge

Community Member State aids directly before the ECJ. See *Kupferberg* (Case 104/81) *European Community Reports* (1982), 3641.

95 Emphasis added. Weiss, 'EC–EFTA Relations', op. cit., at 342–3. See also Wahl, op. cit., at 97.

96 EC–EFTA FTAs, op. cit., Clauses 29(1) and (2), and 30(1) and (2).

97 Ibid., Subclause 23(3)(a).

98 Ibid. See also Bernitz, Ulf, 'The EEC–EFTA Free Trade Agreements with Special Reference to the Position of Sweden and the other Scandinavian EFTA Countries', *Common Market Law Reports* (1986), 23, 567 at 570.

99 EFTA, *Final Report*, op. cit.

100 Curzon Price, op. cit., at 20.

101 Ibid., at 43.

102 Ibid.

103 Bernitz, op. cit., at 570–1.

104 EFTA, 'The EEA Agreement', Pamphlet, (Geneva: EFTA Secretariat, January 1992), at 1.

105 Ibid., at 3.

106 Agence Europe, (3 February 1992), no. 5660, at 7.

107 Agence Europe, (24, 27/8 January 1992), nos. 5653–55, at 5.

108 EFTA, 'EEA', op. cit., at 10.

109 Commission of the European Community (CEC), *Proposal for a Council Decision on the Conclusion of the Agreement on the European Economic Area between the European Communities, their Member States, and [Member States of the EFTA]*, SEC (92) 814 Final, (Luxembourg: Office of the Official Publications of the European Communities, 28 April 1992).

110 EFTA, 'EEA', op. cit., at 10.

111 CEC, *Proposal. . .*, op. cit., Clause 27(a).

112 Ibid., Clause 27(f).

113 Agence Europe, (6 February 1992), no. 5662, at 7.

114 Agence Europe, (13/14 April 1992), no. 5710, at 8.

115 Burrows, Noreen, 'The second EEA Opinion', *European Law Review* (1993), 18, 63 at 65.

116 *The Economist*, 'Lest a fortress arise', (26 October 1991), v.321, no. 7730.

117 Most recently, the EU forced a 60 per cent reduction in investment grants by the government of Austria to an automobile plant in Graz. See CEC, *XXIInd Report on Competition Policy*, (Luxembourg: Office of Offical Publications of the European Communities, 1993), at 210.

118 Agence Europe, (6 February 1992), no. 5662, at 7.

119 Ibid.

4 SUPRANATIONAL REGULATION OF SUBSIDIES

1 *International Legal Materials* (1992), 31, 442.

2 References to Article numbers are to the first Agreement, which has

been significantly revamped. These provisions can be found in the EEA Decision, ibid.

3 Ibid., Article 105.

4 The EEA Decision, op. cit., at 459.

5 See generally *Reports on Competition Policy* published each year by the Commission of the European Communities.

6 Kravis, Irving B., *Domestic Interests and International Obligations*, (Philadelphia: University of Pennsylvania Press, 1963), at 277.

7 Ibid., at 296. See also Article 92 of the Treaty of Rome, in Belford, J., ed., *The European Community: the Single Market*, (loose-leaf service; New York: Oceana Publications, 1988) [Treaty of Rome].

8 Commission of the European Communities, Directorate General for Economic and Financial Affairs, *European Economy no. 48: Fair Competition in the Internal Market: State Aid Policy*, (Luxembourg: Office of the Official Publications of the European Communities, 1989), at 13.

9 Ibid., at 14.

10 Quoted in Evans, Andrew, and Stephen Martin, 'Socially Acceptable Distortion of Competition: Community Policy on State Aid', *European Law Review* (1991), 16(2), 79 at 85–6.

11 Commission of the European Communities, *Eighteenth Report on Competition Policy*, (Luxembourg: Office of Official Publications of the European Communities, 1989), at 150.

12 Commission of the European Communities, *XXth Report on Competition Policy*, (Luxembourg: Office of Official Publications of the European Communities, 1991), at 125.

13 The aversion is, of course, to the involvement of other governments in their own economies. The US government is actively involved in its own economy, principally in the areas of defence spending and bailing out failed financial institutions.

14 Barceló, John J., III, 'Subsidies, Countervailing Duties and Antidumping after the Tokyo Round', *Cornell International Law Journal* (1980), 13, 257 at 278–9.

15 Evans and Martin, op. cit., at 80.

16 Ibid.

17 Commission of the European Communities (CEC), *European Economy*, op. cit., at 15.

18 See Commission of the European Communities, *First Survey on State Aids in the European Community*, (Luxembourg: Office of Official Publications of the European Communities, 1989); *Second Survey on State Aids in the European Community in the Manufacturing and Certain Other Sectors*, (Luxembourg: Office of Official Publications of the European Communities, 1990); *Third Survey on State Aids in the European Community Manufacturing and Certain Other Sectors*, (Luxembourg: Office of Official Publications of the European Communities, 1992). The surveys identified average annual state aids of ECU92 b. in 1986–88, but ECU89 b. in 1988–90, for the Community as a whole. Roughly 40 per cent of this figure, or nearly ECU35 b., goes to the manufacturing sector, 18 per cent is earmarked for the coal mining

industry, and nearly 30 per cent for the transport industry. State aids constitute about 2.2 per cent of the Community GDP, 17.8 per cent of intra-Community export, and 3.3 per cent of value added in the manufacturing sector. This does not include defence expenditure. See also CEC, *European Economy*, op. cit., at 1.

19 See Commission of European Communities, *The Measurement of the Aid Element of State Acquisitions of Company Capital*, (Luxembourg: Office of Official Publications of the European Communities, 1987); Segal Quince Wicksteed Ltd., *Aid Element of Government R & D Contracts*, (Luxembourg: Office of Official Publications of the European Communities, 1990); Belcredi, Massimo, Lounzo Caprio, and Pippo Ronci, *The Aid Element in State Participation to Company Capital*, (Luxembourg: Office of Official Publications of the European Communities, 1988).

20 Evans and Martin, op. cit., at 82. The *Eighteenth Report* stated that criteria are being developed to distinguish the effects of specific programmes coming under Article 92 from general programmes which may distort trade among nations, which come under Articles 101–2; op. cit., at 144.

21 CEC, *European Economy*, op. cit., at 17.

22 Evans and Martin, op. cit., at 82.

23 Ibid., at 85–6.

24 CEC, *European Economy*, op. cit., at 85; Article 92 of the Treaty of Rome, op. cit.

25 Treaty of Rome, ibid., Article 92.2(a).

26 Ibid., Article 92.2(b).

27 Ibid., Article 92.3(a).

28 Ibid., Article 92.3(b).

29 Ibid., Article 92.3(c). Shipbuilding is covered by the Seventh Council Directive, No 90/684. There is a 13 per cent ceiling on operating aid granted to shipyards. There is also a qualified ban on investment aid that may increase a Member State's shipbuilding capacity. Aid for closures, reductions in capacity, or conversion to other activities may be allowed.

30 Treaty on European Union, Title V, amending Article 92.3(d) of the Treaty of Rome.

31 Treaty of Rome, op. cit., Article 92.3(e).

32 The commission's attempt to 'reissue' a Decision following non-compliance by a Member State failed in the ECJ. In *British Aerospace v. Commission*, unreported, the ECJ held that where a Decision of the Commission under Article 93 is not heeded, the Commission may either open a new investigation, or challenge the entity or the State before the Court, but has no other options to enforce its Decision. See CEC, *XXIInd Report of the Commission of the European Community on Competition Policy*, (Luxembourg: Office of Official Publications of the European Community, 1993), at 292.

33 Recent case law has strengthened the investigatory powers of the Commission. See ibid., at 25.

34 Commission of the European Communities, *Competition Rules in the*

EEC and ECSC Applicable into State Aids, (Luxembourg: Office of Official Publications of the European Communities, 1987), at 36.

35 CEC, *XXth Report*, op. cit., at 129.

36 CEC, *XXIst Report of the Commission of the European Community on Competition Policy*, (Luxembourg: Office of the Official Publications of the European Community, 1992), at 122.

37 CEC, *Competition Rules*, op. cit., at 36.

38 CEC, *Second Survey*, op. cit., at 6.

39 Treaty of Rome, op. cit., Articles 101–2; see CEC, *European Economy*, op. cit., at 86.

40 CEC, *XXth Report*, op. cit., at 128.

41 Commission of the European Communities, *Nineteenth Report on Competition Policy*, (Luxembourg: Office of Official Publications of the European Communities, 1990), at 128.

42 Evans and Martin, op. cit., at 102.

43 Ibid., at 14.

44 Cohesion is short form for the policies aimed at bringing the development and living standards of the poorer regions of the Community up to the level of the richer ones. This is similar in principle to the equalisation policies of the Canadian federation.

45 CEC, *Second Survey*, op. cit., at 50.

46 Evans and Martin, op. cit., at 110.

47 CEC, *Competition Rules*, op. cit., at 40.

48 CEC, *Nineteenth Report*, op. cit., at 158.

49 CEC, *XXth Report*, op. cit., at 126. Even EFTA was sensitive to the problems of regional development. A special fund was set up by EFTA countries (principally Sweden and Switzerland) for Portugal after the April 1974 Revolution to help the fledgling democracy. The fund still operated 6 years after Portugal joined the EC. The key conceptual shift was from a beggar-thy-neighbour mentality to one of economic interdependence and co-operation.

50 CEC, *Competition Rules*, op. cit., at 67; Malmgren, Harald, *International Order for Public Subsidies*, (London: Trade Policy Research Centre, 1977), at 14.

51 Evans and Martin, op. cit., at 92–4 and 102.

52 CEC, *Competition Rules*, op. cit., at 41.

53 CEC, *Eighteenth Report*, op. cit., at 146–7; *Nineteenth Report*, op. cit., at 170–1; Evans and Martin, op. cit., at 93–4, 102, 107.

54 Romoli, Aldo, 'Session Two', in Wallace, Don, George C. Spina, Richard M. Rawson, and Brian McGill, eds, *Interface One*, (Washington, DC: The Institute for International and Foreign Trade Law, 1980), at 115.

55 Ibid., at 114.

56 Evans and Martin, op. cit., at 105.

57 CEC, *Aid Element*, op. cit., at 2.

58 Ibid., at 55.

59 CEC, *Second Survey*, *supra* note 282 at 32.

60 Ibid., at 28.

61 CEC, *Nineteenth Report*, op. cit., at 157.

62 CEC, *Third Survey*, op. cit., at 16.

63 CEC, *European Economy*, op. cit., at 13–4.
64 Carson, Ian, 'Who's Subsidising Watt?', *Eurobusiness* (April 1991), 22.
65 Eales, Roy, 'The Hidden Billions', *Eurobusiness* (April 1989), 38.
66 Ibid., at 13.
67 Reports in the EC Bulletin indicate that the Community initiates between 5 to 8 investigations every month. About half are terminated; about a third find unacceptable state aids.
68 Evans and Martin, op. cit., at 110.
69 Kravis, op. cit., at 345.
70 Sir Leon Brittan, 'Industry Council – two items on Competition Policy', Note BIO (91), 371, Aux Bureaux Nationaux (Brussels: 1991).
71 Ibid.
72 CEC, *European Economy*, op. cit., at 66. There are a number of grants and loans for the coal and steel industry. The structural funds include the European Regional Development Fund, the European Social Fund, and various structural measures for fisheries. There also are a number of European-based R & D funds. See generally ibid.
73 Ibid., at 67.
74 Emphasis added; CEC, *XXIst Report*, op. cit., at 22.
75 CEC, *Third Survey*, op. cit., at 1.
76 CEC, *XXIst Report*, op. cit., at 121.

5 UNILATERAL REGULATION OF SUBSIDIES

1 Carroll, Lewis, *The Complete Works of Lewis Carroll*, (London: Penguin Books, 1986), at 35.
2 Romoli, A., 'Session Three', in Wallace, Don, George C. Spina, Richard M. Rawson, and Brian McGill, eds, *Interface One*, (Washington, DC: The Institute for International and Foreign Trade Law, 1980), at 249.
3 Ibid.
4 Malmgren, Harald, 'Session One', in *Interface One*, op. cit., at 27.
5 Thomas, Jeffrey, *Subsidies and Countervailing Duties in the Canada–US Free Trade Agreement: Trends, Critique and Proposals for Rational Reform*, (Toronto: Faculty of Law, University of Toronto, 1989), at 2/22.
6 Scaperlanda, Anthony, ed., *Prospects for Eliminating Non-tariff Distortions*, (Leiden: A.W. Sijthoff, 1973), at 30.
7 Beseler, H.-F., 'EEC Protection Against Dumping and Subsidies From Third Countries', (1968–9), *Common Market Law Reports* 6, 327 at 340.
8 That is, since the trade remedy law reforms of 1979, when the ITA was transferred from the Treasury Department to the Department of Commerce.
9 Since 1984. Before that, initiating a trade remedy investigation was up to the Cabinet.
10 Ibid., at 345. For further elaboration see Romoli, op. cit., at 249; Rivers, Richard and John Greenwald, 'The Negotiation of a Code on Subsidies and Countervailing Measures: Bridging Fundamental Policy Differences', *Law and Policy in International Business* 11, 1447 at 1488.

11 Beseler, ibid., at 344.
12 Ibid.
13 Ibid., at 347. Recent case law has put this test of 'proportionality' under severe strain.
14 Ibid., at 349.
15 Ibid., at 351.
16 Bronckers, M., and R. Quick, 'What is a Countervailable Subsidy under EEC Trade Law?' *Journal of World Trade* 23 (6), 5 at 5.
17 *Ballbearings from Thailand: Exemption from Tariffs on Machinery*, Com. Dec. 90/266/EEC, (1990), OJ L152/59.
18 A 'net–net' approach would calculate the amount of the subsidy, then deduct from it all relevant taxes, costs of complying with the terms of the subsidy, and costs associated with foregoing the benefits of not accepting a subsidy. The most obvious examples are the costs of relocating or locating a factory in a disadvantaged region. More difficult is the tax consequences of accepting a subsidy. For example, if an enterprise leverages the construction of a factory, the costs of the loan will be tax deductible. The enterprise may not, however, claim any deductions if an outright grant is made for the construction of a factory. The benefit to the enterprise, then, is not the amount of the subsidy in the abstract; rather, it is the amount of the subsidy minus the cost of foregoing the tax deduction.
19 Van Bael, Ivo, and J.-F. Bellis, *International Trade Law and Practice of the European Community: EEC Anti-Dumping and other Trade Protection Laws*, (Bicester: CCH Editions Limited, 1985), at 150.
20 Ibid., at 149. These tax exemptions reduce the cost of industrial machinery for certain industries, thus contributing to an overall reduction in the production costs of the industry in question. While the IPI tax exemptions are not directly tied to export enhancement, many products manufactured by these machinery find markets outside of Brazil.
21 Bronckers, M., 'Private Remedies Against Foreign Subsidization: A European View', in Bourgeois, Jacques, H.J., ed., *Subsidies and International Trade: A European Lawyers' Perspective*, (Deventer: Kluwer Law and Taxation Publishers, 1991), at 194; see also van Bael and Bellis, op. cit., at 141.
22 Bourgeois, Jacques H.J., 'Introduction: Law and Policy – Cripple Helping Blind?' in Bourgeois, ibid., at 4.
23 Yi, Seong Deog, and Chong Ju Choi, 'The Community's Unfair Pricing Practices in the Maritime Transport Sector' *European Law Review* (1991), 14, 279 at 279.
24 Bellis, Vermulst, and Musquar argue that the term 'non-commercial advantage' was used because the use of the term 'subsidy' could have involved the GATT. As well, unlike the Community's definition of 'subsidy', a non-commercial advantage may not involve a charge to the public account. See Bellis, J.-F., Edwin Vermulst, and Phillippe Musquar, 'The New EEC Regulation on Unfair Pricing Practices in Maritime Transport: A Forerunner of the Extension of Unfair Trade Concepts to

Services', *Journal of World Trade* (1988), 22 (1), 47 at 49. See also Bronckers, op. cit., at 28.

25 *Regulation on Unfair Pricing Practices in Maritime Transport*, CR 4057/86, (1986), OJ L378/14. Subsidisation or 'unfair' practices by Community Member States are covered by the competition section of the Treaty of Rome.

26 Ibid., Article 2.

27 Ibid., Article 12.

28 Ibid., Clause 13(3).

29 United States International Trade Administration, the body responsible for the determination of the existence and the amount of the subsidy in the US CVD regime.

30 Yi and Choi, op. cit., at 283. There is nothing in the USITA jurisprudence to bar it from imposing a CVD on manufactured goods that benefit from similar government programmes. Should the US decide to extend its trade remedy statutes to cover services, it is likely that all of the above practices, and more, will be caught by the administering authorities. Vermulst has created an interesting catalogue of the practices deemed to be subsidies by the ITA, some of which, as Trebilcock has also noted, are not universally agreed to be, in fact, subsidies. See Vermulst, E., 'Comment', in Bourgeois, op. cit., at 54–5 note 32.

31 (1989) OJ L4/1.

32 Ibid.

33 Ibid., at 4.

34 Ibid., at 5.

35 Ibid.

36 Ibid., at 7. The Council argued that although Hyundai presented an added competitive element for the European market, the Community was not interested in encouraging 'unfair competition based on non-commercial advantages'.

37 Dearden, Richard G., and David Palmeter, *Free Trade Law Reports* (Commentaries on Chapter 18 and 19 procedures), (Toronto: CCH Canadian Limited, 1990), at 31051. Also Article 1902, *Canada–US Free Trade Agreement*, (Ottawa: Ministry of Supply and Services, 1988).

38 Anderson, Andrew, and Alan Rugman, *The Canada–US Free Trade Agreement: A Legal and Economic Analysis of the Dispute Settlement Mechanisms*, Ontario Centre for International Business Working Paper no. 30, (Toronto: University of Toronto, 1989) at 2; Canada–US FTA, ibid., Article 1904.

39 This trend has been outlined extensively by other works too numerous to mention. For one of the more recent histories of US legislative action in this area please see Kaplan, Gilbert, Susan Hagerty Kuhbach, and Ronald Lorentz, 'Antidumping, Countervailing Duty, and National Security Provisions in the 1988 Trade Act,' *George Washington Journal of International Law and Economics* (1989), 22, 553.

40 See Clinton, William J., and Daniel Porter, 'The United States' new Anti-Circumvention Provision and Its Application by the Commerce Department,' *Journal of World Trade* (1990), 24 (3), 101; Bello, Judith, Alan F. Holmer, and Barbara E. Tillman, 'Anticircumvention Masures: Shifting

the Gears of the Antidumping and CVD Laws?' *International Lawyer* (1990), 207. Anti-circumvention provisions have also been enacted in the EU; see for example Torremans, Paul, 'Anti-circumvention duties after the Screwdriver Panel Report', European Law Review 18, 288. The so-called 'Screwdriver' Panel of the GATT ruled that the anti-circumvention provisions of the EC were not GATT-compatible; the EU reluctantly adopted the Report and suspended their application of the anti-circumvention provisions. The EU anti-circumvention measures are sufficiently different from the US measures so that it does not appear that the ruling of the GATT Panel would in anyway affect the legality of the US measures.

41 *Omnibus Trade and Competitiveness Act of 1988*, (1988), Pub. L. No. 100–418, 102 Stat. 1107.

42 See Diamond, Richard, 'A Search for Economic and Financial Principles in the Administration of United States Countervailing Duty Law', and Sykes, Alan O., 'Second-best Countervailing Duty Policy: A Critique of the Entitlement Approach', *Law & Policy Int'L Bus.* (1990), 21, 699. In the recent case of *Roses Inc. v. United States* 774 F.Supp. 1376 (CIT 1991) (*Roses* II) Restani J. examined the statutory framework of the US countervail system and came to the conclusion (at 1377) that in theory, 'countervailing duties subordinate immediate consumer welfare (consumers would naturally prefer the lower prices attached to the good) to the overall health of the economy (unsubsidized domestic firms may be unable to compete with foreign firms)'. He went on to state (at 1382) that 'United States trade laws are not aimed at protecting *every* competitive advantage afforded by government action'. The first comment was unique in that few courts, or ITA or ITC panels, have acknowledged the simple point that consumers do benefit from subsidised imports – a point that academics have been raising for many years without being heard by policy-makers. The second comment is curious, because the trend in US lawmaking has in fact been to extend the reach of US trade remedy laws to nearly every advantage bestowed by foreign governments. See also Nies C.J. of the Federal Court of Appeal in *PPG Industries v. United States* 928 F.2d 1568 (USCA, 1991) (*PPG* III), where he argued (at 1574) that Congress had not intended to countervail all foreign subsidies, and (at 1575) that the protection of domestic industry is not the only purpose of the US countervailing duty law.

43 Perhaps the most startling example of this incoherence and the political nature of trade policy in the US came following the third softwood lumber determination. It was reported that 'three US Senators who led the campaign against Canadian softwood said they would ask the US administration to drop the temporary duty if Canada agrees to end its ban on the export of raw logs to the US'. (Morton, Peter, 'US senators propose softwood lumber deal', *The Financial Post*, 7 April 1992, at 1) Either the ITA has made a positive subsidy determination, or it has not. If it has, then it is problematic that a supposedly objective administrative determination can be overturned on the request of three activist senators. Was the decision of the ITA a coherent analysis of subsidisation in Canada, or was it a frontal assault on Canada's natural resources policies?

44 Committee on Finance, United States Senate, *Report of Committee on Finance on Trade Agreements Act*, (1979), Report no. 249, 96th Congress, 1st session, at 37. See also Guido, Robert, and Michael Monone, 'The *Michelin* Decision: A Possible New Direction for US Countervailing Duty Law', *Law and Policy in International Business* (1974), 6, 237 at 237.

45 Committee on Ways and Means, United States House of Representatives, *Report no. 317, 96th Congress, 1st Session, on Trade Agreements Act of 1979*, (Washington, DC: Government Printing Office, 1979) at 43. See also Feller, Peter Buck, 'Preface: Observations on the New Countervailing Duty Law', *Law and Policy in International Business* (1979), 11, 1439 at 1443.

46 De Kieffer, Donald E., 'When, Why and How to Bring a Countervailing Duty Proceeding: A Complainant's Perspective', *North Carolina Journal of Interntional Law and Commercial Regulation* (1980–1), 6, 363 at 364.

47 *Zenith Radio Corp. v. United States*, 437 US 443 (USSC, 1978).

48 Brown, Craig M., ''Bounty or Grant:' A Call for Redefinition in Light of the Zenith Decision', *Law and Policy in International Business* (1977), 9, 1229 at 1252.

49 Ibid. See also Ehrenraft, Peter, 'The Treasury's Proposed Approach to Imports from State Control Economy Countries and State-owned Enterprises under the Antidumping and Countervailing Duty Laws', in *Interface One*, op. cit., at 77.

50 Quoted in Destler, I.M., *American Trade Politics: System Under Stress*, (Washington, DC: Institute for International Economics, 1986), at 136.

51 Thomas, op. cit., at 3/17–8; Diamond, 'A Search for . . .', op. cit., at 564.

52 Jackson argues that the fairness argument 'is so vague, it is even hard to articulate, much less prove'. See Jackson, John H. *World Trading System*, (Cambridge: MIT Press, 1989), at 254. Lowenfeld believes that absent world-wide harmonisation of wage scales, exchange rates, tax structures, environmental controls, and other socio-economic indicators, 'what is fair and what is unfair is in large part coincidence'. See Lowenfeld, Andreas, 'Fair or Unfair Trade: Does it Matter?' *Cornell International Law Journal* (1990), 13, 205 at 219. See also Gaisford, James D., and Donald McLachlan, 'Domestic Subsidies and Countervail: The Treacherous Ground of the Level Playing Field', *Journal of World Trade* (1990), 24 (4) 55.

53 Diamond, 'A Search for. . .,' op. cit., at 564. See also Jackson, John H., 'Perspectives on Countervailing Duties', *Law and Policy in International Business* (1990), 21, 739 at 750.

54 Cass, Ronald A., 'Trade Subsidy Law: Can a Foolish Inconsistency be Good Enough for Government Work?' *Law and Policy in International Business* (1990), 21, 609 at 641.

55 Thomas, op. cit., at 2/32; Diamond, 'A Search for. . .', op. cit., at 529; Goetz, Charles J., Lloyd Granet, and Warren Schwartz, 'The Meaning of 'Subsidy' and 'Injury' in the Countervailing Duty Law', *International Review of Law and Economics* (1986), 6, 17 at 18.

56 Hufbauer, Gary Clyde, and Joanna Shelton Erb, *Subsidies in International Trade*, (Cambridge: MIT Press, 1984), at 16.

57 From 1980 to September 1989 the US Commerce Department launched 300 countervailing duty proceedings against almost all countries in the world. This number is calculated on a product-by-product, country-by-country basis. See Vermulst, E., 'Comment' in Bourgeois, op. cit., at 54. Between July 1980 and June 1988, the US commenced 264 CVD proceedings, compared with 23, 15, 5, and 1 for Australia, Canada, the EC and Japan respectively. In that period, the US accounted for 58 per cent of all CVD proceedings and 84 per cent of all CVD actions if Chile is not considered. Chile discontinued initiating CVD proceedings following threats of retaliatory measures from its trading partners. See Table 2, Anderson, Andrew, and Alan Rugman, 'Country Factor Bias in the Administration of Antidumping and Countervailing Duty Cases', in Trebilcock, Michael J., and Robert C. York, *Fair Exchange: Reforming Trade Remedy Laws*, (Toronto: C.D. Institute, 1990), at 153–6.

58 Anderson and Rugman, *Dispute Settlement*, op. cit., at 1. Destler called the 'multiple harassment' of importers through the use of legal procedures form of 'legal protectionism'. He suggested that the trade remedy procedures, taken as a whole, constituted a substantial US 'non-tariff barrier'. Destler, op. cit., at 131.

59 Hufbauer, Gary Clyde, 'Subsidies', in Schott, J.J., ed., *Completing the Uruguay Round*, (Washington, DC: Institute for International Economics, 1990), at 95.

60 De Kieffer, op. cit., at 367–8. See also Finger, Michael, and Tracy Murray, 'Policing Unfair Imports: The United States Example', *Journal of World Trade* (1990), 24, (4) 39 at 49; Clinton and Porter, op. cit., at 101; Thomas, op. cit., at 3/13. In *Limousines from Canada*, USITC Pub. 2220 (1989), the market uncertainty caused by the action caused the defendant company's market in the US to dry up. Since the company was entirely export-dependent, it was driven out of business. Interview with Susan Spencer, International Economic Relations Division, Department of Finance, at the Department of National Revenue, Ottawa, (19 February 1992).

61 *USCA* 19, §1671.

62 *USCA* 19, §1671a(a).

63 *USCA* 19, §1671a(b).

64 Spencer, op. cit.

65 See *supra* Chapter 5, Part II.

66 See Anderson and Rugman, op. cit., at 1. Kalt disagrees. He thinks that the ITC is quite diligent in assessing the depth of foreign sector subsidies, offsets US subsidies, takes into account macro- and microeconomic conditions, etc.; Kalt, Joseph, 'The Political Economy of Protectionism: Tariff and Retaliation in the Timber Industry', in Baldwin, Robert, *Trade Policy Issues and Empirical Analysis*, (Chicago: The University of Chicago Press, 1988), at 344. Kalt's analysis is questionable, because the scale of foreign subsidy practices, offsets and the like are determined by the ITA, which has little discretion in analysing offsets and targeted subsidy practices. Anderson and Rugman's argument is more convincing.

67 The Commission of the EU is also responsible for the EU trade policy.

68 *USCA* 19, §1677(5)(A)(ii).

69 *USCA* 19, §1677(5)(B). This merely codified the decision of the Court of International Trade in *Cabot Corp. v. United States*, 620 F.Supp. 722. In *Fresh, Chilled or Frozen Pork from Canada*, the ITA argued that the Tripartite agreements were specific subsidies because, even though nominally generally available, they were used by only a handful of companies. But it was not clear whether the low rate of participation was due to government action or simply business practice; it was also not clear whether it would have made a difference had the lack of participation by private companies been for purely tax or corporate strategy reasons. No analysis was undertaken to determine the cause of low usage of the subsidy. The binational panel accepted the reasoning of the ITA in this area; the case was remanded on other points. See also comments by Houlihan and Romoli re Italian regional development schemes, 'Session Three', in *Interface One*, op. cit., at 206. The issue of specificity came to a head in the binational panel's decision in *Certain Softwood Lumber Products from Canada* (*Softwood Lumber* IV) (1993, USA-92–1904–01) Reviewing *Certain Softwood Lumber Products from Canada* (*Softwood Lumber* III) Fed Reg (28 May 1992, 57, 22570). The Panel quoted the decision of the CIT in *Roses Inc. v. United States* 743 F.Supp. 870 (CIT 1990) (*Roses* I) and Restani J.'s interpretation of *Cabot Corp.* He stated (at 876) that 'in deciding whether a countervailable domestic subsidy has been provided the ITA must always focus on whether an advantage in international trade has been bestowed on a discrete class of grantees despite nominal availability, program grouping, or the absolute number of grantee companies or 'industries'. The panel was of the view that US case law required a far more rigorous analysis of *de facto* specificity than the ITA had undertaken and remanded the decision for further consideration. In *Roses* I and II, the CIT reiterated that nominal general availability does not save a subsidy if it is *de facto* available to a specific industry. However, the court held, although an 'identifiable' sector, the agricultural sector is not a 'specific' industry or company within the meaning of the countervail law. In *Roses* II, Restani J. criticised ITA (at 1380) for 'merely look[ing] at the number of companies that receive benefits under the program. . .'. In *Softwood Lumber* IV, the Panel criticised the ITA for not following its own Proposed Regulations ('Rulemaking').

70 See *supra*.

71 *USCA* 19, §1677(5)(A)(ii).

72 Proposed Rulemaking, Fed Reg (1989), 54, 23366 at 23368. This approach was adopted by the participants in the Uruguay Round of Multilateral Trade Negotiations.

73 The analysis of the ITA reached surrealistic heights when in *Certain Iron-metal Construction Castings from Mexico* it determined a scheme to be specific even though only three highly industrialised cities were exempted from an otherwise general countrywide application.

74 Rulemaking, op. cit., at 23368; the ITA effectively overruled the holding of the CIT in *Cabot Corp.*, op. cit.

75 Ibid., at 23369–70.

76 Ibid., at 23372. This could be problematic. In *Carlisle Tire and Rubber*

Company the CIT had cautioned the ITA against an activist policy in this area, especially in regard to natural resources; Hufbauer, op. cit., at 96.

77 *Certain Softwood Lumber Products from Canada* (*Softwood Lumber* I) Fed Reg (1983), 48, 24159 at 24182–3.

78 See especially *Carbon Black from Mexico*, Fed Reg (1986), 51, 13269. A proposed amendment to the *1988 Trade Act* moved by Rep. Gibbens would have deemed any provision of a natural resource below a 'market determined price' to constitute a subsidy even if numerous and diverse industries benefited from it; Kaplan, Kuhbach, and Lorentz, op. cit., at 562. See also *PPG Industries, Inc. v. United States* (*PPG* III) 928 F.2d 1568 (Fed Cir 1991), where the Circuit Court of Appeal also alluded to that episode and took the failure of the proposed amendment as meaning that Congress made a specific policy decision not to countervail against widely available natural resources subsidies. In *Softwood Lumber* IV the binational panel revisited the classical Ricardian natural resources economic theories and argued that the normal principles of supply and demand are not applicable to the market for natural resources. The panel stated (at 53) that the 'price set for the natural resource does play a key role in determining how the financial value – the economic rent – of the resource will be divided between owner and purchaser. It does not, however, have any market distorting impact on the output of the resource and thence on the amount and price of downstream products'.

79 Rulemaking, op. cit., at 23374.

80 Diamond, 'A Search for . . .,' op. cit., at 538; Cass, op. cit., at 659.

81 Fed Reg (1986), 51, 15037. The company under investigation argued that if it had not accepted the investment grant, it would have borrowed the capital, the interest on which would have been deducted from its taxable profits. It argued that in assessing the rate or amount of the effective subsidy, the ITA should take into consideration the benefits the company has forgone in accepting the subsidy in question. The ITA rejected this argument without any analysis. To be fair to the ITA, it must be said that at least a consistent line is being followed here. The ITA, for example, does not consider how much of the subsidy is paid back to government in the form of corporate taxes.

82 Diamond, 'A Search for . . .', op. cit., at 537.

83 Carroll, op. cit., at 23.

84 Congress exercises considerable influence by virtue of its position as the chief lawmaking body in trade matters. In the past, through amendments to the US trade remedy legislation, Congress has been an active participant in trade policy-making, and has proven its resolve to advance its trade policy interest regardless of possible opposition from the Executive Branch. Inattention to Congressional demands by organs of the Executive could raise the ire of Congress and cause a further diminution of executive and administrative discretion in trade policy matters.

85 Kalt, op. cit., at 349.

86 Destler, op. cit., at 136.

87 Trebilcock, M.J., 'Is the Game Worth the Candle?' *Law and Policy in*

International Business (1990), 21, 723 at 731–2. An editorial in *The Financial Post* (9 March 1992 at S-1) called the CVD on softwood lumber a 'clear violation of the terms of both the General Agreement on Tariffs and Trade, and the Canada–US free trade agreement': 'Resource pricing isn't subject to countervail duties under the GATT. . .'.

As Trebilcock points out, this has not stopped the US from slapping CVDs on Canadian products. This is hardly surprising; the US has always expected other countries to behave according to an American code of conduct, even if the US itself does not abide by it. There is little point in decrying the injustice of American moral imperialism; it is important, however, to recognise this tendency when devising DRMs.

88 Thomas, op. cit., at 2/25; Guido and Monone, op. cit., at 251.

89 Guido and Monone, ibid., at 258.

90 *Special Import Measures Act*, S.C. (1984), c. 25 as am.; *Special Import Measures Regulations*, SOR/84–927 (1984). *Agreement on the Interpretation and Application of Articles VI, XVI and XXIII of the General Agreement on Tariffs and Trade*, 1189 *United Nations Treaty Series* 204, GATT BISD 26th Supp. 56 (1978–9) ('The Subsidies Code'). The Subsidies Code was drafted in large part to satisfy US interests and to maintain the US trade remedy law in place. The similarity of a GATT-consistent SIMA to the US law can be easily understood in this light.

91 This way, at least at the preliminary stages of the investigation, an attempt is made to link the subsidy to the injury. The ITC's preliminary injury investigation must either assume the existence of a subsidy, or determine the existence of an injury abstracted from the subsidy determination. This is at best conceptually incoherent.

92 Interview with Ron Walker, Senior Policy Analyst, MNR-Customs and Excise, at the Department of National Revenue, Ottawa, 19 February 1992. In Canada, the Regulations came into force with the Act. In the US, however, the Rulemaking proposals have been many years in the making and codify the past practice of the ITA, instead of shaping it for the future.

93 Department of National Revenue, *Departmental Manual, v.II: Special Import Measures Act*, §1, pt.X, sec.A, ¶7 (1.X.A.7).

94 'Methodology Appendix', *Certain Steel Products from Belgium*, Fed Reg (1982), 47, 39304 at 39319.

95 *Final determination of subsidizing respecting grain corn in all forms, excluding seed corn, sweet corn and popping corn, originating in or exported from the United States of America*, (2 July, 1986), MNR.

96 It is not expected that this provision will be used much. It is, it seems to me, at best an escape door for politically sensitive cases.

97 MacMillan, Katie, 'Comment,' on Anderson and Rugman, 'Country Factor. . .', in Trebilcock and Robert, op. cit., at 192.

98 Tougas, Frances, 'Softwood Lumber from Canada: Natural Resources and the Search for a Definition of Countervailable Domestic Subsidy', *Gonzaga Law Review* (1988–9), 24, 135 at 140.

99 Spencer, op. cit.

100 This may be changing, however. Although primarily dumping cases, the most recent trio of cases in the steel sector indicate some influence on

part of the *Free Trade Agreement* and the binational review process on Canada's trade remedy mechanism. In *High Strength and Low Alloy Plate* (NQ-92–007) the CITT found material injury caused by dumping from all sources except American exporters, even though the margin of dumping for American steel in Canada was as high as – if not higher than – all other imported steel. The steel industry lost across the board in *Hot Rolled Sheet* (NQ-92–008), but won in *Cold Rolled Sheet* barely a month later (*The Globe and Mail*, 30 July 1993, at B-4; NQ-92–009). The evidence of injury was stronger in the first two cases and there is reason to suspect that the CITT may have been somewhat rattled by the strong decision of the panel in *Machine Tufted Carpets Originating in or Exported from the United States* (CDA-92–1904–02). Both *Plate* and *Hot Rolled Sheet* are now subject to judicial review by the Federal Court of Appeal of Canada and the binational panel.

101 Spencer, op. cit.; Walker, op. cit.

102 NAFTA removes the provision relating to the negotiations over a subsidies code and makes the binational panel review process a permanent feature of the trilateral trading regime. However, there does seem to be a new commitment on part of the Parties to at least try to arrive at a reasonable compromise on a subsidies code.

103 Dearden and Palmeter, op. cit., at 31304. *Machine Tufted Carpets* may have changed this. Relying on a recent and closely divided decision of the Supreme Court of Canada, the majority of the panel in *Carpets* seemed to argue that the standard of review was the 'sufficient evidence' test, as opposed to the 'patent unreasonability' test enunciated by a number of earlier Supreme Court decisions. The analysis of the panel is at best suspect; John D. Richard's strong dissent may yet form the basis for the restoration of the legal *status quo ante*. For a thorough discussion of the standard of review in both Canada and the US please see Boddez, Thomas M., and Michael J. Trebilcock, *Unfinished Business* (Toronto: C.D. Howe Institute, 1993), as well as *Softwood Lumber* IV.

104 Spencer, op. cit.

105 *The Free Trade Observer* 21:311; *Fresh Chilled or Frozen Pork from Canada* (ECC-91–1904–01 USA). The ECC stated in *Pork* that an extraordinary challenge is not intended to function as a routine appeal; its role is to 'review Binational Panel decisions in only exceptional circumstances', (at 13) The ECC reiterated its function in *Live Swine from Canada* (ECC-93–1904–01 USA), although it did venture to set some guidelines for the binational panel.

106 Dearden and Palmeter, op. cit., at 31052.

107 Ibid., at 29256.

108 Ibid.

109 NAFTA has been approved by all the signatories, although Canadian concerns about the Working Group on subsidies remain outstanding.

110 Gil Winham, Conference on NAFTA, Toronto, (23–25 June 1993).

111 *North American Free Trade Agreement* (Ottawa: Minister of Supply and Services, Canada, 1992).

112 Assuming Canada is successful in breathing life into the dormant Subsidies Working Group.

113 For a thorough analysis of the ethical and economic arguments for these policies, please see Trebilcock, Michael J., Robert Howse, and Marsha Chandler, *Trade and Transition*, (London: Routledge, 1990).
114 USA-92–1904–01, Re-remand pursuant to redetermination, (17 December 1993).
115 USA-92–1904–01, Redetermination pursuant to Remand, (10 September 1993).
116 Ibid., at 6.
117 Op. cit., at 161.
118 Fed Reg (1990), 55, 40212.
119 Op. cit., at 161.

6 THE URUGUAY ROUND

1 Hufbauer, Gary Clyde, 'Subsidies', in Schott, J.J., ed., *Completing the Uruguay Round*, (Washington, DC: Institute for International Economics, 1990), at 101, 104, 106; Steenbergen, Jaque, Guido De Clerque, and René Foqué, *Change and Adjustment*, (Deventer: Kluwer Law and Taxation Publishers, 1983), at 193.
2 'EEC Overall Approach to Uruguay Round', III.B, in Simmonds, Kenneth, and Brian H.W. Hill, *Law and Practice under the GATT*, (New York: Oceana Publications, 1991), at 29.
3 The Agreement on Subsidies and Countervailing Measures, MTN/FA II/13, should be read along with the Agreement Establishing the Multilateral (World) Trade Organization, MTN/FA II, and Understanding on Rules and Procedures Governing the Settlement of Disputes , MTN/FA II-A2.
4 'Launching the Uruguay Round', III.A, in Simmonds, op. cit., at 17.
5 General Agreement on Tariffs and Trade, Negotiating Group on Subsidies and Countervailing Measures, 'Communication from Canada: Framework for Negotiations', UR-89–0117, (Geneva: GATT Secretariat, 1989), at 3.
6 Ibid.
7 Ibid.
8 Ibid. See also *supra*, Chapter 5, *The Canada–US Free Trade Agreement*.
9 Ibid., at 4. A cost to government approach reduces the likelihood of governments' regulatory practices being targeted as potential subsidy or subsidy-like schemes, whereas a 'benefit to corporations' approach would be fraught with analytical uncertainties. As Dearden and Weiler observe in their dissent in *Softwood Lumber* IV, (USA-92-1904-01-Canada–US FTA Chapter 19 panel), at 162, 'there is absolutely no intrinsic limitation to the scope of government actions that can be alleged to be subsidies to the extent they generate cost savings for specific groups of industries.' They note that any reduction in tariffs, for example, could potentially confer a benefit on a specific industry. Such a wide application is not analytically sustainable. On the other hand, a cost to government approach would shield government-induced private sub-

sidies (through loan regulations, for example, or as in Korean maritime shipping practices) from anti-subsidy actions.

10 GATT, 'Communication. . .', ibid., at 5.
11 Ibid., at 6. Emphasis in the original.
12 Ibid., at 10–11.
13 Romoli, A., and Ch. Pelletier, Information Report of the Section for External Relations, *Trade and Development Policy on Resumption of the GATT/Uruguay Round Negotiations*, (13 June 1991), (Brussels: EC–Economic and Social Committee, 1991), at 13.
14 Commission of the European Communities, 'Background Report on GATT Negotiations', (11 March 1991), ISEC/B6/91 (London), at 19.
15 Romoli and Pelletier, op. cit., at 15.
16 Ibid., at 19; also CEC, 'Background Report', op. cit., at 19.
17 'Economic and Social Committee Opinion on the GATT/Uruguay Round Negotiations', in Simmonds, op. cit., at 4–5. As to how such the GATT DRM could be strengthened while keeping the political nature of the process was not elaborated. A possible interpretation is that as always, the EC was primarily concerned with CVDs and not with subsidies. Strengthening the dispute resolution mechanism in this context means strengthening the controls on CVDs.
18 Simmonds, 'Launching. . .', op. cit., at 17–8.
19 GATT, Agreement, op. cit., Part I, Article 1.
20 Ibid., Article 2.
21 Ibid., Subclause 2.1(c).
22 Ibid., Clause 2.1.
23 Ibid., Clause 2.4.
24 Ibid., Subarticle 14(a).
25 Ibid., Subarticle 14(b).
26 Ibid., Subarticle 14(c).
27 Ibid., Subarticle 14(d). Significantly, the provision would take into account 'price, quality, availability, marketability, transportation and other conditions of purchase and sale'.
28 Ibid., Part IV, Subclause 8.1(a).
29 These are R&D expenditures at the very early stages of research and are considered to have a minimal impact on international trade.
30 GATT, Agreement, op. cit., Clause 8.2.
31 Hufbauer, op. cit., at 99.
32 GATT, Agreement, op. cit., Part III, Article 5.
33 Ibid., Clause 6.1.
34 Ibid., Clause 6.3.
35 Ibid., Part II, Article 3.
36 Ibid., Part II, Article 4, and Part III, Article 7.
37 GATT, Understanding, op. cit., Clause 4.3.
38 GATT, Agreement, op. cit., Part II, Clauses 4.1–3, 7.1–3.
39 Ibid., Clause 4.4, 7.4.
40 GATT, Understanding, op. cit., Clause 2.1.
41 Ibid., Article 6; Agreement, op. cit., Articles 4 and 7.
42 GATT, Understanding, ibid., Article 8.

43 Ibid., Clause 8.9.
44 Ibid., Article 11.
45 Ibid., Article 13.
46 Ibid., Article 16.
47 Ibid., Article 17 and Clause 17.3.
48 Ibid., Clause 17.6.
49 Ibid., Article 19.
50 Ibid., Clause 21.3.
51 Ibid.
52 GATT, Agreement, Clause 24.3.
53 Ibid., Part VI, Clause 24.3.
54 Ibid., Clause 4.5.
55 Ibid., Clause 4.12.
56 Ibid., Clause 7.8.
57 Ibid., Clause 9.4.
58 Establishing a causal link before an investigation is launched may be difficult in countries where the process is bifurcated. In Canada and the EU this problem does not arise, at least at the preliminary stage; however, in the US the process is divided at the very beginning. See ibid., Part V, Clause 11.1.
59 In the US this is done through a voluntary questionnaire. In fact, some investigations such as *Softwood Lumber* III may proceed despite strong opposition from a large segment of the domestic industry.
60 GATT, Agreement, op. cit., Article 14.
61 See Chapter 2. The argument revolves around efficiency and cost recovery. When governments provide businesslike services for business without charging all the costs to the business, then a net transfer of benefit has occurred.
62 GATT, Agreement, op. cit., Clause 19.2.
63 Ibid. The EU CVD Regulations are discretionary, as opposed to the US regime which requires the imposition of a CVD upon a finding of subsidisation and 'injury that is not immaterial . . .'.
64 Ibid.
65 Ibid., Part VII, Article 25.
66 Ibid., Clause 25.7.
67 See Romoli's discussion of the Italian subsidies to its Mezzogiorno industries, Romoli, Aldo, 'Session Two', in Wallace, Don, George C. Spina, Richard M. Rawson, and Brian McGill, eds, *Interface One*, (Washington, DC: Institute for International and Foreign Trade Law, 1980), at 115.
68 Export subsidies are considered *per se* distortive because the link between the production and export on the one hand, and subsidisation on the other, is clear. No such direct relation exists between domestic subsidies and effects in foreign markets: subsidies may be diverted to shareholders' or managers' pockets, they may offset other costs imposed by government regulation or taxation, or have extra-economic objectives. The counterfactual that needs to be created for the purpose of linking the subsidy to an injury in the importing country's market

cannot simply rest on the magnitude of the subsidy per unit of output or export.

69 For further elaboration see Chapter 2.

70 In preparing its *Third Survey on State Aids*, the Commission was unable to receive any co-operation from the Greek Government, and in the end it had to rely on consultants' reports. *Third Survey on State Aids in the European Community in the Manufacturing and Certain Other Sectors*, (Luxembourg: Office of Official Publications of the European Communities, 1992).

7 CONCLUSION

1 Quoted in Morgenthau, Hans, and Kenneth Thomson, *Politics among Nations: The Struggle for Power and Peace* VI Edition (New York: Alfred Knopf, 1985), at 10.

2 See for example Thomas, Jeffrey, *Subsidies and Countervailing Duties in the Canada–US Free Trade Agreement: Trends, Critiques and Proposals for Rational Reform*, (Toronto: Faculty of Law, University of Toronto, 1989), or Sykes, Alan O., 'Countervailing Duty Law: An Economic Perspective', paper presented at the Law and Economic Workshop Series at the Faculty of Law, University of Toronto, (1989).

3 See Trebilcock, Michael J., Robert Howse, and Marsha Chandler, *Trade and Transition*, (London: Routledge, 1990); Thomas, op. cit.

4 Trade sanctions have been used to advance non-economic national interests or enforce international law since the Greek army blockaded Troy. While some wars have purely economic objectives (thus providing trade sanctions and blockades with an economic logic) the strategic importance of trade sanctions go beyond mere economic imperatives. Therefore, when the dictates of free trade clash with strategic imperatives, it is no surprise that the former are ignored.

5 Thus raising cries of irrationality or cynicism. Undoubtedly elements of both exist in the EU. However, it is doubtful that the Commission is devoid of rationality or goodwill, or that free trade economists are the only guardians of reason.

6 This is particularly important in light of the original reasons for the development of the EU. The EEC and the ECSC were created to reduce the chances of another European war by integrating the war-making industries of Europe (coal and steel), and also its economic structure. Thus, free trade was primarily politically driven. This was also recognised by the ECJ in its *Opinion Regarding the Draft Agreement between the European Communities and the European Free Trade Association Relating to the Creation of the European Economic Area, International Legal Materials* (1992), 31, 442, at 459, where the ECJ stated that 'the provisions of the EEC Treaty on free movement and competition, far from being an end in themselves, are only means for attaining' European unity.

7 ECJ, *Opinion*, ibid., at 459.

8 The same can be said of the US conduct of the trading relations with its

largest trading partner, Canada. The extent to which the market uncertainties caused by repeated legal and administrative harassment of trading partners reduce world welfare is a matter to be determined by economists. However, there is little doubt that if trade disputes were resolved more peacefully, i.e. if the US were willing to negotiate (in good faith) more and litigate less, the world would be much better off.

9 Emphasis added; Schelling, T.C., 'The Diplomacy of Violence' in Art, Robert, and Robert Jervis, eds, *International Politics*, (Boston: Little, Brown and Company, 1985); at 171.

BIBLIOGRAPHY

Agence Internationale D'Information Pour La Presse – 'Europe', (new series), Bruxelles, various issues, (29 Nov 1991: 17 Dec 1991; 15, 24, 28 Jan 1992; 4, 6, 13, 14, 18 Feb 1992; 4 Mar 1992; 14, 24, 25 Apr 1992; 1, 4 May 1992; 17 Nov 1992; 12, 15, 23, 28 Jan 1993; 3, 9, 10, 13, 17, 20 Feb 1993; 12 Mar 1993; 18 May 1993; 17, 25, 29 June 1993; 26 Nov 1993).

Alessandrini, S., 'Subsidies, Strategic Trade Policies and the GATT', in Bourgeois, ed., *Subsidies and International Trade: A European Lawyers' Perspective*, (1991).

Anderson, Andrew, and Alan Rugman, *The Canada–US Free Trade Agreement: A Legal and Economic Analysis of the Dispute Settlement Mechanisms*, Ontario Centre for International Business Working Paper no. 30, (Toronto: University of Toronto, 1989).

——, 'Subsidies in the US Steel Industry: A New Conceptual Framework and Literature Review', *Journal of World Trade* (1989), 23 (6), 59.

——, 'Country Factor Bias in the Administration of Antidumping and Countervailing Duty Cases', in Trebilcock and York, eds, *Fair Exchange: Reforming Trade Remedy Laws*, (1990).

Applebaum, Harvey, and A. Paul Victor, eds, *United States Import Relief Laws*, (Washington, DC: Practicing Law Institute, 1985).

Art, Robert, and Robert Jervis, eds, *International Politics*, (Boston: Little, Brown and Company, 1985).

Aux Bureaux Nationaux, 'Industry Council – two items on Competition Policy', Note BIO (91) 371, (Brussels: 1991).

——, Note BIO (91) 161, (Brussels: 1991).

van Bael, Ivo, and Jean-François Bellis, *International Trade Law and Practice of the European Community: EEC Anti-Dumping and other Trade Protection Laws*, (Bicester: CCH Editions Limited, 1985).

Balassa, Bela, *Competitive Advantage: Trade Policy and Economic Development*, (London: Harvester Wheatsheaf, 1989).

——, ed., *Subsidies and Countervailing Measures: Critical Issues for the Uruguay Round*, (Washington, DC: The World Bank, 1989).

Baldwin, Robert, Carl B. Hamilton, and André Sapir, eds, *Issues in US–EC Trade Relations*, (Chicago: The University of Chicago Press, 1988).

Baldwin, Robert, ed., *Trade Policy Issues and Empirical Analysis*, (Chicago: The University of Chicago Press, 1988).

Baldwin, Robert, and Paul Krugman, 'Industrial Policy and International Competition in Wide-Bodied Jet Aircraft', in Baldwin, ed., *Trade Policy Issues and Empirical Analysis*, (1988).

Barceló, John J. (III), 'Subsidies and Countervailing Duties – Analysis and a Proposal', *Law and Policy in International Business* (1977), 9, 779.

——, 'Subsidies, Countervailing Duties and Antidumping after the Tokyo Round', *Cornell International Law Journal* (1980), 13, 257.

——, 'An "Injury-only" Regime (for imports) and Actionable Subsidies', in Wallace *et al.*, eds, *Interface Three*, (1984).

Barnes, Christopher, 'New and Improved Awards without Discussions or Foreign Competition', Public Contract L.J. (1991), 20, 532.

Belcredi, Massimo, Lounzo Caprio, and Pippo Ronci, *The Aid Element in State Participation to Company Capital*, (Luxembourg: Office for Official Publications of the European Communities, 1988).

Bello, Judith, Alan F. Holmer, and Barbara E. Tillman, 'Anticircumvention Measures: Shifting the Gears of the Antidumping and CVD Laws?', *International Lawyer* (1990), 24, 207.

Bellis, J.-F., Edwin Vermulst, and Phillipe Musquar, 'The New EEC Regulation on Unfair Pricing Practices in Maritime Transport: A Forerunner of the Extension of Unfair Trade Concepts to Services', *Journal of World Trade* (1988), 22 (1), 47.

Bence, Jean-François, 'Analysis of Provincial Transfer Payments to Business in Canada', *International Economic Issues* (April 1990), 25.

Bence, Jean-François, and Murray G. Smith, 'Subsidies and Trade Laws: The Canada–US Dimension', *International Economic Issues* (April 1989), 1.

Bernitz, Ulf, 'The EEC–EFTA Free Trade Agreements with Special Reference to the Position of Sweden and the other Scandinavian EFTA Countries', *Common Market Law Reports* (1986), 23, 567.

Beseler, H.-F., 'EEC Protection Against Dumping and Subsidies from Third Countries', *Common Market Law Reports* (1968–9), 6, 327.

Bhagwati, Jagdish, 'Fair Trade, Reciprocity and Harmonization: The Novel Challenge to the Theory and Policy of Free Trade', (August 1991) mimeo, Columbia University.

Bhaskar, Krish, *The Effect of Different State Aid Measures on Intra-Community Competition: Exemplified by the Case of the Automotive Industry*, (Luxembourg: Office of Official Publications of the European Communities, 1990).

Boddez, Thomas M., and Michael J. Trebilcock, *Unfinished Business*, (Toronto: C.D. Howe Institute, 1993).

Bourgeois, Jaques H.J., 'Introduction: Law and Policy – Cripple Helping Blind?', in Bourgeois, ed., *Subsidies and International Trade: A European Lawyers' Perspective*, (1991).

——, ed., *Subsidies and International Trade: A European Lawyers' Perspective*, (Deventer, Holland: Kluwer Law and Taxation Publishers, 1991).

Brittan, Sir Leon, 'Competition Policy in the Light of the Agreement Creating the European Economic Area', (Walras Conference, Switzerland, 8 November 1991).

——, 'Industry Council – two items on Completion Policy', Note BIO (91), 371, Au Bureau Nationaux (Brussels: 1991).

Bronckers, M., 'Private Remedies Against Foreign Subsidization: A European View', in Bourgeois, ed., *Subsidies and International Trade: A European Lawyers' Perspective*, (1991).

Bronckers, M., and R. Quick, 'What is a Countervailable Subsidy under EEC Trade Law?', *Journal of World Trade* (1989), 23 (6), 5.

Brown, Craig M., '"Bounty or Grant:" A call for Redefinition in Light of the *Zenith* Decision', *Law and Policy in International Business* (1977), 9, 1229.

Bruce, Neil, *Measuring Industrial Subsidies: Some Conceptual Issues*, Working Paper no. 75, (Paris: OECD, Department of Economics and Statistics, 1990).

Buchan, David, 'EC–EFTA near deal on single market', *Financial Times* (15 February 1992).

Burrows, Noreen, 'The second EEA Opinion', *European Law Review* (1993), 18, 63.

Cantin, Frederic P., and Andreas Lowenfeld, 'Rules of Origin, the Canada–US FTA, and the *Honda* Case', *American Journal of International Law* (1993), 87, 375.

Carson, Ian, 'Who's Subsidising Watt?', *Eurobusiness* (April 1991), 22.

Cass, Ronald A., 'Trade Subsidy Law: Can a Foolish Inconsistency be Good Enough for Government Work?', *Law and Policy in International Business* (1990), 21, 609.

Clinton, William J., and Daniel Porter, 'The United States' new Anti-Circumvention Provision and Its Aplication by the Commerce Department', *Journal of World Trade* (1990), 24 (3), 101.

Coffield, Shirley, 'Using Section 301 of the Trade Act of 1974 as a Response to Foreign Government Trade Actions: When, Why and How', *North Carolina Journal of International Law and Commercial Regulation* (1981), 6, 381.

Commission of the European Communities, 'Background Report on GATT Negotiations', (London: 11 March 1991), ISEC/B6/91.

——, *Bulletin of the European Communities* (Luxembourg: Office of Offical Publications of the European Communities, 1991), various issues.

——, *Bulletin of the European Communities (Supplement 4/92), The Challenge of Enlargement: Commission opinion of Austria's application for membership* (Luxembourg: Office of Offical Publications of the European Communities, 1992).

——, *Bulletin of the European Communities (Supplement* 5/92), *The Challenge of Enlargement: Commission opinion of Sweden's application for membership* (Luxembourg: Office of Offical Publications of the European Communities, 1992).

——, *Competition Rules in the EEC and the ECSC Applicable into State Aids*, (Luxembourg: Office of Official Publications of the European Communities, 1987).

——, Directorate General for Economic and Financial Affairs, *European Economy no. 48: Fair Competition in the Internal Market: State Aid*

Policy, (Luxembourg: Office of Official Publications of the European Communities, 1991).

——, Directorate General for Information, *Europe Information – External Relations* no. 61/82.

——, *Eighteenth Report on Competition Policy*, (Luxembourg: Office of Official Publications of the European Communities, 1989).

——, *First Survey on State Aids in the European Community*, (Luxembourg: Office of Official Publications of the European Communities, 1989).

——, *Information*, (22 November 1989).

——, *The Measurement of the Aid Element of State Acquisitions of Company Capital*, (Luxembourg: Office of Official Publications of the European Communities, 1987).

——, 'Ministerial Dinner between EC and EFTA Ministers: 13 May 91', (Brussels: Note 14 May 1991).

——, *Nineteenth Report on Competition Policy*, (Luxembourg: Office of Official Publications of the European Communities, 1990).

——, *Ninth Annual Report of the Commission on the Community's Anti-Dumping And Anti-Subsidy Activity* (1990).

——, 'Report on United States Trade Barriers and Unfair Practices 1991', (Services of the Commission of the European Communities), (1992).

——, *Second Survey on State Aids in the European Community in the Manufacturing and Certain Other Sectors*, (Luxembourg: Office of Official Publication of the European Communities, 1990).

——, *Third Survey on State Aids in the European Community in the Manufacturing and Certain Other Sectors*, (Luxembourg: Office of Official Publication of the European Communities, 1992).

——, 'Uruguay Round: Etat de la Situation à l'Issue de la Conference Ministerielle de Bruxelles', (Comité 113 Réunion 11 January 91).

——, *XXth Report on Competition Policy*, (Luxembourg: Office of Official Publications of the European Communities, 1991).

——, *XXIst Report on Competition Policy*, (Luxembourg: Office of Official Publications of the European Communities, 1992).

——, *XXIInd Report on Competition Policy*, (Luxembourg: Office of Official Publications of the European Communities, 1993).

Committee on Ways and Means, United States House of Representatives, *Report no. 317, 96th Congress, 1st Session, on Trade Agreements Act of 1979*, (Washington, DC: Government Printing Office, 1979).

Corbet, Hugh, and David Robertson, *Europe's Free Trade Area Experiment: EFTA and Economic Integration*, (Oxford: Pergamon Press, 1970).

Cullen, Robert, 'The True Cost of Coal', *The Atlantic Monthly* (December 1993), 38.

Curzon, Victoria, *The Essentials of Economic Integration: Lessons of EFTA Experience*, (London: Macmillan, 1974).

Curzon Price, Victoria, *Free Trade Areas: The European Experience*, (Toronto: C.D. Howe Institute, 1987).

Dearden, Richard G., and David Palmeter, *Free Trade Law Reports* (Commentaries on Chapter 18 and 19 procedures), (Toronto: CCH Canadian Limited, 1990).

Deardorff, Alan V., and Robert Stern, *Methods of Measurement of Non-Tariff Barriers*, (UNCTAD, 1985).

Delegation of the Commission of the European Communities–Ottawa, *European Community News* (30 October 1991).

——, 'US Government Support to US Commercial Aircraft Industry During the Past 15 Years Exceeds $33 Billion', *European Community News* (16 December 1991).

Depayre, G., and P. Petriccione, 'Definition of Subsidy', in Bourgeois, ed., *Subsidies and International Trade: A European Lawyers' Perspective*, (1991).

Destler, I.M., *American Trade Politics: System Under Stress*, (Washington, DC: Institute for International Economics, 1986).

Diamond, Richard, 'A Search for Economic and Financial Principles in the Administration of United States Countervailing Duty Law', *Law and Policy in International Business* (1990), 21, 507.

——, 'Economic Foundations of Countervailing Duty Law', *Virginia Journal of International Law* (1988–9), 29, 767.

Eales, Roy, 'The Hidden Billions', *Eurobusiness* (April 1989), 38.

Earl, Victor, 'Who Needs It?', *Eurobusiness*, (September 1990), 31.

Eberstadt, George, 'Government Support of the Large Commercial Aircraft Industries of Japan, Europe, and the United States,' prepared for the Office of Technology Assessment, *Competing Economies; America, Europe, and the Pacific Rim* (Washington, DC: Congress of the United States, 1991).

The Economist, 'Coming Together, coming apart'; 'EC Summit: On the eve'; 'Mind over Maastricht', (7 December 1991), v. 321 no. 7736.

——, 'EEC Regional Aid', (15 July 1989), v.312, no. 7611.

——, 'European Economic Area: A short shelf-life'; 'Lest a fortress arise', (26 October 1991), v.321, no. 7730.

——, 'Europe's Dutch Treat'; 'The deal is done'; 'What's in a deal', (14 December 1991), v.321, no. 7737.

——, 'Europe's Trade Policy', (2 September 1989), v.312, no. 7619.

——, 'Unequal Partners', (13 January 1990), v.313, no. 7631.

Ehrenraft, Peter, 'The Treasury's Proposed Approach to Imports from State Control Economy Countries and State-owned Enterprises Under the Antidumping and Countervailing Duty Laws', in Wallace *et al.*, eds, *Interface One*, (1980).

European Free Trade Association, *1984 Twenty Fourth Annual Report of the EFTA*, (Geneva: EFTA, 1985).

——, *1987 Vingt-septième Rapport annuel de l'Association européen de libre-échange*, (Geneva: EFTA, 1988).

——, *1988 Twenty-eighth Annual Report of the EFTA*, (Geneva: EFTA, 1989).

——, *1989 Twenty-ninth Annual Report of the EFTA*, (Geneva: EFTA, 1990).

——, Economic Committee, Working Party on Government Aids, *Final Report*, (Geneva: EFTA, 1986).

——, 'The EEA Agreement', (Pamphlet), (Geneva: EFTA Secretariat, January 1992).

——, 'The EEA Agreement', *EFTA Bulletin* (July-December 1991), 32 (3–4), 1.

——, 'EFTA Agreement on Goverment Aid', *EFTA Bulletin* (Octover 1968), 9 (7), 17.

——, *Government Aid in 1988: Annual Report by Secretariat*, (Geneva: EFTA, 1989).

——, *Regional Development Policies in EFTA*, (Geneva: EFTA, 1968).

——, *State Aid in EFTA in 1990: Fifth Annual Report by the Secretariat*, (Geneva: EFTA, 28 January 1992).

Ems, Emil, 'Tendency in EFTA Countries: Government Aid Decreasing', *EFTA Bulletin* (June 1990), 31 (2), 18.

Eskridge, William N., Jr., 'Dynamic Interpretation of Economic Regulatory Legislation (Countervailing Duty Law)', *Law and Policy in International Business*. (1990), 21, 663.

European Communties' Spokesman's Service, IP(91), (22 May 1991), no. 451: (27 November 1991), nos 1043, 1044, 1045, 1048.

European Parliament News, 'Delight over EFTA Agreement', (October 91).

European Trends, (London: *The Economist* Intelligence Unit, 1990–91).

Evans, Andrew, and Stephen Martin, 'Socially Acceptable Distortion of Competition: Community Policy on State Aid', *European Law Review* (1991) 16 (2), 79.

Fallows, James, 'How the World Works', *The Atlantic Monthly* (December 1993), 60.

Farber, Daniel, and Philip Frickey, *Law and Public Choice: A Critical Introduction*, (Chicago: The University of Chicago Press, 1991).

Feenstra, Robert C., ed., *Trade Policies for International Competitiveness*, (Chicago: The University of Chicago Press, 1989).

Feller, Peter Buck, 'Preface: Observations on the New Countervailing Duty Law', *Law and Policy in International Business*. (1979), 11, 1439.

Committee on Finance, United States Senate, *Report of the Committee on Finance on Trade Agreements Act, 1979*, Report no. 249, 96th Congress, 1st Session, (1979).

Finger, J. Michael, and Tracy Murray, 'Policing Unfair Imports: The United States Example', *Journal of World Trade* (1990), 24 (4), 39.

Finger, J. Michael, and Julio Nogués, 'International Control of Subsidies and Countervailing Duties', *The World Bank Economic Review* (1987) 1 (4), 707.

Ford, Robert, and Wim Suyker, *Industrial Subsidies in the OECD Economies*, Working Paper no. 74, (Paris: OECD, Dept. of Economics and Statistics, 1990).

Fry, Earl H., 'The Economic Development Policies of US State and Local Government: Implications for the Canada–US Free Trade Agreement', *International Economic Issues*, (April 1990), 41.

Gaisford, James D., and Donald L. McLachlan, 'Domestic Subsidies and Countervail: The Treacherous Ground of the Level Playing Field', *Journal of World Trade* (1990), 24 (4), 55.

Gardener, E.P.M., 'The European Free Trade Association and the European Community', *International Lawyer* (1991), 25, 187.

Globerman, Steven, and Michael Walker, *Assessing NAFTA: A Trinational Analysis* (Vancouver: The Fraser Institute, 1992).

Goetz, Charles J., Lloyd Granet, and Warren Schwartz, 'The Meaning of 'Subsidy' and 'Injury' in the Countervailing Duty Law', *International Review of Law and Economics* (1986), 6, 17.

Greenwald, J.D., 'US Law and Practice', in Bourgeois, ed., *Subsidies and International Trade: A European Lawyers' Perspective* (1991).

Grey, Rodney de C., 'Some Notes on Subsidies and the International Rules', in Wallace *et al.*, eds, *Interface Three*, (1984).

Griffin, Ronald, 'The European Dream Come True: What Will Become of American Business (Boeing) After EEC '92', *Northern Kentucky Law Review* (1991), 18, 431.

Guido, Robert, and Michael Monone, 'The Michelin Decision: A Possible New Direction for U.S. Countervailing Duty Law', *Law and Policy in International Business* (1974), 6, 237.

Halberstam, David, *The Best and the Brightest*, (New York: Penguin, 1969).

Hart, Michael, *The Canada–US Working Group on Subsidies: Problem, Opportunity or Solution?*, (Ottawa: Centre for Trade Policy and Law, 1990).

Hemmendinger, Noel, and William Baninger, 'The Defense of Antidumping and Countervailing Duty Investigations under the Trade Agreements Act of 1979', *North Carolina Journal of International Law and Commercial Regulation* (1980–81), 6, 427.

Hindley, Brian, 'Subsidies, Politics and Economics', in Wallace *et al.*, eds, *Interface Three*, (1984).

Horlick, Gary N., Judith Bello, and Michael Levine, 'The Countervailability of Subsidies: Specificity', in Applebaum and Victor, eds, *United States Import Relief Laws*, (1985).

Hudec, Robert, 'GATT Dispute Settlement After the Tokyo Round: An Unfinished Business', *Cornell International Law Journal* (1980). 13, 145.

——, 'Regulation of Domestic Subsidies under the MTN Subsidies Code', in Wallace, *et al.*, eds, *Interface Three*, (1984).

——, '"Mirror, Mirror on the Wall" The Concept of Fairness in United States Trade Policy', paper presented at the 1990 annual meeting of the Canadian Council of International Law, Ottawa, (19 October, 1990).

Hufbauer, Gary Clyde, 'Procedures for Monitoring and Disciplining Government Aids,' EFTA Economic Affairs Dept. Occasional Paper no. 30, (Geneva: EFTA, 1989).

——, 'Subsidies,' in Schott, ed., *Completing the Uruguay Round*, (1990).

Hufbauer, Gary Clyde, and Joanna Shelton Erb, *Subsidies in International Trade*, (Cambridge: MIT Press, 1984).

International Trade Administration, US Department of Commerce, *A Comparative Assessment of the US General Aviation Aircraft Industry*, (Washington, DC: 1986).

Jackson, John H., 'United States Policy Regarding Disruptive Imports from State Trading Countries or Government-owned Enterprises,' in Wallace *et al.*, eds, *Interface One*, (1980).

——, *The World Trading System*, (Cambridge: MIT Press, 1989).

——, 'Perspectives on Countervailing Duties', *Law and Policy in International Business*. (1990), 21, 739.

Johns, R.A., *International Trade Theories and the Evolving International Econonmy*, (London: Frances Pinter Publishers, 1985).

——, *Subsidy and Subsidylike Programs of the US Government*, (Washington D.C.: US Goverment Printing Office, 1960).

Joint Economic Committee – Sub-committee on Priorities and Economy in Government, US Congress, *Federal Subsidy Programs*, (Washington, DC: US Government Printing Office, 1974).

Jones, Ronald W., and Peter B. Kenen, eds, *Handbook of International Economics*, (Amsterdam: North Holland, 1984).

Kalt, Joseph, 'The Political Economy of Protectionism: Tariffs and Retaliation in the Timber Industry', in Baldwin, ed., *Trade Policy Issues and Empirical Analysis*, (1988).

Kaplan, Gilbert, Susan Hagerty Kuhbach and Ronald Lorentzen, 'Antidumping, Countervailing Duty, and National Security Provisions in the 1988 Trade Act', *George Washington Journal of International Law and Economics* (1989), 22, 553.

Katz, Lawrence, and Lawrence H. Summers, 'Can Interindustry Wage Differentials Justify Strategic Trade Policy?', in Feenstra, ed., *Trade Policies for International Competitiveness*, (1989).

de Kieffer, Donald E., 'When, Why, and How to Bring a Countervailing Duty Proceeding: A Complainant's Perspective', *North Carolina Journal of International Law and Commercial Regulation* (1980–1), 6, 363.

Knox, Francis, *Towards 1992: State Aids to Industry*, (London: Trade and Tariffs Research, 1989).

Komoroski, Kenneth, 'The Failure of Governments to Regulate Industry: A Subsidy under the GATT?', *Houston Journal of International Law* (1988), 10, 189.

Koteen, Lisa B., 'GATT Dispute Settlement of Anti-Dumping and Countervailing Duty Cases: A Primer', in Willkie, ed., *The Commerce Department Speaks 1990*, (1990).

Kravis, Irving B., *Domestic Interests and International Obligations*, (Philadelphia: University of Pennsylvania Press, 1963).

Krueger, Anne O., 'The Political Economy of the Rent-Seeking Society', *The American Economic Review* (1974), 64, 291.

Kuttner, Robert, 'Clinton Is Wrong to Launch His Missiles at Airbus', the *International Herald Tribune*, (26 February 1993).

Lanner, James, 'Aspects of Regional Policy in EFTA', *EFTA Bulletin* (1984), 25 (2) 13.

——, *The Problems of the Textiles and Clothing Industries in the EFTA Countries*, (Geneva: EFTA Occasional Paper no. 2, no date).

Laursen, Finn, 'The EC and its European Neighbours: Special Partnerships or Widened Membership?', *International Journal* (Winter 1991–92), 47, 29.

Leamer, Edward, *Sources of International Comparative Advantage – Theory and Evidence*, (Cambridge: MIT Press, 1984).

Lorentzen, Ronald, 'Antidumping and Countervailing Duty Issues in the Uruguay Round of Multilateral Trade Negotiations', in Willkie, ed., *The Commerce Department Speaks 1990*, (1990).

Lowenfeld, Andreas, 'Fair or Unfair Trade: Does it Matter?', *Cornell International Law Journal* (1980), 13, 205.

Macey, 'The Theory of the Firm and the Theory of Market Exchange', *Cornell Law Review* (1988), 74, 43.

Malkin, Lawrence, 'Airbus Flap: Washington Says What It Wants', the *International Herald Tribune*, (24 February 1993).

Malmgren, Harald, *International Order for Public Subsidies*, (London: Trade Policy Research Centre, 1977).

Malmrose, Roy, A., 'Interest Rate Benchmarks in Countervailing Duty Proceedings', in Willkie, ed., *The Commerce Department Speaks 1990*, (1990).

Manchester, William, *The Last Lion – Visions of Glory*, (New York: Dell Publishing Inc., 1983).

Marcuss, Stanley, 'Understanding Direct and Indirect Subsidies: Are the Problems Negotiable or Incurable?', in Wallace *et al.*, eds, *Interface Three*, (1984).

Mauer, Laurence Jay, and A.J.W. van de Gevel, 'Non-tariff Distortions in International Trade: A Methodological Review', in Scaperlanda, Anthony, ed., *Prospects for Eliminating Non-tariff Distortions*, (Leiden: A.W. Sijthoff, 1973).

McLean, Iain, *Public Choice: An Introduction* (Oxford: Basil Blackwell Ltd, 1987.

Michel, Ann A., Larry I. Good, Terry Bolger, Ellen Sweet, W.M. Taylor and Andrew R. Moroz, *An Annotated Inventory of Federal Business Subsidy Programs in the United States*, (Ottawa: Institute for Research on Public Policy Discussion Paper 8701, 1987).

Middleton, Robert, *Negotiating on Non-tariff Distortions of Trade: The EFTA Precedent*, (London: The Macmillan Press Ltd., 1975).

Morgenthau, Hans, and Kenneth Thomson, *Politics among Nations: The Struggle for Power and Peace* 6th edn, (New York: Alfred Knopf, 1985).

Morris, James, *Heaven's Command*, (London: Penguin, 1973).

Morton, Colleen S., *Subsidies Negotiations and the Politics of Trade*, (Washington, DC: National Planning Association, 1989).

Morton, Peter, '"Options to fight US are limited"', *The Financial Post* (11 March 1992), 1.

——, 'US seeks to rewrite pact, group says', *The Financial Post* (7 April 1992), 3.

——, 'US senators propose softwood lumber deal', *The Financial Post* (7 April 1992), 1.

——, 'US wood and wine targets for trade probe', *The Financial Post* (12 March 1992), 3.

Mueller, Dennis, *Public Choice* II, (Cambridge: Cambridge University Press, 1989).

Mundheim, Robert, and Peter Ehrenraft, 'What is a "Subsidy"? A Discussion Paper', in Wallace, *et al.*, eds, *Interface Three* (1984).

National Revenue – Customs and Excise, *Customs Notice*, (no date).

National Revenue, *Introduction to Subsidies and Guidelines on Identification of Subsidies*, (Departmental Manual), (no date).

Organization for Economic Cooperation and Development (OECD),

Internationalisation of Industrial Activities: Case Study of the Aerospace Industry, (Paris: 10 January 1990).

OECD, *The Role of Indicators in Structural Surveillance*, Working Paper no. 72, (Paris: OECD, Dept. of Economics and Statistics, 1990).

Patience, Allan, *The Bjelke-Petersen Premiership* (Malaysia: Longman Cheshire, 1985).

Pedersen, Thomas, 'Community Attitudes and Interests', in Wallace, ed., *The Wider Western Europe: Reshaping the EC/EFTA Relationship*, (1991).

Pescatore, Pierre, William Davey, and Andreas Lowenfeld, *Handbook of GATT Dispute Settlement*, (Ardsley-on-Hudson: Transnational Juris Publications, Inc., 1991).

Pono, Giuseppe, 'Government Aids: The Rules in EFTA, the EC and GATT', *EFTA Bulletin* (1982), 23 (4), 13.

Porter, Michael E., *The Competitive Advantage of Nations*, (New York: The Free Press, 1990).

Posner, R., and William Landes, 'The Independent Judiciary in an Interest-Group Perspective', *Journal of Law and Economics* (1975), 18, 371.

Powell, Stephen, J., and John D. McInerney, 'Globalization of the Production Forces and the Unfair Trade Laws,' in Willkie, ed., *The Commerce Department Speaks 1990*, (1990).

Rekola, Esko, 'Subsidies as a Barrier to Foreign Trade', *EFTA Bulletin* (1982), 23 (1), 17.

Report from Brussels, 'EC, EFTA and the European Economic Area', (November 1991).

Reynolds, Alan, *The Political Economy of a North American Free Trade Agreement*, (Vancouver: The Hudson Institute and The Fraser Institute, 1993).

Rivers, Richard, and John Greenwald, 'The Negotiation of a Code on Subsidies and Countervailing Measures: Bridging Fundamental Policy Differences', *Law and Policy in International Business* (1979), 11, 1447.

Romoli, A., and Ch. Pelletier, *Information Report of the Section for External Relations, Trade and Development Policy on the Resumption of the GATT/Uruguay Round Negotiations, 13.6.1991*, (Brussels: EC–Economic & Social Committee, 1991).

Rugman, Alan, 'The Softwood Lumber Decision of 1986: Broadening the Nature of U.S. Administered Protection,' *Review of International Business Law* (1987), 2, 35.

Rugman, Alan, and Samuel Porteus, *Canadian Unfair Trade Laws and Corporate Strategy*, (Toronto: Ontario Centre for International Business Working Paper no. 8, 1988).

Scaperlanda, Anthony, ed., *Prospects for Eliminating Non-tariff Distortions*, (Leiden: A.W. Sijthoff, 1973).

Schelling, T.C., 'The Diplomacy of Violence' in Art and Jervis, eds, *International Politics*, (1985).

Schott, Jeffrey J., ed., *Completing the Uruguay Round*, (Washington, DC: Institute for International Economics, 1990).

Schreiner, John, 'Canada Vows to Fight US Lumber Industry', *The Financial Post* (9 March 1992), 3.

Schrybman, Steven, Conference on NAFTA, (Toronto, 23–25 June 1993).

Schwartz, Warren, and Eugene Harper, 'The Regulation of Subsidies Affecting International Trade', *Michigan Law Review* (1972), 70, 831.

Segal Quince Wicksteed Ltd., *Aid Element of Government R & D Contracts*, (Luxembourg: Office of Official Publications of the European Communities, 1990).

Simmonds, Kenneth, and Brian H.W. Hill, *Law and Practice under the GATT*, (New York: Oceana Publications, 1991).

Smith, Margaret, *Subsidies and United States Trade Law: The Application to Canada*, (Ottawa: Law and Government Division Research Branch, Library of Parliament, 1989).

Smith, Murray G., 'Overview of Provincial and State Subsidies: Their Implications for Canada–US Trade', *International Economic Issues* (April 1990), 1.

Spencer, Barbara, 'Countervailing Duty Laws and Subsidies to Imperfectly Competitive Industries', in Baldwin *et al.*, eds, *Issues in US–EC Trade Relations*, (1988).

Steenbergen, Jacque, 'Regulation of Subsidies in International Trade', in Bourgeois, ed., *Subsidies and International Trade: A European Lawyers' Perspective*, (1991).

——, Guido De Clercq, and René Foqué, *Change and Adjustment*, (Deventer: Kluwer Law and Taxation Publishers, 1983).

Sykes, Alan O., 'Countervailing Duty Law: An Economic Perspective', paper presented for the Law and Economics Workshop Series, (Toronto: Faculty of Law, University of Toronto, 1989).

——, 'Second-best Countervailing Duty Policy: A Critique of the Entitlement Approach', *Law and Policy in International Business.* (1990), 21, 699.

Thomas, Jeffrey, *Subsidies and Countervailing Duties in the Canada–US Free Trade Agreement: Trends, Critiques and Proposals for Rational Reform*, (Toronto: Faculty of Law, University of Toronto, 1989).

Tougas, Frances, 'Softwood Lumber From Canada: Natural Resources and the Search for a Definition of Countervailable Domestic Subsidy', *Gonzaga Law Review* (1988–9), 24, 135.

Trebilcock, M.J., 'Is the Game Worth the Candle', *Law and Policy in International Business.* (1990), 21, 723.

——, 'Throwing Deep: Trade Remedy Laws in a First-Best World', with comments by Michael M. Hart, 'Idealism v. Pragmatism,' and Jonathan Fried, 'The Art of the Possible: A Comment', in Trebilcock and York, eds, *Fair Exchange: Reforming Trade Remedy Laws*, (1990).

——, 'The Future of the World Trading Regime: Multilateralism or Regionalism? Fair Trade or Free Trade?' Working Paper no. 42, The Ontario Centre for International Business, (Toronto: Faculty of Law, University of Toronto, 1992).

Trebilcock, M.J., and Robert C. York, eds, *Fair Exchange: Reforming Trade Remedy Laws*, (Toronto: C.D. Howe Institute Policy Study 11, 1990).

Trebilcock, Michael J., Douglas Hartle, Robert Prichard and Donald Dewees, *The Choice of Governing Instrument*, (Ottawa: Economic Council of Canada, 1982).

Trebilcock, M.J., R. Howse, and M. Chandler, *Trade and Transition*, (London: Routledge, 1990).

Torremans, Paul, 'Anti-circumvention Duties after the Screwdriver Panel Report', *European Law Review* (1993), 18, 288.

Toulin, Alan, and Laura Fowlie, 'Ottawa Won't Bow to US Lumber Offer', *The Financial Post*, (8 April 1992), 3.

Tuchman, Barbara, *The March of Folly*, (New York: Ballantine Books, 1984).

United States International Trade Commission, *Global Competitiveness of US Advanced-Technology Manufacturing Industries: Large Civil Aircraft*, Publication 2667, (Washington, DC: USITC, 1993).

'US, EC Finalize Controversial Accord Limiting Aircraft Subsidies, Officials Say', *International Trade Reporter* (1992), 9, 826.

'US Tactics demand strong rebuke', Editorial, *The Financial Post*, (9 March 1992), S-1.

'US wants it all its own way', Editorial, *The Financial Post*, (8 April 1992), 10.

Vernon, Raymond, and Debora Spar, *Beyond Globalism: Remaking American Foreign Economic Policy*, (New York: The Free Press, 1989).

Verrill, Charles O., Jr., 'State-owned Enterprises and the Countervailing Duty Law: Where, Oh, Where to Draw the Line', in Wallace *et al.*, eds, *Interface Three*, (1984).

Victor, A. Paul and Michelle S. Benjamin, 'Major Decisions of the Court of International Trade and the Court of Appeals for the Federal Circuit', in Applebaum and Victor, eds, *United States Import Relief Laws*, (1985).

Völker, E.M., *Protectionism and the European Community*, (Deventer: Kluwer Law and Taxation Publishers, 1987).

Wahl, Nils, *The Free Trade Agreements Between the EC and EFTA Countries*, (Stockholm: Institute for Intellectual Property and Market Law, 1988).

Wallace, Don, George C. Spina, Richard M. Rawson, and Brian McGill, eds, *Interface One*, (Washington, DC: Insitute for International and Foreign Trade Law, 1980).

Wallace, Don, Frank J. Loftus, and Van Krikorian, eds, *Interface Three: Legal Treatment of Domestic Subsidies*, (Washington, DC: International Law Institute, 1984).

Wallace, Helen, ed., *The Wider Western Europe: Reshaping the EC/EFTA Relationship*, (London: Frances Pinter Publishers, 1991).

Walther, R., 'Comment', in Bourgeois, ed., *Subsidies and International Trade: A European Lawyers' Perspective*, (1991).

Weiss, Freidl, 'The European Free Trade Association after Twenty-five years', *Yearbook of European Law* (1985), 5, 287.

——, 'EC–EFTA Relations: Towards a Treaty Creating a European Economic Space,' *Yearbook of European Law* (1989), 9, 329.

——, 'The Legal Issues', in Wallace, ed., *The Wider Western Europe: Reshaping the EC/EFTA Relationship*, (1991).

Wieser, Thomas, 'Government Aids to Industry in EFTA', *EFTA Bulletin* (1987), 28 (2), 13.

Willkie, Wendell L., II, ed., *The Commerce Department Speaks 1990: The*

Legal Aspects of International Trade, (Washington, DC: Practicing Law Institute, 1990).

Wilson, James Q., *American Government*, (Lexington: D.C. Heath and Company, 1983).

Winham, Gil, Conference on NAFTA, Toronto, (23–25 June 1993).

Yi, Seong Deog, and Chong Ju Choi, 'The Community's Unfair Pricing Practices in the Maritime Transport Sector', *European Law Rev* (1991), 14, 279.

York, Robert C., 'A Level Playing Field: Toward a Canada–US Trade Law', in Trebilcock and York, eds, *Fair Exchange: Reforming Trade Remedy Laws*, (1990).

Interviews

Ron Walker (Senior Policy Analyst, Department of National Revenue) and Susan Spencer (International Economic Relations Division, Department of Finance), at the Department of National Revenue, (19 February 1992).

Authorities

Austria–EC Free Trade Agreement, (1972) OJ L300.

Ball Bearings from Thailand, Commission Decision 90/266/EEC, (1990) OJ L152/59.

Cabot Corp. v. United States, 620 F. Supp. 722, (Ct. Intl Trade 1985)(US).

Canada–US Free Trade Agreement, (Ottawa: Ministry of Supplies and Services, 1988).

Carbon Black from Mexico, Fed Reg (1986), 51, 13269 (Preferentiality Appendix)(US).

Certain Steel Products from Belgium, Fed Reg (1982), 47, 39304 (Methodology Appendix no. 2)(US).

Certain Softwood Lumber Products from Canada (*Softwood* I), Fed Reg (1983), 48, 24159 (US).

Certain Softwood Lumber Products from Canada (*Softwood* II), Fed Reg (1986), 51, 37543 (US).

Certain Softwood Lumber Products from Canada (*Softwood Lumber* III) Fed Reg (28 May 1992), 57, 22570 (US).

Certain Softwood Lumber Products from Canada (*Softwood Lumber* IV) (USA-92–1904–01)(Canada–US FTA), (1993).

Certain Softwood Lumber Products from Canada (*Softwood Lumber* V) (USA-92–1904–01), Redetermination by the USITA pursuant to Remand, (10 September 1993).

Certain Softwood Lumber Products from Canada (*Softwood Lumber* VI) (USA-92–1904–01), Re-remand by the binational panel, (17 December 1993).

Cold Rolled Sheet, (NQ-92–009)(Canada), (15 June 1993).

Cold Rolled Carbon Steel Flat-Rolled Products from Argentina, Fed Reg (1984), 49, 18006 (Methodology Appendix)(US).

European Communities, Commission Regulation no. 2423/88 on Countervailing Duties on Third Country Subsidised Products, (1988) OJ L209/1.

——, Commission Decision no. 91/500/EEC, (1991) OJ L262/29.

Finland–EC Free Trade Agreement, (1973) OJ L328.

Fresh Chilled or Frozen Pork from Canada (ECC-91-1904-01 USA) (Canada–US FTA), (1991).

General Agreement on Tariffs and Trade, 61 Stat. A3, TIAS No. 1700, 55 *United Nations Treaty Series*, (1947), 187.

General Agreement on Tariffs and Trade, Agreement Establishing the Multilateral (World) Trade Organization, MTN/FA II, (15 December 1993).

——, Agreement on Interpretation and Application of Articles VI, XVI and XXIII of the General Agreement on Tariffs and Trade (The Subsidies Code), 1186 *United Nations Treaty Series*, 204, GATT BISD 26th Supp. 56 (1978–9).

——, Agreement on Subsidies and Countervailing Measures, MTN/FA II/13, (15 December 1993).

——, Chairman of the Trade Negotiations Committee at Official Level, 'Stocktaking of the Uruguay Round', (Geneva: GATT Secretariat MTN.TNC/W/89, 1989).

——, Negotiating Group on Subsidies and Countervailing Measures, 'Communications from Canada: Framework for Negotiations', (Geneva: GATT Secretariat UR-89–0117, 1989).

——, Understanding on Rules and Procedures Governing the Settlement of Disputes, MTN/FA II-A2, (15 December 1993).

High Strength and Low Alloy Plate (NQ-92–007)(Canada), (21 May 1993).

Hot Rolled Sheet (NQ-92–008)(Canada), (15 June 1993).

Hyundai Shipping, Council Regulation no. 15/89, (1989) OJ L4/1.

Iceland–EC Free Trade Agreement, (1972) OJ L301.

Industrial Phosphoric Acid from Belgium, Fed Reg (1986), 51, 43761 (US).

Leather from Argentina, Fed Reg (1990), 50, 40212 (US).

Kupferberg (Case 104/81) European Community Reports (1982), 3641.

Live Swine from Canada (ECC-93–1904–01 USA)(Canada–US FTA), (1993).

Machine Tufted Carpets Originating in or Exported from the United States (CDA-92–1904–02)(Canada–US FTA), (1993).

North American Free Trade Agreement (Ottawa: Minister of Supply and Services, Canada, 1992).

Norway–EC Free Trade Agreement, (1973) OJ L171.

Oil Country Tubular Goods from Canada, Fed Reg (1986), 51, 15037 (US).

Opinion Regarding The Draft Agreement between the European Community and the European Free Trade Association Relating to the Creation of the European Economic Area, International Legal Materials (1992), 21, 442 (Court of Justice of the European Communities).

PPG Industries v. United States 928 F.2d 1568 (USCA, 1991) (*PPG* III)(US).

Proposal for a Council Decision on the Conclusion of the Agreement on the European Economic Area between the European Communities, their Member States, and [Member States of the EFTA], SEC (92) 814 Final, (28 April 1992).

Proposed Rulemaking, Fed Reg (1989), 54, 23366; 19 *CFR* 355.42–65 (US).

Pure and Alloy Magnesium from Canada, (USA-92–1904–03)(Canada–US FTA), Review of redetermination on remand, (14 December 1993).
Regulation on Unfair Pricing Practices in Maritime Transport, Council Regulation no. 4057/86, (1986) OJ L378/14.
Roses Inc. v. United States 743 F.Supp. 870 (CIT, 1990) (*Roses* I)(US).
Roses Inc. v. United States 774 F.Supp. 1376 (CIT, 1991) (*Roses* II)(US).
Special Import Measures Act, S.C. (1984), c.25 as am.
Special Import Measures Regulations, SOR/84–927, (22 November 1984).
Steel Bars from Brazil, Commission Decision 80/552/EEC, (1980) OJ L139/30.
Sweden–EC Free Trade Agreement, (1972) OJ L300.
Switzerland–EC Free Trade Agreement, (1972) OJ L300.
Trade Agreements Act of 1979, Pub. L. No. 96–39, tit. 1, 93 Stat. 144 (1979) (codified as amended at *19 USC* §§ 1671–1677g (1988)(US).
Treaty Establishing the European Free Trade Association, *United Nations Treaty Series* (1960), 1.
Treaty on European Union, Agence Europe no. 1759/60, (7 February 1992).
Treaty of Rome, in Belford, J., *The European Community: The Single Market*, (New York: Oceana Publications, 1989) at I.A.
Turkish Polyester Fibres and Yarns, Council Regulation no. 2834/91, (1991) OJ L272/3.
Zenith Radio Corp. v. United States, 437 US 443, (USSC, 1978).

INDEX

actionable (countervailable) subsidies 134, 136, 137; dispute settlement on 144; in framework of Uruguay Round 139–40

Adams case (Switzerland) 69

adjudication: in international trade 154; in multilateral trade negotiations 79–80

Agreement on Subsidies and Countervailing Measures 5, 6, 133–4, 136–50

agriculture, state aid in EU 92

Airbus 152; and Boeing, case study 30–2; derogations in EU 88–9; state aid by EU 93

aircraft production, subsidies in 30–2, 152

Anderson, A. 105, 108, 125

Appellate Body, dispute settlements (Uruguay Round) 142, 149

arbitration, in EEA 75

Austria 67

Automobile industry, state aid in EU 92

aviation industry in EU: derogations in 88–9; as 'matter of interest' 91; state aid for 92

Baldwin, R. 30–2

Ballbearings from Thailand report 101

Barceló, J.J. III 18, 27

Barnes, C. 32

benefits: frustration of, EFTA 60–1; to industry, Uruguay Round of MTN 139

Bhagwati, J. 15

'Big Business': and Canada–US free trade agreement 38

bilateralism in trade negotiations 78–80

Boeing *see* Airbus–Boeing war

Bourgeois, J.H.J. 102

Brazil 116; IPI tax exemptions 102

British Aluminium Smelter case 64, 65

Brittan, Sir Leon 93

Brown, C.M. 107

Cabot Corp. case 110, 127

Canada: communication to Uruguay Round of MTN 134–5; exporters, problems of 3–4; on US use of CVDs 133, 146

Canada–US Free Trade Agreement 7, 38, 48, 105–29; chapter 18 procedures 121–2; chapter 19 procedures 118–21; CVD law, Canada 113–18; CVD law, USA 105–13; potential for harassment 125–6; potential for judicial abuse 126–8; potential for legislative abuse 128–9

Canada–US Trade Commission 121

Canadian countervailing duty (CVD) law 113–18; analysis of law 116–18; case law in 116; institutional aspects 113–14; legal differences with USA 116;

practical differences with USA 115; substance of 115
Canadian International Trade Tribunal (CITT) 113–14, 116
Cantin, F.P. 7
capital, free movement of: in classical free trade theory 8–9
Cass, R.A. 108
Chandler, M. 59
chapter 18 procedures, Canada–US Free Trade Agreement 121–2; commission for 121; panels for 122
chapter 19 procedures, Canada–US Free Trade Agreement 118–21; binational panels 119–20, 123; *per se* exclusion rule 120–1
Choi, C.J. 103
classical free trade theory 8–10; analysis 22–4; comparative advantage 9; comparative advantage, modified in 18–20; competitive advantage 20–2; critique of 15–24, 151; imperfect markets in 16–18
Clinton, Bill (US president) 4
coal industry, state aid in EU 92, 93
Commerce, Department of (USA) 108–9
Commission of the European Union 5; and EC–EFTA FTAs 69; and EEA 82–3; on imperfect competition 17; state aid policy 86–8, 92, 95; subsidies, defined 84–5
Committee on Subsidies and Countervailing Measures (GATT) 53, 143, 150
comparative advantage: in classical free trade theory 9, 18–20; in Uruguay Round of MTN 137
competitive advantage: and shipbuilding 21–2; and state aid in EEA 73
conceptual frameworks on subsidies: EFTA 57–9; European Union 84–6; GATT Subsidies Code Track II 51–2
conciliation in GATT Track II 53
consultation: in Canada–US FTA 120; in GATT Track II 53; in Uruguay Round 140
consumer demand: and comparative advantage 19; in imperfect markets 16
countervailing duty (CVD) 97–8; amount of (Uruguay Round) 145–6; criteria for (GATT) 98; and EC-EFTA FTAs 69–70; and GATT Code Track I 98–9; imposition of in EU 101; imposition of (Uruguay Round) 146; regulations of EU 99–104; Subsidies Group (Uruguay Round) 135; in Uruguay Round of GATT 145–6; US law on 105–13
Court of International Trade (CIT, USA) 108, 110, 114, 119, 127
Court of Justice of the European Union (ECJ) 71, 72, 73, 75, 79; and supranationalism 81, 83
Curzon Price, V. 60, 64, 66, 70–1

Dearden, R.G. 120, 122
defence procurement programmes (USA) 19–20, 31
Defense, Department of (USA) 31
Denmark: and EC-EFTA FTAs 69
derogations in European Union 88–91; 'matters of interest to the community' 91; regional aid schemes 89–90
Diamond, R. 107
dispute resolution mechanisms (DRM): in EEA 77; in EFTA 61; evaluation in Canada–US FTA 123–9; GATT Track I as 51, 99; potential for harassment 125–6; potential for judicial abuse 126–8; potential for legislative abuse 128–9
Dispute Settlement Body (Uruguay Round) 141, 149
dispute settlements: and agreement on subsidies 143–4; Appellate Body 142; bodies specific to agreement 143; consultations in

140–1; DSB in 141; by EEA 82; elements of (Uruguay Round) 140–3; in GATT Track II 53–4; panels for 141–2; recommendations and rulings in 142–3; by Subsidies Group (Uruguay Round) 136; by supranational agents 81

EC–EFTA Free Trade Agreements 48, 155; analysis 71; and EEA 67, 68–71; institutional framework 70–1; regulatory framework 69–70
economic strategy: and subsidies 28–32
EEA Court 82–3
EEA Court of First Instance 82
EFTA Court 74, 75, 76
EFTA Standing Committee 74
EFTA Surveillance Authority (ESA) 73–4, 76; and supranationalism 82, 95
Ehrenraft, P. 23
electronics, state aid in EU 92
Euratom 48
European Coal and Steel Community (ECSC) 47–8, 57
European Community: and GATT Track II 55; *see also* EC–EFTA Trade Agreements
European Economic Area (EEA) 57, 66; EFTA Surveillance Authority (ESA) in 73–4, 76; evaluation of 76–8; false start of 82–4; institutional framework 72–4; Joint Committee 75; regulatory framework 72–3; and subsidy regulation 67–78
European Economic Community (EEC) 48
European Free Trade Association (EFTA) 5, 48; conceptual framework on subsidies 57–9; dispute resolution mechanisms (DRMs) in 62–4; evaluation 65–7; failures in 65–6; frustration of benefits 60–1; and GATT complaint procedures 62–4; institutional framework on subsidies 61–4; regulatory framework on subsidies 59–61; subsidy regulation in 56–67; surveillance mechanisms in 65–6; *see also* EC–EFTA Trade Agreements *and entries beginning* EFTA
European Parliament 68, 72
European Union 4, 48; conceptual considerations 84–6; countervailing duty regulations 99–104; derogations 88–91; evaluation 92–5; GATT Subsidies Code Track I 99–104; imposition of countervailing duty 101; institutional framework on subsidies 86–8; interests of 152–3; as model for GATT 154–5; notification procedures 149; regulatory and institutional framework 100–2; report to Uruguay Round of MTN 135–6; state aid in 84–95; unfair practices in maritime transport 102–4; on US use of CVDs 133, 135, 146; *see also* EC–EFTA Trade Agreements
Evans, A. 91–2
Examining Committee of EFTA 63
exchange rates, and imperfect competition 17–18
expert panel on Subsidies and Countervailing Measures (GATT) 53, 143
externalities: in imperfect markets 16–17; of markets in economic management 26–7
Extraordinary Challenge Committee (Canada–US FTA) 119–20, 126

fair trade practices: in EFTA 58–9; and *laissez faire* 23; and subsidies 12–14
Fallows, J. 13
Farber, D. 37, 39–41
Federal Court of Appeal (Canada) 119

Finland: in EU 67; competitive advantage in shipbuilding 22
fisheries, state aid in EU 92
France: state aid in 92
free markets: in EFTA 58–9; theory of 23
free trade agreements (FTAs): Canada–US 7, 38, 48; EC–EFTA *see* EC–EFTA Free Trade Agreements; NAFTA *see* North American
free trade *see* classical free trade theory
Frickey, P. 37, 39–41
frustration of benefits, EFTA 60–1

GATT Subsidies Code Track I 51, 98–105; analysis of 104–5; CVD regulations of EU 99–104
GATT Subsidies Code Track II 50–6; conceptual and regulatory framework 51–2; conciliation in 53; consultation in 53; difficulties in 54–5; dispute settlement in 53–4; DRM 54, 149; and EFTA complaint procedures 63–4; evaluation 54–6; institutional framework 52–4; lawsuits in 55; notification in 52–3
General Agreement on Tariffs and Trade (GATT) 6, 47; and Canadian CVD law 117; failures of 153–4; Subsidies Code 47, 109, 117; Tokyo Round 47, 51; Uruguay Round *see* Uruguay Round of MTN; *see also* GATT Subsidies Code Track I & II
Germany: state aid in 92
Great Britain: British Aluminium Smelter case 64, 65; and EC–EFTA FTAs 69; free trade in 9–10; state aid in 92
Greenwald, J. 10, 13
Guido, R. 112

Harper, E. 25
Harris, R. 32
Heckscher, E. 9
Hindley, B. 14, 27
Howse, R. 59
Hudec, R. 13, 15, 26, 55–6, 129
Hufbauer, G.C. 12, 29, 61–2, 64, 108
Hungary: subsidies in 25
Hyundai, maritime transport penalites 103–4

imperfect competition in classical free trade theory 17–18
imperfect information in markets 17
imperfect markets in classical free trade theory 16–18; Airbus–Boeing war case study 30–2; economic management in 26–8; externalities 16–17; and imperfect competition 17–18; subsidies in 24–32
import-substitution 60
institutional framework of Uruguay Round of MTN 140–6
institutional framework on subsidies: Canadian countervailing duty (CVD) law 113–14; EC–EFTA FTAs 61–4; EEA 72–4; EFTA 61–4; European Union 86–8, 100–2; GATT Subsidies Code Track II 52–4; United States countervailing duty (CVD) law 108–9
interest groups and public choice theory 36–7
interests: as motives 151–3; non-economic 151–2; pursuit of in international trade 155–6
international trade, interests governing 152–3
International Trade Administration (ITA, US) 25, 31–2, 59; and CVDs 108–12, 114, 120, 126, 128
International Trade Commission (ITC, US) 106, 109, 112, 128
investment: benefits to industry, Uruguay Round of MTN 139; and classical free trade theory 9;

and comparative advantage 19; strategic objectives of 28–9
Ireland: research and development (R&D) 30
Italy: derogations in EU 89, 90; state aid in 92

Jackson, J.H. 13
Japan: competitive advantage in shipbuilding 22
Johns, R.A. 12, 15, 17, 23, 151
judicial abuse, potential for, Canada–US FTA 126–8

Kalt, J. 112
de Kieffer, D.E. 107, 108
Korea: competitive advantage in shipbuilding 21–2; maritime transport penalites 103–4
Krugman, P. 30–2

labour: in classical free trade theory 8–9
laissez faire theory 15, 23
Lanner, J. 59
lawsuits in GATT Track II 55
Leather from Argentina report 127
legislation and public choice theory 34–5, 40
legislative abuse, potential for, Canada–US FTA 128–9
List, Friedrich 20
Lowenfeld, A. 7
Luxembourg 90

Malmgren, H. 17, 44, 100
manufacturing, state aid in EU 92
manufacturing costs, and subsidies 11
maritime transport, unfair practices in EU 102–4
markets: in free trade theory 23; subsidies as corrective mechanisms in 25–6
Marshall Plan 57
Martin, S. 91–2
McLean, I. 39–40
Messerschmidt–Bölkow–Blohm (MBB) 91
Mexico, in NAFTA 128
Michelin case (USA) 112, 135
Middleton, R. 61
multilateralism in trade negotiations 78–80; failure of 104–5; and national interests 153
Mundheim, R. 23

National Revenue, Department of (MNR, Canada) 113–14, 116, 118
negotiating framework of Uruguay Round of MTN 134–6
Nineteenth Report on Competition Policy (EU) 88
non-actionable subsidies (Uruguay Round) 139; dispute settlement on 144
non-prohibited subsidies 134, 136, 137
North American Free Trade Agreement (NAFTA) 4, 6, 7; and chapter 19 procedures 122–3
Northern Ireland 89
Norway: and EC–EFTA FTAs 69; in EU 67; and British Aluminium Smelter case 64, 65
notification procedures: in Canada–US FTA 120; in EFTA 62; in EU 87–8; in GATT Track II 52–3; Uruguay Round of MTN 147, 149
Nyerges, J. 22–3, 25

Ohlin, B.G. 9
Oil Country Tubular Goods from Canada 111
Olson, M. 34
operating grants in EU 90
Organization for Economic Cooperation and Development (OECD) 56
Organization for European Economic Co-operation (OEEC) 56–7

Palmeter, D. 120, 122
panels: at Appellate Body (Uruguay Round) 142; binational, chapter 19

procedures, Canada–US FTA 119–20, 123; chapter 18 procedures, Canada–US FTA 122; for dispute settlements (Uruguay Round) 141–2; expert, on Subsidies and Countervailing Measures (GATT) 53, 143
Pelkmans, J. 28
Pelletier, Ch. 135
per se exclusion rule, Canada–US FTA 120–1
Permanent Group of Experts (PGE, GATT) 143
Philip Morris case 85
policy-making under GATT 154
political economy of subsidies 32–41; analysis of 38–41; empirical evidence on 36–7; and public choice theory 33–6
pollution, as externality in imperfect markets 16
Pono, G. 59
Pork decision 120, 126, 138
pork-barrelling: and public choice theory 37
Porter, M.E. 19–22, 29, 43, 151
Portugal 65; derogations in EU 89
potential for harassment, Canada–US FTA 125–6
price in imperfect markets 16
product costs, and subsidies 11
production, factors of: in classical free trade theory 9
production aid schemes in EU 90
prohibited subsidies 134, 136, 137; dispute settlement on 143–4; in framework of Uruguay Round 140
protectionism: and public choice theory 38–9; state aid as 86, 93; and subsidies 12; of United States 3–4
public choice theory: empirical evidence on 36–7; in subsidisation 33–6; weaknesses 40–1
pulp and paper industry, state aid in EU 92

quotas: and public choice theory 37

regional aid schemes: in European Union 83, 89–90; in report to Uruguay Round of MTN 135–6, 138; in USA 110
regulatory framework of Uruguay Round of MTN 136–47
regulatory framework on subsidies: EC–EFTA 69–70; EEA 72–3; EFTA 59–61; European Union 100–2; failures of 153; GATT Subsidies Code Track II 51–2
Reich, R. 29
Rekola, E. 58–9
rent-seeking behaviour 34–5, 36–7
research and development (R&D): aid for in EU 91, 93–4; and aircraft production 31–2; in EEA 82; as externality in imperfect markets 16–17; strategic objectives of 28–9
resource allocation: in economic management 26–7; subsidies as distortion of 11–12
Reynolds, A. 37, 39
Ricardo, David 9, 13, 58
Rivers, R. 10, 13
Rome, Treaty of 48, 72, 84, 86, 94; and maritime transport 102
Romoli, A. 90, 110, 135
Rugman, A. 105, 108, 125
Rulemaking proposals (USA) 110–11
rules for competition: in EU 84–5

Scandinavia: competitive advantage in shipbuilding 21–2
Schelling, T.C. 155
Schlozman, K.L. 37
Schwartz, W. 25
Second Survey of State Aids (EU) 88, 91
Shelton Erb, J. 12
shipbuilding industry: competitive advantage in 21–2; state aid in EU 92
Shorts Brothers plc 89

Smith, Adam 9, 13, 58
social policy: in EEA 82; in Europe 84
Softwood Lumber I 110, 125, 138
Softwood Lumber II 111, 112, 125–6, 127
Softwood Lumber III 125, 127
Softwood Lumber IV 125, 126, 127
Softwood Lumber V 125, 126
Softwood Lumber VI 125
Soustelle, J. 57
Special Import Measures Act (SIMA, Canada) 113, 115–17
specificity in Uruguay Round of MTN 137–8
Standards of Review (Canada–US FTA) 119
state aid: differences, Canada & USA 115; EEA, prohibition in 72–3; in EU 84–8; evaluation of in EU 92–5; forms of 59–60; proportionality of in EU 89–90; in Stockholm Convention 57
Stockholm Convention 48; and EFTA 57, 59–61
Structural funds, in EU 90, 93
subsidies: to aircraft production 30–2; defined 10, 101–2, 109; determination under GATT Code Track I 100–1; dispute settlements on 143–4; as distortion of resource allocation 11–12; and EC–EFTA trade 71; in economic management 26–7; effectiveness and meaning 42–4; in imperfect markets 24–32; imposition of countervailing duties 101; investigation under GATT Code Track I 100–1; as market corrective mechanisms 25–6; multilateral regulation of 50–80; and multilateralism in trade negotiations 79–80; and national interests 153; political economy of 32–41; strategic objectives through 28–32; supranational regulation of 81–96; as trade barriers 10–15; traffic light approach to (Uruguay Round) 134, 136; as unfair trade practices 12–15; unilateral regulation of 97–130
Subsidies Code (Uruguay Round) 133, 138; institutional framework 140, 149
Subsidies Group (Uruguay Round) 134; traffic light approach to subsidies 134, 136
substantive framework of Uruguay Round of MTN 137–40
supranationalism 154–5; bureaucracy and 95–6; regulation of 81–96
Supreme Court (USA) 108
surveillance mechanisms: in EEA 82; in EFTA 65–6; in Uruguay Round of MTN 147
Sweden: and EC–EFTA FTAs 67, 71
Switzerland: and EC–EFTA FTAs 69, 71; in EEA 67; research and development (R&D) 30
Sykes, A.O. 12, 25

tariffs: between EC and EFTA 71
Thurow, L. 29
Tierney, J.T. 37
Tokyo Round of Multilateral Trade Negotiations 47, 51, 99
Tougas, F. 117
Trade Act (USA, 1988) 106
Trade Agreements Act (USA, 1979) 106
trade barriers: subsidies as 10–15
trade liberalization, in Europe 69
trade wars, risks of 79
transport, state aid in EU 92
Trebilcock, M.J. 24, 28, 35, 38, 42, 56, 59, 112

unfair trade practices: Canada and US 118; maritime transport, EU 102–4; subsidies as 12–15
unilateralism: Canada–US Free Trade Agreement 129–30; regulation of subsidies 97–130
United States: on control of subsidies 133, 146; defence

procurement programmes 19–20, 31; free trade in 9–10; as GATT litigant 55; protectionism of 3–4; research and development (R&D) 29–30; subsidies defined 109; and unfair trade practices 12–14. *see also* US countervailing duty (CVD) law

Uruguay Round of Multilateral Trade Negotiations 5, 48–9, 121, 129, 133–50; analysis 147–50; benefit to industry 139; Canadian Communication 134–5; European Union report 135–6; institutional framework 140–6; negotiating framework 134–6; notification and surveillance 147, 149; regulatory framework 136–47; specificity in 137–8; subsidies, classes of 137; substantive framework 137–40; traffic light approach to subsidies 134, 136

US countervailing duty (CVD) law 105–13; conceptual considerations 106–8; institutional aspects 108–9; legal differences with USA 116; practical differences with Canada 115; practice, analysis of 111–13; substance of 109–11; use of in Uruguay Round 133, 135

Völker, E.M. 52, 56

voluntary export restraints (VERs): and public choice theory 37

Weiler, P. 127

welfare reducing actions and public choice theory 36

Yi, S.D. 103

Zenith case (USA) 107